A HISTORY OF CHILDREN'S TELEVISION IN ENGLISH CANADA, 1952-1986

by

F. B. Rainsberry

The Scarecrow Press, Inc.
Metuchen, N.J., & London
1988

ACKNOWLEDGMENTS

The author gratefully acknowledges permission to reprint the following material:

Excerpts from Mr. Rogers Talks to Parents, by Fred Rogers and Barry Head. Copyright © 1983; reprinted by permission of The Berkley Publishing Group.

Excerpts from "Remember Uncle Chich?" by Ed Hausmann; "The Bananas," by Ed Hausmann; Sandor Stern's quote in "The Show Is ... Read a Note!" by Ralph Thomas; column by Michele Landsberg. Reprinted with permission--The Toronto Star Syndicate.

Excerpts from the book The Disappearance of Childhood, by Neil Postman. Copyright © 1982 by Neil Postman. Reprinted by permission of Delacorte Press.

Lyrics by Cliff Braggins reprinted with his permission.

Quote by Gian Carlo Menotti used with his permission.

Excerpts about Circle Square syndicated television series used by permission of Circle Square.

Excerpts from CBC Times by Alfred Harris reprinted by permission of the author.

Quotes about The Kids of Degrassi Street by Linda Schuyler and Kit Hood used by permission of Linda Schuyler.

Quotes about Matt and Jenny by Ralph Ellis used with his permission.

Excerpts from Let's Play TV in the Classroom, prepared by Lynne Hyne and Jack Livesley, and quotes about Read All About It! 2 reprinted by permission on TVOntario.

(continued on next page)

Library of Congress Cataloging-in-Publication Data

Rainsberry, F. B. (Fred B.), 1915-
A history of children's television in English Canada, 1952-1986 / by F. B. Rainsberry.
p. cm.
Bibliography: p.
Includes index.
ISBN 0-8108-2079-X
1. Television programs for children--Canada--History. I. Title.
PN1992.8.C46R35 1988
791.45'09'099282--dc19 87-28773

Manufactured in The United States of America

Quotes about *The New Music* used by permission of CITY TV, Toronto.

Quotes about *The Bananas*, excerpts from *Children's Programs: CBC Background* and from CBC's "Departmental Policy" used by permission of the Canadian Broadcasting Corporation.

Material by David and Janis Nostbakken used with their permission.

Quotes about *The Friendly Giant* by Robert Homme used with his permission.

Excerpts from the Children's Television Workshop contract with the CBC regarding *Sesame Street* used by their permission.

Excerpts from the "Broadcast Code for Advertising to Children" reprinted by permission of Canadian Advertising Foundation, Standards Division.

Excerpts from Dennis Braithwaite's column in the Toronto *Globe & Mail* reprinted by permission of the author.

Quotes from "Is Your Child a TV Junkie?" published by the Children's Broadcast Institute, used by permission of the Institute.

Material by Barry Duncan used with his permission.

Excerpts from *Education in the Primary and Junior Division*, 1975, pp. 38-39, used by permission of the Ministry of Education.

Excerpts from "The Evidence So Far," by G. Comstock, and "A Suggested Research Strategy," by B. Fawles and B. Horner, reprinted by permission of *Journal of Communications*.

Excerpts from "Against the Grain," by George Comstock, in *Television Advertising and Children*, J. F. Esserman, ed. (New York: Child Research Services, 1981), reprinted by permission of the author.

Excerpts from *Children and Television*, by Gerald S. Lesser (New York: Random House, 1974). Copyright © 1974 by Gerald S. Lesser. Reprinted by permission of the publisher.

Quotes from The Australian Children's Television Foundation used by permission of the Foundation.

Photographs provided by the Canadian Broadcasting Corporation, Department of Communications, used with their permission.

Excerpts from "Television and Young Children," by Alice S. Honig in *Young Children* (May 1983) reprinted by permission. Copyright © by The National Association for the Education of Young Children.

Excerpts from *The Hurried Child*, by David Elkind (Reading, MA: Addison-Wesley Publishing Company, Inc.), © 1981, reprinted with permission.

DEDICATED TO

the producers, directors, writers, and performers whose creative talents made possible the program achievements in this book.

CONTENTS

List of Illustrations vii
Preface ix

I. The Early Years, 1952-1954 1

II. Policy for Program Development and Production, 1954-1986 14

III. The Major Daily Shows 37

IV. Magazine Programming and Continuity in Children's Programming 64

V. Information Programming for Children 78

VI. Drama and Storytelling 117

VII. Variety Programming for Children 139

VIII. Pre-School Programming 162

IX. Developing Relations in Programming Between Two Cultures -- English and French 194

X. Private Television and Children's Programs 207

XI. Advertising in Children's Television 213

XII. The Issue of Visual Literacy 219

XIII. Children, Television, and Research 236

XIV. Conclusions and Recommendations About Thirty Years of Television for Children 243

Appendixes
A. Annotated References 273
B. List of Interviewees 278
C. Source Companies and Associations 287

Index 293

LIST OF ILLUSTRATIONS

1. Uncle Chichimus and Hollyhock. 6

2. Franz Kraemer, Frank Fice, and Norman Campbell on the set of Uncle Chichimus. 8

3. Ed McCurdy in Ed's Place, with Joe Austin as the Postman and, superimposed, as the Fireman. 11

4. Howdy Doody. 38

5. Peter Mews as Timber Tom with Howdy Doody in the Canadian Howdy Doody Show. 40

6. Alfie Scopp as Clarabell the Clown in the Howdy Doody Show. 45

7. Ross Snetsinger and Jean Cavall in Whistletown. 49

8. Al Hamel, Howard the Turtle, and Michelle Finney in Razzle Dazzle. 51

9. Wonderstruck, with Bob McDonald. 88

10. The Mighty Mites, in Owl TV. 91

11. Howard Green and Jennifer Gibson host What's New? 94

12. The Spirit Bay Braves, in Spirit Bay. 131

13. Megan Follows and Richard Farnsworth in Anne of Green Gables. 133

14. Megan Follows and Dame Wendy Hiller in Anne of Green Gables--The Sequel. 133

15. Alex Trebek, original host of Music Hop. 143

16. An elephant and Eric Nagler join Sharon, Lois and Bram, and children on The Elephant Show. 150

17. A new Canadian series, Vid Kids. 151

18. Steve Aiken and Susanne McGillivray, the young hosts of CTV's Don't Stop Now. 158

19. Bob Homme in The Friendly Giant. 165

20. Ernie Coombs and friends, in Mr. Dressup. 169

21. Fred Penner's Place, a CBC pre-school series. 177

22. The Silver Basketball, with host Ron Oliver. 179

23. Nursery School Time, with original hostess Teddy Forman and producer Rena Elmer. 181

24. The Canadian edition of Sesame Street. 186

25. TVOntario's Polka Dot Door. 190

26. Niki Kemeny and Nicole Skoffman in DeGrassi Junior High. 252

PREFACE

The author is most indebted to the Explorations Program of the Canada Council for the grant which made it possible to undertake this study. I am also indebted to the Council for the use of the facilities at Stanley House in order to convene a group of senior personnel who had long associations with children's television.

I express my thanks to the Canadian Broadcasting Corporation for support given in the supply of the tape recorder and the audio tapes which made possible the recording of the interviews which form the backbone of much of the content of this history. It is with pleasure that I return these tapes to the Public Archives for future reference. In particular I wish to thank Ms. Nada Harcourt, the former Head of Children's Television at the CBC, Ms. Angela Bruce, the present Head, and Dr. Deborah Bernstein, her able assistant, for continuing support during this arduous undertaking; and Mr. A. W. Ross, the Corporate Program Supervisor, Ottawa, under whose aegis this study was first initiated.

I wish to acknowledge the generous support given by Dr. David Nostbakken and Dr. André Caron in permitting the use of valuable documentation in their report, Children and Television: Programs, People, Policies, submitted to the Federal Task Force on Broadcasting Policy, January 1986. Many of their conclusions and recommendations complement the thought process which shaped this study.

The task of collecting data and matching records concerning policy, programs and schedules was greatly facilitated by Deborah Lindsay, Senior Clerk in Program Resources, who diligently located copies of programs from the early days of children's television to the present. Robert Clarke, Senior Clerk in Central Records and Archives, coordinated and delivered to one center all the available correspondence and program data filed over a 30-year period. Victoria Wilcox, Public Relations Assistant in Audience Relations, provided invaluable help in compiling the daily schedule of programs. Ms. Gayle Jabour of the Canadian Radio and Television Commission procured valuable documentation to assist in the development of the project.

I commend especially Elizabeth Jenner, Supervisor of Reference and Design Libraries, and her staff, for the remarkable collection of program information which was made available to me.

At TVOntario, I received valuable assistance from Ruth Vernon, Supervisor of Children's Programs, Ms. Kay Duggan, Research Officer, and Mr. Jack Livesley, host of The Academy.

To Michael Saunders, I give my thanks for his intelligent and diligent care in the final assembly of the program schedule and for the organization of the print materials which provided essential elements in the text which follows.

Margaret McCaffery edited the text with intelligence, patience and understanding, contributing much to the ready comprehension of this history.

Special thanks are extended to Mrs. Rosalee Monk and Mrs. Peggy Stevenson of the Children's Broadcast Institute for their continuing support, and to Janis and David Nostbakken for their interest and concern.

It was Kate Hamilton and Ann Phelps of Facilities for Writers in Toronto whose diligence and patience with a word processor made possible the delivery of this monograph.

I am especially indebted to Mr. John Twomey, Professor at Ryerson Polytechnical Institute, for his support and his special undertaking in preparing the section on research in the final chapter.

I wish to thank all those who took time from their busy schedules to submit to interviews and to provide me with materials which made it possible to give as accurate a record as I have been able to assemble here. To each and all, my deepest gratitude. I owe especial thanks to Margaret Collier,

National Executive Director, Writers, of the Association of Canadian Television and Radio Actors (ACTRA) for much help in locating former writers and performers of children's television.

F. B. RAINSBERRY

Toronto, Canada
November, 1986

Chapter I

THE EARLY YEARS, 1952-1954

The annals of broadcasting in any developed country are usually to be found in the record of the programs which were produced in radio, television, or film. The nerve center of a broadcasting organization is to be found among the producers and directors who execute the programs for presentation on air. Policy, by its very nature, is a function of the environment in which the broadcasting organization has its roots. In a country with either a long history of cultural tradition and/or a centralized national authority in government, policies will be much more clearly set forth for the broadcasting organization to follow. In North America, where democratic government in the United States and Canada is organized on a federal basis, in each case constituting a union of provincial or state jurisdictions, national policy with respect to broadcasting is much more loosely defined and in many instances no clear directions are to be found.

In Canada, broadcasting policy is the responsibility of the Ministry of Communications at Ottawa, and federal/provincial agreements have to be worked out in order that each province which wishes to set up its own broadcasting authority may do so. The provinces--in particular, Quebec, Ontario, Alberta, and British Columbia--all operate under the Ministry of Education in each province. Since education is a state/provincial jurisdiction, the extension of education into the broadcasting realm necessitates some modus vivendi between the constitutional authority of the federal government to control broadcasting, on the one hand, while educational broadcasting is acknowledged to be a proper responsibility for individual provinces.

Because policy was largely determined within the program units of the Canadian Broadcasting Corporation, in this case children's programming has its own unique history. It is the purpose of this monograph to trace the development of that policy as it was manifested in the programs which were developed and presented over thirty years.

Programs are classified under several genres/formats so that the concerns unique to children's programs may be readily identified and development towards a meaningful and mature policy may be traced. While the CBC remains the major producer of children's programs in Canada, programs produced for children by both the provincial broadcasting agencies and the private broadcasters are included.

On November 2, 1986, the CBC reached its fiftieth anniversary. As part of the commemoration of this occasion, the CBC has lent its support for the past five years, in both a financial and an advisory capacity, to an oral history project being conducted by the Institute of Canadian Studies at Carleton University.

The CBC Oral History Project was inaugurated in 1981 because of concern that an important part of Canada's cultural heritage would be lost forever if recollections of the people associated with the CBC through the years were not soon recorded for posterity. Dr. Ross Eaman of the School of Journalism at Carleton University in Ottawa was selected as Research Director for the project.

Those involved in starting the project included Ernest Dick of the Public Archives of Canada; Professor Sidney Wise, the then Director of the Institute of Canadian Studies; Donald Lytle and William A. Ross of Corporate Program Services at the CBC, and Davidson Dunton, Chairman of the CBC Board of Governors from 1945 to 1958.

Using a team of graduate students in the Canadian Studies program, the CBC Oral History Project has conducted approximately two hundred interviews with CBC programming, administrative, and engineering personnel across the country. All of these interviews, along with those done by the author with key personnel concerned with children's television, have been deposited with the Public Archives of Canada and are available for research purposes.

The availability of this collection has already borne fruit in terms of research on the CBC. It has contributed significantly to several graduate dissertations on subjects such as the Montreal producers' strike, the evolution of CBC sports programming, and women in public affairs programming at the CBC.

Over the last couple of years, the CBC Oral History Project has become less of an oral history project and more of a history project; that is, an increasing amount of time has been spent researching archival records and other non-oral source materials. This trend is likely to continue during the next few years as researchers pursue plans to produce a series of scholarly monographs on selected aspects of the CBC's history.

When the Canada Council approved a grant for the writing of the history of the children's enterprise in television programming, it was agreed by the CBC that oral interviews should be undertaken with full support. For this reason, much of the information contained within this volume is derived from interviews themselves. As one might expect, many of those interviewed had failed to remember vital elements in the continuity of development over the years. To supplement these discrepancies, use was made of CBC's reference library, particularly at Toronto, where files had been kept on programs as they were originally announced. As well, newspaper critics often wrote evaluations of the programs seen, or feature stories were written about the characters in the shows as well as about the directors who were responsible for the presentations. In addition, there were statements of policy made by the supervisory group which served as guidelines for those who produced the shows within the limits of the children's television department. By and large, these are the sources of information which document this history.

Long before television began in Canada in 1952, the CBC children's department in the English services division dated back to 1938 when Mary Grannan produced the first popular children's radio program, known as Just Mary. Miss Grannan was a teacher from Fredericton, New Brunswick, who first launched her program on the local private station. Later, it was picked up as a network program by the CBC and Mary became responsible for its presentation from Toronto. A decade later Dorothy Jane Goulding devised a program known as Kindergarten of the Air, which began in 1947. Dorothy Jane Goulding was the presenter; the scripts were prepared by two pre-school specialists, the Misses Hazel Baggs and Gladys Dickson. In addition, two other notable personalities of the early days of radio were responsible for Sports College (Lloyd Percival) and The Stamp Club (Doug Patrick). Folk singer Alan Mills and storyteller Frosia Gregory also contributed significant elements to the radio schedule.

A national television service for Canada began in Montreal and Toronto in September, 1952. As with radio, there was to be a CBC-owned and operated station and production center in each of the main regions of Canada. Extensive training programs for producers were undertaken in Montreal and Toronto. For two years, the managers of the two stations were to be free to develop programming strategies which would make the most of the training and creative endeavor of the television producers.

On March 29, 1954, at the invitation of the Chief Producer Mavor Moore, and his associate Stuart Griffiths, the Program Director, I accepted the position of Supervising Producer of Children's Television at station CBLT of the Canadian Broadcasting Corporation in Toronto.

Before my arrival, Joanne Hughes and Peggy Nairn had been appointed producer-directors for children's programs. These two producers were responsible for a limited schedule of children's programs which appeared in the late afternoon each weekday. Up to this point no clear policy had been delineated to guide the producers and the whole of television was developing in an experimental atmosphere at this stage in its history. The producers of children's programs were therefore free to try out their own ideas, gathering talent where it was available and trying to discover who would make the best performers for children's television.

As Montreal was the only other station on the air at this time, it was natural that the schedule would be made up of contributions from both Toronto and Montreal. The first children's program was scheduled at 5:30 p.m. on September 7 with the French production of Pepinot & Capucine under the direction of Jean Paul Ladouceur. The characters, puppets created by Edmondo Chiodini, were involved in a story recounting the adventures of a boy and girl who lived in the village of Trois Pommes but who traveled to far-distant lands, accompanied by their friends, Mr. Black, Mr. White, Mr. Panpon, and Bruin, the pet bear. However, an uninvited guest, the villainous Powpow, caused constant trouble. Reginald Boisvert was so successful in developing the character that Powpow became a hero to young viewers, bringing complaints from parents--and a revision of the character. On December 26, 1954, Powpow fell asleep and dreamed that one of the shepherds represented the birth of Christ in the stable. Powpow was so impressed that he resolved to change his ways. With the help of a small-scale reproduction of himself (Powpow's conscience!), he learned to live a better life. Every time Powpow was tempted to be a troublemaker, his conscience appeared to challenge him.

The series was filmed in Montreal, where the sound track was dubbed separately in English and French. The characters Pepinot and Capucine first appeared in _Français_, a Montreal French-language newspaper, as a comic strip written by Reginald Boisvert and Jean Paul Ladouceur.

Slowly the shape of a regular schedule for children's television began to emerge, with the addition of a children's newsreel from Montreal along with Frank Heron's _Children's Corner_ (later known as _Small Fry Frolics_). The program consisted of a child audience participating in quiz games and in discussion of problems such as babysitting and how to keep a bank account. On the English side, _Uncle Chichimus_ was developed by John Conway as part of the regular evening magazine entitled _Let's See_. The success of _Uncle Chichimus_ depended largely on the wit and whimsy of John Conway, who managed to combine elements of both fantasy and satire in his conceptions of the relationship between Chich and Hollyhock. While the program was essentially adult in its conception and appeal, children were attracted by the puppets and the element of fantasy in the story.

At the suggestion of Norman Jewison, the original producer of _Uncle Chichimus_, a live character, Larry Mann, was added and the show was made into a 15-minute program. In Conway's subtle imagination, Chich developed into a parody of aristocratic old Ontario and the suffix "-imus"--the Latin form for the superlative--suggested the ultimate in pride, arrogance or disdain, or, as Conway says, "Chichimus was a

Uncle Chichimus and Hollyhock

scholar of arcane lore!" The script was developed in rehearsal; Conway interacted with Larry Mann, the producer (first Norman Jewison, then Norman Campbell), Frank Fice, the studio director and members of the crew, sometimes voicing the puppets. Suzanne Mess dressed the puppets and the whole enterprise was known as the Chichimus Broadcasting Corporation, comprehending the whole universe within the acronym "C.B.C."! The series continued until 1955.

On January 20, 1954, Uncle Chichimus and Hollyhock were "kidnapped" during the early hours of the morning from Conway's unlocked car parked on King Street West. Since "Chich" and "Holly" had won the hearts of thousands of viewers, there was a public outcry about their disappearance. Indeed, the Toronto Daily Star ran a banner headline about the "kidnapping" on the front page of its first edition. As Ed Hausmann observed, "it was the only time before or since that any television performers, Canadian or otherwise, ever warranted such headline treatment. No ransom note was found nor were the culprits ever apprehended. To this day the case remains in those dusty files marked 'unsolved.'" (Star Week, July 11-18, 1970).

Since Conway had no duplicates of the puppets, he appeared on camera with Larry Mann to stage a mock investigation. Mann played several roles as the investigation went on, such as a private detective and a news dealer. In this last role, he was about to tell where Chich and Holly could be found when he was "shot down" in a rain of machine gun bullets, thus preventing the crime from being solved.

Ed Hausmann gives a reporter's account in The Toronto Star of the relationship between Hollyhock and Uncle Chichimus which captures the spirit of the show very effectively:

> Like the Peanuts comic strip up to two or three years ago, it had two levels of humor and appeal--a sophisticated one for adults and smarter children, and another for young, less cynical children. The show was done ad lib from the beginning. A rough outline was talked out beforehand and with only the sketchiest rehearsal and no script, Conway and Mann went before the cameras, in a day when such things were done live.
>
> Chichimus was a "balding Canadian curmudgeon" and Hollyhock a "hatchet-faced re-creation of a retired private secretary with a horsetail hairdo made from a string mop," as one writer described the pair. Chich was an idea man, constantly thinking up things to do that were bound to make him rich and famous. He was mischievous, bumbling, egotistical, imprudent, bombastic and headstrong, a likeable little creature who reflected the foibles of everyman.
>
> Hollyhock was the restraining, ever-practical conservative influence; she was the worrier, the nag, the I-told-you-so, but always, way down, deeply enamoured of Chichimus.
>
> Most of Chich's schemes were inspired by the news of the day, so that his adventures were, in effect, satires of things that were going on in the real world of serious adults. The daily show was a serial with each adventure lasting a week or two and usually ending in disaster for Chich, but each disaster was easily over-shadowed by Chichimus' next great plan.

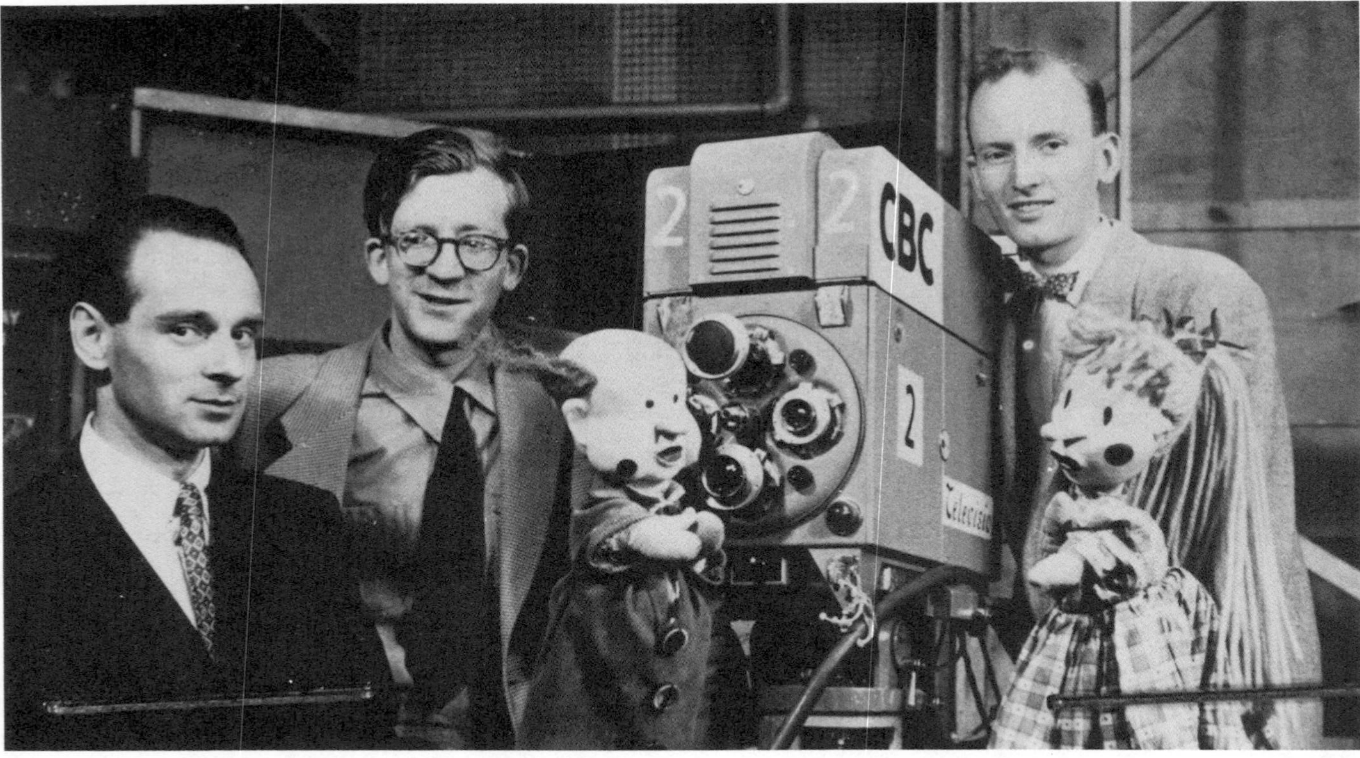
CBC
2

> Chichimus did many things--he once flew to the moon, he was a detective, he was an actor, hockey coach, and anything else that Conway and Mann could poke fun at. It was a clever and witty show, but it was something more--it was the only properly done show of gentle satire ever aired on Canadian television that reached out and was acclaimed by the public at large. (Star Week, July 11-18, 1970).

In 1958, Conway returned to C.B.C. to do 26 episodes of The Adventures of Chich in which Conway made fun of fairy tales through the medium of Uncle Chichimus. Still later, Conway moved to Ottawa, where under the direction of Bill Swaffield he continued the program of puppets intermixed with cartoons as a regular production of CJOH-TV until 1966.

Concurrently the schedule included serialized production of Jules Verne's 20,000 Leagues Under the Sea and The Mysterious Island, along with Thomas Raddall's Roger Sudden. An original science fiction series, Space Command, was devised by Alfie Harris.

When Joanne Hughes (Soloviov) and Peggy Nairn (Liptrot) were appointed as producer-directors, the schedule of children's programs was already in place. With no training, they simply moved from the role of script assistant to the director's chair. Using techniques observed while they were script assistants, with cooperation from the cameramen and technical crew, they learned by doing. The program director had selected obvious formats such as science demonstration, crafts, pets, folk singing and puppet shows. Much depended upon the personality and skill of the presenter. Percy Saltzman, as host of How About That, was an urbane, disarming and well-informed presenter who always showed respect for his audience. The program emphasized almost exclusively demonstration of simple scientific phenomena with less emphasis on exploration or the stimulation of a child's curiosity.

Like How About That, Hobby Workshop focused on the use of practical materials available in the home. Tom Martin's personality as host was very different from Percy Saltzman's.

[Opposite:] Left to right, Franz Kraemer, Frank Fice, and Norman Campbell (producer) on the set of Uncle Chichimus.

He was less dynamic, but was able to use his skills as an art educator to organize the activities of both the children on the set and his young viewers to make the learning experience pleasurable. While he was a most competent art educator, the show rarely revealed the relationship between the "busy work" of the children at the craft tables and the excitement of creative activity, the joy in completing a creative endeavour.

Pet Corner relied entirely on staff announcer Rick Campbell's competence with a variety of pets, and guests who commented on their behavior and the care of these pets.

Planet Tolex was an original story series designed by Leo and Dora Velleman, who used their puppets. As the title indicates, the action took place in an extra-terrestrial realm. Blumper, a white elephant, and Timothy, a leprechaun, made contact with Planet Tolex in outer space, a realm inhabited by creatures with no facial expression--they had "coils" for heads. The society of Planet Tolex was fantastically hierarchical and it was difficult to comprehend its function. The show lasted only a short time because the Vellemans found it difficult to accommodate themselves to the demands of television production, where so many artistic decisions have to be shared. Presently they operate the only permanent puppet theatre in Canada, at Chester, Nova Scotia.

Ed's Place featured folk singer Ed McCurdy, who operated from a "place" which had a door that would not open. Entry was possible only by sliding down a coal chute. The "Place" included a Moosehead which talked and a shadow which philosophized, both voiced by Joe Austin. Joe also played the roles of both the postman and the fireman, with whom Ed would ad lib. For example, the fireman would tell of how many lives he had saved in a great fire many years ago; Ed said he had never read of such an event. Joe replied, "You wouldn't have been able to because the newspaper burned to the ground." The Shadow usually appeared on a music cue three minutes before the end of the show, uttering such wisdom as:

> The thing that goes the farthest and
> Was making life worthwhile
> That costs the least and does the most
> Is just a pleasant smile.

Ed McCurdy in Ed's Place, with Joe Austin as the Postman and, superimposed, as the Fireman.

Two other programs made up the total weekly offering on this first schedule: Telestory Time and Let's Make Music. Telestory Time will be discussed later, under programming for younger children in Chapter VII, and Let's Make Music in Chapter IV.

Obviously, much had yet to be done to provide a wide spectrum of programs for children and to raise the professional standard at the same time. Children's programs traditionally have never received funding which adult programming receives and it was usually considered a fairly simple task to fill the time required to entertain children. On my arrival I met with the creative staff to determine policy for the future scheduling of children's programs on CBC television.

Several factors played a significant role in our choice of direction. Management had given the two stations, Toronto and Montreal, freedom to experiment without supervisory constraints from the National Program Office, so that they might learn the techniques of television production. It was planned that a proper authority would eventually be established to determine policy in all program areas. The responsibility of the supervising producers was therefore particularly heavy, since they were for all practical purposes the last port of call in recommending program policy in their respective areas.

Then, fiscal controls were relatively simple and no one seemed to be clearly aware of the real costs involved. The 15 per cent tax on television sets was being directed toward the development of CBC television and the staff tended to think there were unlimited funds available--not necessarily the best operating philosophy. Even in the midst of such affluence, children's programming did not receive grants as substantial as those awarded to other departments such as outside broadcasts, drama or news. Nothing has changed in this regard. Despite the problems we faced as novices, we had a rare opportunity to experiment with a new medium for entertainment and creative expression.

At that first meeting with the creative people, I particularly recall insisting, as a good educator should, that professionals have input into program planning. I wanted to draw upon the authority of respected librarians, musicians and other experts with whom we would be expected to work. Many months later, I discovered that the producers apparently looked at one another and asked themselves, "Well, if these are professional people, what are we?" I came to have a very healthy respect for the creative endeavor of the many talented professionals with whom I worked. Early in my tenure I saw the common denominator of creativity in education and creativity in television production: both are professional in this sense of the word.

By the fall of 1954 a revised schedule of children's programs had been developed under a policy which took into consideration the informal viewing needs of children. Instead of a catch-all of whatever might be available, each program had been carefully planned for the slot it occupied.

In addition to Hidden Pages and Let's Make Music, which were produced from Toronto, Let's Go to the Museum was presented as a remote telecast from the Ottawa museum under the direction of Marion Dunn, while Frank Heron continued his presentation of a children's variety show, Small Fry Frolics, from Montreal.

Chapter II

POLICY FOR PROGRAM DEVELOPMENT AND PRODUCTION, 1954-1966

When television was instituted in Canada in 1952, the Canadian Broadcasting Corporation adopted a policy of building stations in Montreal and Toronto only. For the first two years, those who were in charge of these two stations were left to develop their own strategies for program planning and production. The authority of the national program office which shaped the policy for radio programs across the country was instructed by management at Ottawa not to interfere with the television operation during this period of time. When I arrived in March 1954 as the first head of children's television for English Canada, I was unaware that in fact there was a national program office responsible for children's programming. Slowly, after the termination of the two-year period and the gradual spread of CBC-owned and operated television stations in Winnipeg, Vancouver, and Halifax, the national program office began to exercise its authority. The issue of program policy was controversial, since a policy of the national program office might readily interfere with decisions taken by the television program unit.

An example comes to mind: I was asked to address the national association of home and school and parent-teacher federations in Toronto shortly after my appointment in 1954. I was anxious to draw attention to the concerns which one should have with respect to values in programming for children.

Many parents had been clamoring against the frequency of "cowboy serials" for children and favoring programs that dealt with nature. As part of my address, I drew attention to the fact that in a program like *Lassie*, which was so popular because of sentimental attachment to dogs as pets, the scriptwriters often resorted to plot lines which were full of anxiety and tension, somewhat harmful to young children who might be watching television alone. On the other hand, cowboy serials were quite predictable. Children were not frightened by the "action-motion matrix" because the action was always predictable. Yes, there were guns and chases of that sort; but the good always won out in the end, and the hero was usually a wholesome model for children, simple though his character might be. In short, the case I made was that often nature films could be more harmful to children by creating anxiety than the simplistic plots of cowboy serials which were unlikely, in my view, to lead children down the path of violence and destruction.

The next day the local newspaper published an account of my address with a five-column banner headline: "Lassie Bad For Children, Doctor Says." No attempt was made to clarify the fact that the word "doctor" was pertinent to the degree of doctor of philosophy, not of medicine; but the casual reader would quickly assume that a medical doctor had lent his customary authority to this statement.

In due time I was summoned to the head of the department responsible for children's programs at the national level, and asked about my statement. He claimed that there really was no policy on the part of the CBC, except for the fact that we should produce programs which were pleasing to parents and not disturbing to children. At the same time, he questioned the right of a supervisor to make a public criticism of programs which were scheduled by the CBC.

While his intentions were of the best, he did not fully understand how policy is developed. The matter was quickly forgotten, and we proceeded to develop a policy which would serve as a guideline for those responsible for production and scheduling of programs for children at the CBC.

This was a challenging time to undertake the task of developing a policy for children's television, since parental concern about the impact of the medium on children was widespread. At the outset, we undertook the responsibility of speaking to a great number of parent groups in the Toronto area and, as far as travel allowances would permit, in other parts of Canada. I was ably assisted in this task by Ms. Joy

Simon, who was herself trained as a specialist in early childhood education and was a most articulate and responsible speaker. From the feedback we got from parents, we learned a great deal about how to handle the concerns and anxieties they had, and to focus their attention more appropriately on the techniques of television production rather than on content alone. The example of Lassie and the cowboy serials was a classic illustration of the problem we constantly faced.

Perhaps the most significant advice we could give to parents was the strong opinion that they should spend time watching television with their children. This shared experience served a double purpose. On the one hand, elements in a program which might be frightening to some children were immediately overcome by the reassuring presence of a loving and concerned adult. On the other hand, when parents saw things of which they did not approve, they could share with their children their concerns, and the beginnings of a critical awareness of how to use television would be developed.

At the outset, being an educator, I was anxious to ensure that viewing for children out of school hours would not be inconsistent with the creative learning experience which they should be having in school. There was wide concern about reading. Would television divert children from reading? Long after these early days, it was established with a fair degree of truth that children were not diverted from reading by television if parents exercised reasonable control over the access to the television set and if the experience of learning reading at school was a challenging and dynamic one.

Nevertheless, we quickly found ways to relate storytelling on television to reading itself. The early and very successful program Hidden Pages, with Ms. Beth Gillanders, herself an experienced librarian and teacher as well as a charming presenter, undertook to refer children to books in the library. The first ten minutes of the program dealt with books for young children, picture books, which were shown and the story read, much in the fashion of The Friendly Giant. The remainder of the show was given over to novels for older children. Beth combined narrative with integrated dramatic sequences. Since funds limited us to two additional performers, sometimes making a quick costume change in order to play a second role. Not until several weeks into the series did the program planners, producers and accountants realize that "below the line" costs such as design, graphic and technical support cost far more than the addition of one or two actors to the show. This series ran for several seasons from Toronto and three seasons from Vancouver. It became clear, within a very short time, that the stimulus of television caused a run on the books at the library. In many cases, the librarians were unable to meet the demands of the children to read the books shown on Hidden Pages for several weeks after the program had been seen.

While the effort which went into this pro-social endeavor (to encourage the use of public libraries and to foster the art of reading) was noble indeed, it was some time before we realized that a more essential enterprise was the promotion of original writers, of a wider range of performers and of an artistic use of the television medium. Nevertheless, independent stations across Canada continued to develop single programs about books for children. The following examples reflect the continuing tendency to make TV respectable by an emphasis on books.

Bookshop presents 52 half-hour programs produced by CKY-TV Winnipeg for children up to 12 years of age. Each episode is built around a theme which is the focus of the story along with craft exercises and the exchanges which take place among such characters as Witchkin and Piccadilly the Clown.

In a similar vein, Rogers Cable TV of Calgary has presented over 200 episodes of The Children's Club in which a retired couple tell stories to children in the basement of their home.

Genesis Storytime consists of over 200 fifteen-minute episodes of story-telling using computer graphics in order to bring children's storybooks alive. The programs are presented without sound so as to encourage reading aloud.

Storytime is a combination of variety with storytelling, ten half-hour programs produced by Fundy Cablevision of Saint John, New Brunswick. In each episode, piano accompaniment is provided for children to play their instruments. As well, two stories are read in each program by the children.

Library Storytime is produced in short 4-5 minute

episodes from CKBI-TV in Prince Albert, Saskatchewan; the series provides libraries with the opportunity to read short stories and to inform young viewers of events happening at their local library.

Cuddle Up and Listen is designed as a pre-school storytelling series of 13 fifteen-minute programs produced by Burlington Cablenet of Burlington, Ontario. The series focuses on books for pre-school children and stories are both read and discussed.

One could say that this early concern reflected, on the part of program planners, including myself, a lack of awareness of the intrinsic esthetic value of television itself. In short, television was being prostituted to institutional causes. The program Let's Make Music was CBC's first music show for children. While its presenter, David Ouchterlony, himself a distinguished organist and musicologist, selected the music very carefully and in an ingratiating manner presented performers of the highest level of quality, he nevertheless concentrated on didactic elements about music and did not really face the challenge which television presented: how best to make a musical experience meaningful in visual terms.

Somewhat later, the program, which was one-half-hour in length, was reduced to 15 minutes and retitled Mr. O. Every day Mr. O would appear on the program with charming puppets designed by John and Linda Keogh, in such personifications as Clarence the Clarinet and Chelly the Cello. He would engage in dialogue with the puppets and a whole visual sequence was developed which was intrinsically pleasant to look at, while at the same time the musical values were indirectly communicated to children.

As time went on, we learned to use television for its own sake and there was less emphasis on trying to make television respectable in terms of other media of communication. In short, we encouraged the producers to treat the medium as an opportunity for creative expression. This was not inconsistent with any educational elements a program might contain, since we believed that education itself was a creative experience. The question of the nature of such creativity remained a continuing challenge.

In reviewing 30 years of television programming for

children one can only be impressed by the immense diversity, the concern, and the range of quality--from the simplest and most hastily prepared programs to those with which creative writers, performers and producers have taken great care. In speculating on the history of children's television, Fred Rogers observed that

> ... if we were setting out today to do what we started more than twenty-five years ago, I wonder if we would find a place on a national broadcast network. Mister Rogers' Neighborhood has a slow pace compared to most other programs and I think it would have a very difficult time justifying that pace and explaining the series content to many network executives. Even a passionate plea that a little bit of television time be devoted to young children's emotional growth would most likely work against us. A West Coast writer-producer told me, 'You must never show that you care about an idea that you're presenting, because if you do, management decision-makers will be afraid you will expend too much effort on content and not enough on demographics and ratings. Consequently, they'll turn you down.'
>
> --Fred Rogers and Barry Head, Mister Rogers Talks With Parents (New York: Berkley Books, 1983, p. 164.)

Regardless of quality, and wrong though they may have been in many cases about their concepts of child development, their treatment of children and their understanding of creativity as it affects growth and development, the producers and performers of children's TV were for the most part caring people. As has been demonstrated thus far, the effort that was put into coordination and planning of programming and the integral development of policy did much to ensure that the caring endeavor of those who undertook to do children's programming would produce the best results.

Sociologist and media ecologist Neil Postman has said that "the idea of childhood is disappearing, and at a dazzling speed. The dividing line between childhood and adulthood is rapidly eroding" (Neil Postman, The Disappearance of Childhood. New York: Delacorte Books, 1982, p. xii). Postman is quick to choose television programming as one of the forces which is causing the idea of childhood to disappear. He is worried that television has made children more materialistic, more sexually precocious and sophisticated, with adult tastes in fashion and music, and maybe even in crime. "To stand back and wait as the charm, malleability, innocence and curiosity of children is degraded and then transmogrified into the lesser features of pseudo-adulthood is painful and embarrassing and, above all, sad" (p. xiii). Fred Rogers continues in a similar vein, indicating that there has been

> some improvement in children's programming over the past decade, but most of the improvement has come about through outside pressures rather than from the deep conviction of programmers themselves. Until change comes from within the industry, television will continue to have a negative effect on children, family life, and human relationships in general. Often, the kindest thing one can say about a television program these days is that it is a waste of time. Much of television, though, is degrading, reducing important human feelings to the status of caricature or trivia. Some of it, in my opinion, even encourages pathology. Yet here it is, for hours a day, part of the intimacy of family life, an influence on family values, a growing part of family tradition, and an accessory of family education. We parents need to think hard about how television is affecting our children and, in turn, our grandchildren to come. We need to think harder still about what to do about it. (Rogers, p. 164.)

In advancing suggestions and recommendations based upon the experience of over 100 interviews with broadcasters to children, and upon the review of all the programs mentioned, it is my intention to support the continuing creative endeavor of those presently responsible for providing children's television programming. While some observations may seem critical, the reader should interpret them as supportive rather than condemnatory. Since very few people will undertake an enterprise in children's television without some commitment, they deserve the opportunity to share the insights of others who may have had more experience or even a different experience. The very matching of differences alone will contribute to insights which a producer working alone might not realize in the productions which he creates.

First, a word to parents and professionals who work

with children. The literature of the past 30 years is full of criticisms of television production which often reflect little or no understanding of its techniques or of contemporary values in society. In the western world adults have become accustomed to a very high standard of material existence. We cherish the image of the best of all possible worlds, a world we believe to be getting better all the time. We wish our children to grow up in an environment free of violence and conflict, while all around us we see violence in the news, in human relations, and even in families, even though most of us pretend that it is not there. An attempt to screen our children from such conditions is likely to make them hostile --or at least to make them aware of our hypocrisy. And in the face of such hypocrisy they are not likely to take us very seriously.

To offset this false idealism, we must develop an awareness of the esthetic qualities of a good television production. We do not scorn violence in Shakespeare; we have idolized him as the paragon of literary achievement. We deplore the seamy violence of cheap novels, and we seem somehow to know the difference. In television, we usually make the blanket assumption that all of it is bad. Distinctions between good and bad can be made only by those who have some appreciation of its style and of the techniques employed to create the effects we see. If television is as bad as many say it is, it is that way because no one protests in favor of better production.

We must also realize that television costs a great deal of money to produce. If we therefore put it exclusively in the category of entertainment and fail to realize the importance of spending enough money to make it culturally significant, then we deserve what we get. I hope that some of these suggestions will be realized, especially to provide us all with an opportunity to contribute to the improvement of television for children and for society as a whole.

Perhaps the outstanding perception gained from this intensive review of children's television is the increasing awareness of a need for a community of TV producers to devote themselves exclusively to meeting the needs of children. This implies that there should be very strong support, both within and without the Canadian Broadcasting Corporation, for a good children's television department. This in no way implies criticism of leaders past and present, who in every instance committed themselves far beyond the call of duty to realize what was best for children.

A simple illustration of the problem arises when economic recessions force cutbacks in federal funds provided to the Canadian Broadcasting Corporation. The tendency is to make the cut across the board. The point of diminishing returns is reached when an already low budget, such as that of children's television, is cut to the point where little or nothing can be done to create a climate of growth and significant creative development. Recently the cutbacks have been sufficiently severe to prevent the expansion of facilities to meet the increasing demands of the public for program fare. Consequently, studios are in short supply and the children's department rarely has regular access to CBC-owned and -operated studios for its productions. Some programs are therefore accumulated in large numbers to be produced at moments when the studios are free. This packing of programs into a short period of production cuts down on thoughtful, creative production. Whatever money is left over has been spent working with private film producers or in the use of outside studios. While the participation of producers who work outside the Corporation is commendable, it is imperative that there be carefully produced inside productions which enable the supervisor to communicate to the outsider how he sees the policy being implemented effectively.

Above all, with a strong children's department there is likely to be a community of well-intentioned, thoughtful people exchanging ideas frequently, and working together as a team to improve children's television. Any outside producer contracted to work with such a team automatically becomes a part of that team, enhancing his commitment to his endeavor. While the independent producer has already demonstrated his ability to produce programs of high quality, there is no reason in the world why that endeavor would not be improved by exchange with others whose daily task is constantly concerned with the development of policy and the realization of programs in terms of that policy.

Policy in this context should be thought of in terms of creative guidelines for writers and producers. It should <u>not</u> be conceived as a set of restrictive rules which would inhibit fresh, creative endeavour. A good policy enables dialogue, which enhances freedom of expression, and allows for thoughtful evaluation of every idea advanced. Only in this way can the initial endeavor of a creative person be given the kind of social relevance which makes for good programming for children. Dialogue of this sort automatically provides social content for every creative idea advanced, and prevents the product from reflecting only the single-minded will of its creator. Moreover, many young producers, lacking experience, gain greatly from the support of a policy which reflects the experience of those who have worked together in a common cause for a long time.

In short, a policy should not be etched in stone; rather, it should be a living entity which provides supportive guidelines for critical evaluation of any idea advanced by an independent producer. The producer-director has full control over the material he produces once he enters the control room, and much of what he happens to achieve, the creative result--a good program--comes about through thoughtful planning and creative endeavor in the studio itself. However, pre-planning is essential in order that studio time will be productive. Fred Rogers comments that he and his associates

> have been more fortunate than most people in the world of television programming, because we have had the luxury of time--time to grow in our work, and time for our work to grow into what it has become. But was time to develop really a "luxury"? I think it's been a <u>necessity</u>. It seems that all living things need time if they are to grow in a healthy way. They need to pass through certain stages before they can move on to the next stages of their growth. This is certainly true for human beings, and I think it may be true for any work that human beings do together--from running a government to producing a television program. Something else that humans need for healthy individual growth and worthwhile joint enterprise is caring relationships. We have been greatly fortunate in being surrounded by these, too. (Rogers, p. 164.)

These remarks distill the long and intense experience that brought about the achievement of Fred Rogers as a writer, performer and producer. They also reflect the close affinity between a thoughtful policy on the one hand, and the community of caring people who developed it on the other. Such communities inspire confidence in the public at large, and set examples for those outside who will work with them. A community is not a closed corporation; it suggests interaction, interrelationships, dialogue, and communication.

Throughout its history, the Children's Department at the CBC has been fortunate in the leadership it has had. While my own tenure was the longest of any, those who succeeded me carried with them the ideals we had cherished in earlier days. At the same time, each supervisor made further changes in policy depending upon budgets and general program policy from within the Corporation as well in response to changes in audience reception. While we were very different in temperament and background, each of us has made a valiant attempt to realize creative programming for children. Since the 1970s the CBC, like many public corporations, has suffered from the effects of rapidly rising inflation and funding cutbacks. I know of no western country where a children's department was adequately funded from the beginning of its establishment. Therefore, as I have already explained, when cuts are made on a percentage basis the effect is likely to be more disastrous than if an operating minimum were set, below which no further cuts would be made. During the 1970s the supervisors faced difficulties which were unknown in the 1950s and '60s. A close examination of the schedule during the late '60s will reveal that many brave attempts to launch new concepts for children's programs were terminated because either facilities or adequate monies were unavailable.

Decisions made by managers concerning enterprises like children's television are often subtle reflections of what they believe the general attitude of the public to children's television to be. While we all profess to be deeply concerned about the impact of television upon our children, managers of broadcasting generally feel that any cuts in adult programming in favor of children's programming would be unacceptable.

By 1966 the general policy for the development of children's programs and the criteria for the selection of syndicated film programs or films produced by other companies had been well established. At no point were the statements of policy intended to be absolute; rather, they were to serve as guidelines for the producers so that, on the one hand, the material could be relevant and would be above casual criticism by parents and professionals; on the other hand, the guidelines were intended to support the producers in the development of the most creative programming possible. For all practical purposes, given the budgets and the nature of scheduling at that time, the children's department of the CBC was internationally recognized for its achievements, both through awards which the programs received and through the recognition given to producers, who were called upon to give advice and counsel to other broadcasting agencies across the world.

In 1966, after 14 years of service, I left the Corporation to undertake an assignment first with the Instructional Television Trust in Israel, and secondly with the Eastern Educational Network in Boston. I was succeeded by Dan McCarthy, who picked up where I left off to meet new challenges of a sort that had not been anticipated.

McCarthy brought to the leadership of the department experience both as a radio and as a television producer. He was thoroughly familiar with the policy of the department and sought to implement it to the best of his ability.

Already pressures were coming from the adult schedule which were to change the shape of the scheduling of children's programs. The Sunday afternoon period gave way to the commitment to sports activities for adults. Studio space for the production of children's television, as well as for the production of experimental programming, gradually became more difficult to obtain. A greater reliance on film began to come about because the studios were overtaxed with the demands of adult programming. Because of pressures on the budget, the CBC was required to bring in more and more commercial revenue. This entailed an "invasion" of the late afternoon period, when the program director was required to purchase children's programs produced in the United States on syndicated film in order to win the right of first release for a new adult program which had just been produced. And so the policy which normally applied to the selection of films for children was suspended in order to schedule these American syndicated films.

In the early 1970s, the CBC committed itself to the concept of management by objectives. Part of this enterprise entailed extra money being offered to program departments in successive years. The enterprise lasted about three years, with public affairs, drama and light entertainment being first in line. When it came time for children's programs to be given the green light for expansion and development, funds were suddenly unavailable. Indeed, the program of management by objectives was itself abandoned.

At the same time, public affairs broadcasting was rapidly expanding, culminating in the production of the ten o'clock news and The Journal. Presently this area of programming uses most of the facilities and experienced crew available, leaving children's programming to be produced on an occasional basis or to be produced by outside agencies under supervision of the area head. As studio facilities became more difficult to obtain, children's programs were assigned to the regions. The Canadian segments of Sesame Street were produced in Montreal and Winnipeg, with some animation being done in Vancouver. The prize-winning program Pencil Box was produced in Ottawa until its development reached the point where it was overtaxing the studio facilities there. Further funds requested from the network to continue the enterprise were refused. By 1979 the budget cuts were becoming critical and access to studios even more difficult. At that time the then head, Dodi Robb, made the decision to abandon the late afternoon period for children and to concentrate all her efforts on production of a few well-executed dramas combined with carefully selected films from agencies such as the Children's Film Foundation.

Obviously it is difficult to maintain the kind of tradition which had been established earlier. Nevertheless, in spite of these handicaps the CBC is still producing programs of high quality for children.

While the CBC accepted the acknowledged worth of Sesame Street as valid entertainment and as a highly researched device for teaching reading and the numeration system, Neil Postman's thesis about the impact of television on the minds of children is interesting. He sees television as one of the major forces breaking down the boundaries between childhood and adulthood. Communication used to depend on oral communication or on the ability to read.

> The book culture of the sixteenth through the twentieth centuries created another knowledge monopoly--this time separating children and adults. A fully literate adult had access to all of the sacred and profane information in books, to the many forms of literature, to all of the recorded secrets of human experience.

> Children, for the most part, did not. Which is why they were children. And why they were required to go to school. (Postman, p. 76.)

Postman, like McLuhan, recognizes television as first and foremost a visual medium. His use of this perception leaves something to be desired. His prejudice emerges in

> recalling what Lewis Carroll's Alice says just before beginning her adventures. Having nothing to do on a lazy day, Alice peeks at a book her sister is reading. But the book contains no pictures or conversations, by which Alice means stories. 'And what is the use of a book,' Alice thinks, 'without pictures or conversations!' Lewis Carroll is making the obvious point that the pictorial and narrative mode is of a lower order of complexity and maturity than the expository. Pictures and stories are the natural form in which children understand the world. Exposition is for grown-ups. (Postman, p. 117.)

But the producers of *Sesame Street* "have accepted without reservation the idea that learning is not only *not* obstructed by entertainment but, on the contrary, is indistinguishable from it" (Postman, p. 116). Using all of television's visual technology, a rapid-fire succession of images is employed to evoke from young viewers automatic responses designed to develop correct habitual responses to numeration and the alphabet so that the difficulty of learning in the early stages of reading and mathematics will be overcome. Depending upon what research report one reads, the producers have been more, *or less*, successful than they claim to be. The conflict "raged" between Gerald Lesser and Dorothy and Jerome Singer about whether fast pacing enhanced or hindered the development of cognitive skills.

No matter how one looks at the program, deservedly acclaimed though it is, both the defenders and the critics seem to miss the real opportunity presented by television. If television is "first and foremost a visual medium," then why not exploit its esthetic possibilities to the fullest extent? While Postman is right to say that television is unsuited for the development of skills of ratiocination and logic, he is wrong to suggest that a creatively conceived and imaginative sequence of visual images is an experience inferior to the skills of grammar and mathematics.

In 1974 McCarthy decided to resign and take over full responsibility as the project director for Sesame Street. In his place, John L. Kennedy was appointed as the area head of children's television. He had been trained in the children's department in the early days, and had become an accomplished television producer. When he took on the responsibility, he devoted his attention to children of the middle years. Many of the problems which beset the era of Dan McCarthy continued to plague the efforts of Kennedy and his associates. By this time studio space was becoming increasingly difficult to obtain even in the regions, and in a case like the program Pencil Box, designed to foster creative expression in writing from young people, the cost of its production and the demands on studios in Ottawa, its point of origination, became so great that Ottawa was unable to continue with the production without help from the network office. This the network refused to do, because its budget was already committed to other major program areas. The same phenomenon began to develop in other parts of the country as well, forcing even further the production of children's programming on film, acquisitions from abroad, and limitations on the expansion of the schedule.

In 1978 Dodie Robb was appointed head. She took over the position knowing full well that good intentions were continually nursed during the quarter-century of children's television, but that at no time was there any assurance of funds to achieve a level of excellence in production over an extended period. During the seventies, budget cuts became more severe. Faced with such restraints, Dodi Robb took a bold decision: to give up the regular daily period at 4:30 p.m. and devote most of her available funds to an hour-long weekly drama, Saturdays at 12 noon. The dramas were scheduled two to three weeks apart, depending on the production schedule, alternating with outstanding films produced by the Children's Film Foundation in Britain, Walt Disney and others. The series was entitled W.O.W. (Wonderful One-of-a-kind Weekend show). The shows were produced on location across Canada, on film and in studio when available. The series included original dramas such as The Popcorn Man by Pat Patterson and produced by Bob Gibbons, The Stowaway by Gordon Ruttan and produced by Denis Hargrave, an original opera, Chip and His Dog, by Gian Carlo Menotti, produced by Stan Swan, and a special: Sharon, Lois, and Bram Downtown.

Later, Dodie Robb was able to recover the 4:30 period, but by this time she had been asked to take on other responsibilities within the CBC. In 1981 she was succeeded by Nada Harcourt.

At this juncture another change had taken place in policy for the CBC as a whole, owing to the implementation of the Applebaum-Hébert Report, where a heavy emphasis had been placed upon the development of individual producers and creative artists. To implement this policy, the federal government created the Canadian Film Development Corporation as an instrument for the funding of artists.

The Minister of Communications placed some $35 million at the disposal of the Canadian Film Development Corporation for a new enterprise known as the Canadian Broadcast Program Development Fund. Within five years, the fund will rise to $60,000,000. The purpose of the fund is to encourage private or independent film producers to undertake production in the areas of drama, light entertainment and children's programs. Up to half of the money is to go for productions in the CBC network and the remainder for productions on independent networks. Grants are made to independent producers on a matching fund basis (producers 2/3, CFDC 1/3) and grants will be made only when the networks have agreed to schedule the programs.

The purpose of the fund is to stimulate creative endeavor among Canada's film producers and to increase the volume of Canadian productions seen on television and in the cinemas of Canada. The purpose is a noble one indeed, and the government of Canada is to be praised for its gesture. My concern is that there is no coordinated focus or policy to guide film and television producers in the kind of programming needed for young people. I have the same concern about the well-meaning intentions of those who see a children's channel as the panacea for the shortage of good television programming for children. Unless careful research is undertaken to assess the needs of children and unless a team of thoughtful, creative producers work together in developing a comprehensive policy to shape a schedule of programs which will meet the needs of young viewers, I am concerned that much creative effort supported by the Fund will not have a significant impact on the available audience of young Canadians.

There is a crying need for a recognized national public agency to represent writers, producers, parents and professionals who are concerned with children's media needs. Presently several organizations aim to meet these needs from different perspectives.

Nada Harcourt quickly seized upon the policy and proceeded to develop a schedule of programs which were to be funded by the Film Development Corporation. This meant that internal development of programming in the fashion of the fifties and sixties, and to some extent the seventies, was almost completely abandoned. To be sure, programs like Mr. Dressup and The Friendly Giant continued, along with Sesame Street, but to all practical purposes the schedule of programs was made up of productions done outside the Corporation but under the Corporation's seal of approval.

In 1984 the work which Nada Harcourt had done with independent production achieved considerable momentum, and she left the children's department to take on full responsibility for independent productions in the drama department. The dramas which had been produced for children continued under her supervision.

In the meantime, the Corporation reappointed Ms. Dodie Robb to fill in for one year prior to her retirement, thus giving themselves a longer period of time to choose a successor. Within this short term, Dodie Robb turned her attention to the needs of the pre-school group. She introduced the Owl TV show and the versatile talents of Sharon, Lois, and Bram described elsewhere in this work. In addition, she introduced the Fred Penner show and a new science program, Wonderstruck. Basically, her concern was with the growth and development of children and she used the talents of new and vital performers who had a special interest in these areas.

In 1985, Dodie Robb retired and was succeeded by Angela Bruce, who set about reshaping the policy for program development in the context of the now powerful Canadian Broadcast Program Development Fund. At the same time, a new challenge was presented in the recommendations of the Caplan-Sauvageau Report, which had major implications for broadcast programming across Canada.

The reader will have observed that most of the

programming developed, particularly at the CBC, in the past thirty years has taken place in the context of well-defined departmental enterprises--drama, variety, children's, sports, news, etc. Each of these departments over the years developed a staff of producers and program planners who worked closely in the development of policies which shaped the nature of the programs produced. There is little question that such a strategy was successful for many years. While the majority of programs produced by the CBC over the years were in-house productions, the policies developed within the several program departments served as guidelines for independent producers whom the Corporation from time to time employed for the implementation of the schedule. As time has passed, the demand for Canadian programming has increased rapidly. The cost of provision for studio programming has also increased, and a tendency developed for the Corporation to depend more fully on independent producers to meet the demands of the program schedule. At the same time, the artistic community in Canada from coast to coast had developed a keen sense of national pride and an enthusiasm for creative expression through the media that was unmatched in previous history. As might be expected, the private broadcasters had been slow to respond to the challenges presented by this new renaissance in creative programming, and, as always happens with a small country adjacent to a large one like the United States, there was a pattern of Canadians showing preference for American programs produced in Hollywood. On the other hand, the charter of the CBC was clearly to present Canadian material as far as possible. At the same time, the Corporation had to depend on commercial revenue for a good portion of its budget, and for this reason it was caught in the same bind as the private broadcasters in the pressure to provide American adult entertainment for prime-time audiences.

The Applebaum-Hébert Report on Cultural Policy made recommendations for the increased support of independent producers of programming in order to support a flourishing creative endeavor across the country. There were indications that Applebaum and Hébert were not satisfied with the way in which the Canadian Broadcasting Corporation was dealing with the renaissance in independent production. To this end, they recommended that a separate body be created, now known as the Canadian Broadcast Program Development Fund. The Canadian Broadcast Program Development Fund is administered by a board of directors of the Canadian Film Development

Corporation, in accordance with a memorandum of understanding entered into on February 21, 1983, by the Fund and the Minister of Communications. The primary purpose of the Fund was to increase the quantity of high-quality Canadian television productions in the categories of drama, Children's programming, and variety. The intention was to encourage the development of a vigorous program production industry in Canada, within the private sector, to supply programming called for in the broadcasting strategy for Canada. In the national interest, appropriate measures were taken to insure that there should be an appropriate balance for the investment of the fund across the regions of Canada. Approximately one-third of the Fund would be disbursed in the French-language television productions, and two-thirds of the Fund in English-language television productions. At least one-half of the monies from the Fund were to be applied to television productions intended to be exhibited by private over-the-air broadcasters in Canada, and up to one-half applied to productions intended to be exhibited by the Canadian Broadcasting Corporation/Société Radio-Canada.

While it was the intention to foster primarily Canadian production, the Corporation kept in mind that Canada had co-production agreements with five countries, and therefore allowed that the production of film under a co-production agreement entered into between Canada and another country would qualify for financial support from the Fund.

In making application to the Fund for money to support production, an independent producer must file a letter of intent from a television broadcaster indicating the level of its financial participation, together with its intention to schedule broadcast of the production within 24 months after the completion of production, and in accordance with the guidelines contained in the memorandum of understanding referred to above. The television broadcaster at the same time is contractually bound, through a licensing agreement to the producer, with respect to both its financial participation in the project and the intended time/date for the broadcast, before the Fund will advance any monies to the producer.

Among the criteria for approval of projects, a new thrust was indicated in the desire to have the exhibition of the programs on air between the hours of 7 p.m. and 11 p.m. While the Fund specifies particularly drama and variety programming, the CBC in particular has aimed to reach a family audience with its children's dramas, produced in cooperation with the Fund, by scheduling them in the early evening hours of prime time. It is further noteworthy that, regardless of what broadcasting organization undertakes to cooperate with the Fund and an independent producer, the project must act in conformity with the Canadian Association of Broadcasters' Code of Ethics, and other Canadian programming standards endorsed by the Canadian Radio and Television Commission, usually those dealing with the portrayal of sexual violence and sexual exploitation. Care was taken to ensure that monies from the Fund would be directed to new productions and should not replace existing expenditures by broadcasters for established program commitments. A review of projects which have been approved during the past two to three years indicates that many of the programs are produced either on film or video tape, and are either stand-alone programs or series of a somewhat longer nature.

Since the creation of the Fund on July 1, 1983, more than 630 hours of production have been logged, mostly geared to prime-time audiences. By March 31, 1985, Telefilm Canada had approved of some 25 projects, with budgets totaling more than $30 million, nearly $10 million of which was supplied by Telefilm Canada. The projects funded included 19 series of various lengths and six features, ranging from 24 minutes to one at 120 minutes.

There is little doubt that the advent of Telefilm Canada has diverted large sums of money from the support of public broadcasting to the enterprise of independent production. This in itself is not necessarily a bad thing. The only problem which arises is the question of policy control. Because of the cutbacks, the staff of the CBC has been substantially reduced. Again, this may not in itself be a bad thing, but one is left with the impression that the cuts were made before the policy for leadership could be determined and effective relations established between the new enterprise of Telefilm Canada and the CBC, not to mention other broadcasting organizations. Therefore, the role of the supervisor of children's television becomes an even more significant responsibility. Confronted with proposals from a variety of independent producers, what guidelines should be employed in order to ensure diversity in the children's program schedule as well as some homogeneity in the policy which underlies the entire schedule as it is presented from year to year? Inevitably some film producers will wish to act as much as possible on their own, while others will be looking for direction from experts who know what constitutes good entertainment for children.

In the Caplan/Sauvageau Report, the section on children's programming opens with the challenging statement, "Responding to the developmental and recreational needs of young viewers has always been a difficult task." The Report sums up very succinctly the dilemma which confronts both Canadian viewers and broadcasters. To quote,

> availability is caught in a kind of three-way squeeze involving imports, commercial restraints, financial priorities of our public broadcasters. First, most of the American imports for children are cartoons, with a penchant for strident, often violent action and jingoistic values ("foreigners" are often given funny accents and treated as outsiders). Even imports such as Sesame Street have been criticized for their reliance on "jokes per minute" to transmit educational values, compared to the more serene approach of Canadian program such as Friendly Giant, Mr. Dressup, and Polka Dot Door. As far as viewing by francophone children is concerned, animated programs from Japan seem to have been gaining ground on similar material from the United States.
>
> Second, children's programming is not a reliable source of profits for broadcasters, particularly given the more or less severe restrictions placed on ads directed at children. In Quebec, provincial law prohibits broadcasters entirely from advertising to children. At the behest of the CRTC, the CBC has not allowed advertising on its children's programs since 1975, although older children are certainly a target for advertising carried on rock video shows, sitcoms, and other programs that may also be intended for older viewers. Other scheduling and demographic restrictions, including the complexities of marketing to a group which in itself has little or no discretionary income, have prompted most private broadcasters to regard children's programming as primarily a task for the public broadcaster.

> As a third and final point, however, we note that chronic shortage of funds--or other priorities--has hampered the development of children's programming in the public sector, especially at CBC. Availability by province varies considerably, with Ontario and Quebec enjoying the widest variety of programming because of the efforts of TVOntario and Radio-Quebec, in addition to CBC. The Knowledge Network (KNOW) in British Columbia and ACCESS in Alberta have even more limited resources. (Caplan/Sauvageau, pp. 109-110.)

The Report makes two other observations which are a cause for concern among those responsible for leadership in children's programming. At the outset, the researchers for the Caplan-Sauvageau Report discovered that the 6-11 age group was by far the worst served by television. There was virtually no material on the private stations addressed to this sector, leaving them only with American cartoons aimed at the 2-11 age group overall.

Another concern has to do with the fact that although the number of available hours of children's programming per week has risen from 76 in 1976 to 109.5 in 1985, new production is declining. In 1976, there were 247 hours of new programming; by 1985, the figure had dropped to 237, reflecting cutbacks at the CBC which reduced new production there from 100 hours in 1976 to 60 hours in 1985. The rise in overall hours available, therefore, indicates an increased use of repeats and materials from outside resources (Caplan/Sauvageau, p. 111).

The reduction in the amount of new production is directly linked to the cuts which have been suffered by the CBC. It would be difficult to argue that the cuts have freed money for the operation of Telefilm Canada. The fact remains that television and film production costs a great deal of money, and regardless of whether the money goes to the CBC or to Telefilm Canada, the end result is that more money is required in these times of inflation to ensure that the standard as well as the quantity of high-quality production is maintained.

As late as November 15, 1986, the Canadian Radio and Television Commission, dealing with applications for renewing licences to the Global Television Network, issued a tough decision timed to warn the CTV network of the position it was taking. The Global Network was ordered to more than double its expenditures on Canadian dramas, variety shows, musicals, children's programs, and documentaries. No escape was allowed to divert any of this commitment to the news budget, which the Network was instructed to leave at its current level.

Chapter III

THE MAJOR DAILY SHOWS

The Canadian Howdy Doody Show

The major feature of the whole period was the advent of the Canadian Howdy Doody Show. Upon my arrival at CBC in 1954, Stuart Griffiths informed me that the CBC had already made a contract (see Appendix III) to schedule the Howdy Doody Show. I felt that the American version's rather brash and aggressive format, and some of the tasteless old-time movies which were used in each day's show, left much to be desired. However, upon being assured that I could do anything I wished with the show, I set to work with Frank Fice and Clifford Braggins, whom we hired as the senior writer, to build what proved to be a long-running and successful show. Indeed, it was some time before it was generally recognized that Howdy Doody was in fact the first daily dramatic serialized show produced by the CBC. All of this was accomplished from the confined quarters of Toronto's Studio 5 which is now a local news facility.

In developing Howdy Doody we were fortunate to gather some of the finest talent available in the country. The enthusiasm and imagination of Frank Fice, with his dry wit and good judgment, gave a stable base for the development of the show itself. He was ably assisted by Cliff Braggins, the senior writer and composer who devised the script outlines, wrote most of the scripts and most of the music.

The other main writer was the late John Gerrard, whom Braggins acknowledges as the great character-maker for the show. He comments that he himself tended to write his script and plots around Flubadub, while John Gerrard wrote for Dilly Dally, the lovely, pathetic and vulnerable puppet child, along

Howdy Doody

with Willow, the playful witch. Gerrard was greatly admired as a sensitive and talented writer.

They were in turn ably assisted by the great Quentin Maclean as the resident organist in Doodyville, a most inventive and inspired genius with a capacity for innovation that would never again be matched. Braggins gives great credit to Quentin Maclean for having taught him so much about composition. On one occasion, Braggins reports that he tried to trick Quentin by composing a song in seven flats; when the show came, Quentin not only performed it with great facility, but added a fugue as well. When Braggins asked him how he did it, he simply replied, "When I see seven flats, I just think in terms of playing a bassoon and carry on." There were endless tales about his versatility. One day the stage hands had accidentally placed the celeste on the wrong side of the organ. Throughout the half-hour of the show, Quentin simply crossed his hands and kept on going--nothing could really shake his professional calm when it came to invention.

The other regulars on the show were the infinitely patient and talented Hal and Renee Marquette, who were responsible for the puppets; Larry Mann as Captain Scuttlebutt; Alfie Scopp as Clarabelle, and above all, Peter Mews as the host of the show. Alfie Scopp as Clarabelle, Barbara Hamilton as Willow and Drew Thompson as Mendel Mantelpiece Mason, along with Larry Mann as Captain Scuttlebutt, provided much of the show's comedy and fun.

The _Howdy Doody Show_ had its own share of distinguished actors who have made their mark upon the world since the early days of television. The first Timber Tom was William Shatner, the Captain Kirk of _Star Trek_. He had taken the role of Ranger Bob to replace Timber Tom since Peter Mews was unable to arrive for the opening of the show on November 15th, 1954, owing to previous commitments with _Spring Thaw_.

Originally James Doohan had been chosen to play the role of Timber Tom, but he turned it down, partly because he did not wish to commit himself for what appeared to be a long run, and partly because he had asked for more than scale salary, which the producer at that time refused to consider.

Occasionally Robert Goulet replaced Peter Mews in the

Peter Mews as Timber Tom with Howdy Doody in the Canadian Howdy Doody Show.

role of Trapper Pierre when Mews had to be away, and Alfie Scopp had Bernard Slade as his back-up. Toby Tarnow was the alternate for Maxine Miller in the role of the Princess; she in fact was known as Pan of the Forest, discovered by Timber Tom on one occasion in the show.

John Gerrard conceived the charming character Willow, "the witch." However, she was really much more of a friendly fairy than a witch. Conceived in the pantomime tradition, she was frequently sent to fairy godmothering school because she never managed to get anything right. She perceived the role as a mixture of fun and fantasy and spent a good part of her time playing tricks on the actors. The role was first played by Eric House but Barbara Hamilton soon established the role as her own. She delighted particularly in teasing Drew Thompson in his role as the confused and somewhat wacky Mendel Mantelpiece Mason. Mendel Mason was always up in the air, teetering on the precipice of confusion, and Scopp particularly appreciated him as a foil for his mime action.

In addition to the live actors, there were the puppets. Howdy Doody was first played by Claude Rae, a role later taken over by Jackie White in order to give the character a more youthful voice. After Rae was removed from the role of Howdy Doody, he continued to play Phineas T. Bluster and other occasional puppet roles. Jack Mather contributed his skills with over 20 voices through the five and a half years of the show. On one occasion, the script writer didn't know that Mather did so many of the voices, and Jack found he was talking to himself throughout the script!

Part of the performers' talent was realized through their amazing daily interaction. Alfie Scopp as Clarabell loved the show, and was always able to combine his rascality with a high degree of intelligence and sensitivity.

The stories are infinite about the encounters of the cast with the children in the Peanut Gallery--some 30-strong every day--who appeared to witness and participate in the action of the show.

The three great musical contributors were obviously Braggins, Quentin Maclean and Maxine Miller Gerrard, who played the role of Princess Haida. She had been chosen for her unique singing voice and Braggins obviously enjoyed writing music for her to sing.

Quentin Maclean would often try to anticipate Clarabell's mime with counterpoint executed on the organ. Whenever he missed, he would say "You got me that time."

As the composer of most of the songs for the Howdy Doody Show, Cliff Braggins felt that when he was experimenting or showing off he was unable to engage their attention, but when he aimed to relate to the child as a person through the music, he succeeded. The song, "I am an ape, in pretty good shape, see how I crouch, see how I slouch, when you shake hands with me, you say outch," became an imitative game which the children enjoyed playing.

To encourage participation, Braggins conceived lyrics which depended upon simple situations in which children could readily participate. At the same time, he used the old device of double and triple rhyme as a means of achieving a certain kind of rhythm which inevitably attracted young children. An example is the song about Astronaut Homer.

> Oh say have you heard about Homer?
> They tell me he lived ... over there
> Over there where the fir trees grow sideways
> And the wind blows your hat in the air.
> Well Homer, it seems, had the kind of sweet dreams
> That could let him pretend he was many things
> Like a bird or a bee, or a horse or a tree
> Or a cowboy ... a fireman ... well anything.
>
> Chorus:
> He was Astronaut Homer
> And each night he'd roam around
> Half of the town in his wagon
> Dragging at a little dog name O'Bridget
> Who'd bark like an idiot
> Each time Homer's shout in her face
> Come on, dog! We're heading for space!

The analogy of growing up is developed in the Acorn Song. Likewise, in the Bird Song, the lyrics are intended to put children in a happy mood. It could be called a morning song. And so pro-social activity is encouraged in lyrics such as:

If you're lookin' for a cheer-up in the morning,
Every bird has got a chirrup that'll please.
Only listen to him singin' to you,
With a chirp chirp cheep cheep,
Now and then a peep peep,
Chitter-chatter-twitter in the trees,
Chitter-chatter-twitter in the trees.

In making the transition from the American show to the Canadian one, the most basic change was the substitution of Timber Tom for Buffalo Bob. Bob Smith, the emcee of the American show throughout its history, had always banked heavily on his personality to stimulate the enthusiasm of children. His warm but boisterous manner had been sustained throughout each show; his companionship with Howdy Doody was always at a boyish level and much of the fun arose from the absurdity of an adult playing in the manner of a child. In the ups and downs of their adventures, Howdy Doody was often seen to be consoling Buffalo Bob for his mistakes.

In introducing Timber Tom, we were anxious to present a mature character whose name would indicate his familiarity with Canadian folk lore and nature. He was to be a leader, both for the inhabitants of Doodyville and for his wide audience of viewers. An actor was chosen because the policy of the show was to be carried by the script rather than by the immediacy of an emcee's personality. In this way we hoped to stimulate a disciplined and creative response from the youngsters in the Peanut Gallery. It was intended that the children should respond to Timber Tom's leadership in order to develop spontaneous but ordered fun rather than rowdy or disorderly conduct.

In the early stage of the series a new character was introduced in the person of Mr. X. In order to carry out the historical and educational material, Mr. X was conceived as a classical figure of mysterious origin who was possessed of the ability to go back through history to any period of his choice. He was voiced in a rather somber and authoritative tone in order to add a certain dignity and status to his role. The character was not too successful. The desire to develop an educational theme was too self-conscious and produced an abstract and somewhat cold or forbidding character which tended to frighten rather than to entertain or to inform the children. This abstract quality was out of keeping with the warmth and charm of the rest of the characters. The formality was inconsistent with the whimsical strain of the lyrics in the songs and with the script. There were complaints from parents as well as from sponsors, so Mr. X had to be recast in order to keep the element of mystery and imagination. The script-writer therefore turned his attention to a wittier and more imaginative aspect of a character from the past. Mr. X became more of a kindly, wise old man, and less the representation of an idea. The producers were interested to see that the dramatic presentation of abstract ideas without careful attention to the ordered and creative response of the child viewer should stimulate such fear and uncertainty. The reaction of the children was natural, because they were resisting the authoritarian principle of learning, particularly when it appeared in a situation which they expected to be entertaining.

Captain Scuttlebutt was another new character introduced to the Canadian Howdy Doody Show. He was rather boisterous but nevertheless friendly, and his chief characteristic was his incongruous timidity. He was the frequent butt of Clarabell's tricks and was constantly mocked by his companion, Percival Parrot. His entrances into the Clubhouse of Doodyville were always heralded by the children singing the sea shanty, "Blow the Man Down." Larry Mann, who performed the role, used sea jargon, wore the costume of an 18th-century pirate, and generally appeared as a buffoon, much to the delight of the children in the Peanut Gallery. His role was really that of a talking clown, a role that provided frequent sources of comedy as he was the foil for Clarabell.

As part of the attempt to build up the character of Timber Tom as a leader and as a source of reliable information, the content of the film clips in the show was changed. The old-time movies were replaced by nature and travel film clips--a recent UNESCO report on the child film audience had revealed that travel and nature films were by far the most popular among children. Judging from the response of the youngsters in the Peanut Gallery, this theory was confirmed. Instead of trying to maintain the pace of the show with the old-time movies, the travel and nature films were intended to change the pace and relax the viewers. We were fortunate to acquire the rights to the large library of films in this category from the Encyclopaedia Britannica Corporation. We assumed that the youngsters had a keen enthusiasm for knowledge, and we further believed that there was no better time

Alfie Scopp as Clarabell the Clown in the Howdy Doody Show. (Courtesy of the CBC)

to capture their attention than when their sense of pleasure and fun had already been stirred.

As in the NBC show, these film clips were run without sound track and were accompanied by a commentary from Timber Tom or one of the other characters, along with musical accompaniment by the organist. The children in the Peanut Gallery frequently asked Timber Tom interesting questions and expressed their enthusiasm for the educational films.

In the script, any specific separation of education and entertainment was avoided. It had been assumed that if the show stimulated an ordered response from children, it would not be contrary to any educational principle. As previously noted, care has to be taken with the casting in order to ensure that the actors are disciplined and artistic in their performance.

The films were essentially educational. From time to time, interesting factual material could be presented through the medium of characters like the Princess for Indian lore, Timber Tom for nature lore, or Mr. X for historical lore. We hoped that the esthetic integrity of the script and of the performances would be sufficient to stimulate expression among children and to create enthusiasm for knowledge in an entertaining manner.

The didactic element was only rarely admitted to the script. In cooperation with the Canadian Highway Safety Conference, the producers of the Canadian Howdy-Doody Show developed a coloring and cut-out booklet concerning the rules of traffic safety for young children, entitled Follow the Rule. It was believed that a response of creative rather than conforming activity was best for children. Therefore no attempt was made to emphasize the conventional conduct of adults, such as one saw in the NBC show from time to time. The objective was to stimulate spontaneous laughter from comic situations--effectively mimed by Clarabell--or from the whimsical naivete of Dilly Dally. If the child's responses are spontaneous and if his joy arises from the esthetic order of a witty script, a more basic foundation for moral conduct is being established than can be achieved by didactic indoctrination. A child is not essentially educated by moralistic slogans. His true place in society will be determined by the ability to handle crises in a constructive and intelligent manner. If education is effective, the customs of society will become a part of his life because they have become meaningful for him and because they are the result of a creative response to life situations--not because they are the conventional way of doing things among most people.

The ultimate objective of the Canadian Howdy Doody Show was to create a child's world in which joy was the central theme. The antics of Clarabell the Clown may be absurd to an adult, but his art of gesture was an authentic discipline of which many an adult actor should be envious. The simplicity and immediacy with which the emotions of joy and sorrow are expressed are most meaningful to a child. The simple dignity and sincerity of Timber Tom's commentary on the nature films readily invited responses from the youngsters in the Peanut Gallery. Above all, the script writer was constantly aware of the need for a constructive element in the plot. The young viewers responded enthusiastically to the serial element in the story as they anticipated the development of the plot from day to day. But we avoided creating tension or anxiety. The character of Phineas T. Bluster was changed from a dominant hostile character to a garrulous and whimsical crank whose chief characteristic was his unpredictability.

Correspondence from the youngsters indicated that a genuinely entertaining format had been accomplished and that a world of fantasy had been successfully created.

At this early stage in the development of children's television the Children's Television Department had already learned that the program need not be pleasing to an adult in order to be entertaining and instructive for a child. If such simple devices as repetition and action have a fundamental appeal for children, may not those same principles be employed in the communication of educational elements in every other kind of program?

The Canadian Howdy Doody Show ran five days a week for over five years. During this time young Canadians had the privilege of being entertained by a large group of well-known and very talented performers and writers.

Howdy Doody was finally withdrawn from the schedule to make way for new ideas in daily programming for children. The demands of a daily dramatic series were taking their toll on the creative energy of the directors and production staff. As we became more sophisticated in the proper use of television facilities, the limitations of the small studio from which Howdy Doody had been produced since 1954 became more and more obvious. Several of us became uncomfortable with the dependence on a program format which had originated in the U.S. The initial rationale for its adoption--its viability as a vehicle for commercial messages for children--had long since vanished.

When the contract with NBC and the Kagran Corporation was made, it had been thought that the commercial side of the show would be useful revenue for the CBC. In the beginning we were fortunate indeed to attract a fair number of sponsors for whom live commercial messages were produced by Rena Elmer, who worked closely with the show. As the supervisor, it was my task to see that the content of the commercial messages was acceptable by normal standards of good taste and not offensive to parents. We had remarkable cooperation from the advertising agencies, who gave very generously of their time to ensure that the commercial messages were properly conceived and integrated into the plot of the show. The whole enterprise collapsed within a few months when it became obvious, first, that it was much cheaper to bring in filmed commercial messages from sponsors' parent companies in the United States, and second, that audiences for family shows were much larger.

The other complication was the fact that in the United States, merchandising of various toys, hats, replicas of puppets, etc., had become a thriving business for NBC and the Kagran Corporation. By statute the CBC itself was not in the business of merchandising, but it became clear that such merchandising was necessary to extend the popularity of the show and especially its attractiveness to would-be commercial sponsors. In the long run the show continued without commercial messages and made its own contribution by the unique talent of the writers, the production staff and the performers.

As the network of CBC-owned and -operated stations expanded across the country, creative personnel in these stations wanted opportunities to develop programming for the schedule.

Whistletown

The decision to terminate the *Howdy Doody Show* in no way reflected upon the quality of the direction or of the writers and performers, who continued to do a dynamic professional job. In order to explore new directions for a daily program format, we reduced *Howdy Doody* to three days a week (Monday, Wednesday and Friday), and on Tuesday and Thursday we introduced a new show called *Whistletown* which originated with producer John L. Kennedy. Along the main street of Whistletown there was a firehall, a toyshop, the city hall, etc. Action would originate from one or other of these locations each day. Jean Cavall played the mayor, with Ross Snetsinger as the handyman in the Firehall, assistant to fire chief Joe Austin. The Keoghs provided Foster as a puppet who lived in the toyshop and Rex Hagon played himself.

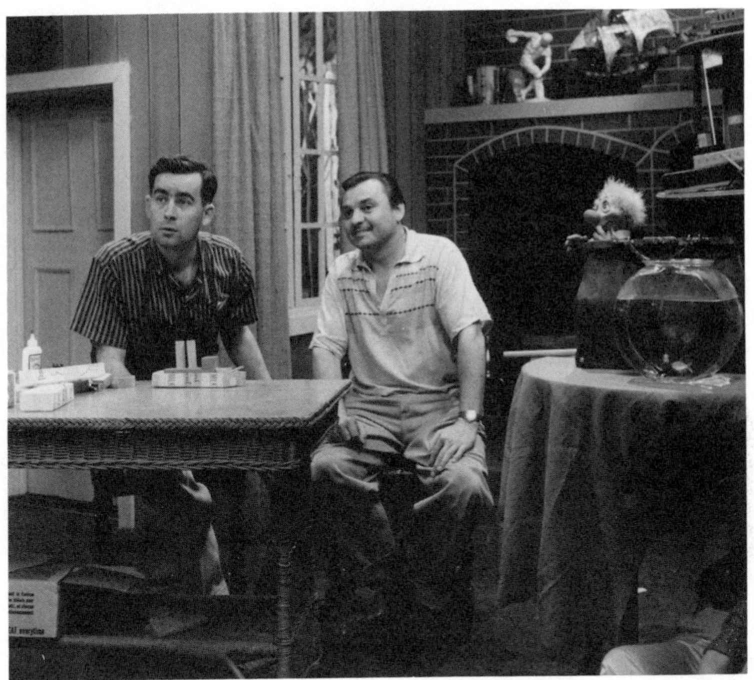

Ross Snetsinger and Jean Cavall in Whistletown.

Junior Roundup

After one year of alternating Whistletown with Howdy Doody, we developed a network show, Junior Roundup, to meet the challenge of network contributions from stations across the country. Producer William Davidson was in charge of the project, which began in January 1961. Murray Westgate was chosen as the main host to link up the network stations. Dave Broadfoot and Jean Templeton served as hosts for Monday's contribution from Toronto. On this occasion a range of variety acts was performed before an audience. On other occasions, Paul Rockett was featured with his skills in photography, Harry Freedman in music, Percy Saltzman on weather and Eric Aldwinckle as master craftsman and artist. The show varied in length from 30 to 60 minutes and included Vancouver's weekly drama, Tidewater Tramp. At the end of six months Roundup Goes Camping became a summer replacement with the regulars from Junior Roundup. During this nine-month period, Davidson mastered a variety of camera techniques and developed an awareness of visual continuity which proved to be invaluable in the advent of Razzle Dazzle.

Razzle Dazzle

By this time it was generally agreed that the climate of TV viewing among young people was changing. As techniques of production improved and audiences became more aware of pacing and timing, the pace of TV viewing stepped up. Davidson, with the help of Sandy Stewart and Francis Chapman, along with writers Cliff Braggins, Ron Krantz and Michael Spivak, set out to create a variety show for young people aged seven and over. The show was to have network appeal with humor, original music and good fun. Like Howdy Doody, Razzle Dazzle was a daily (5:00 p.m., EST) live half-hour English network television program designed to entertain and enlighten "kids and turtles." By the middle of its third year Razzle Dazzle was being viewed and cheered by youngsters from coast to coast. Audience estimates put its daily average of young viewers at over half a million. Eventually over 100,000 children had joined the Razzle Dazzle Club.

Newspapers and magazines such as Liberty and The Star Weekly did cover stories on the show and its stars. Stemming from the program's success and her part in it, Michelle Finney made numerous personal appearances in several provinces and eventually had her own fan club. Razzle Dazzle also received a Liberty award from the hand of Ed Sullivan for being the best children's program in Canada in 1962-63.

Razzle Dazzle was launched in the 1961 fall schedule through a combination of top professional talent, a three-week period of brainstorming and pressure cooker creativity, and a conviction that the CBC could produce a program so solidly entertaining that the kids of Canada would turn forever from rival station programming featuring corny Captain What's-His-Name and his storehouse of third-rate cartoons.

Davidson and his team knew that to win viewer loyalty the new daily 5:00 p.m. show had to have pacing. It had to have a number of attractive ingredients whose action would compel interest. It especially had to have a name that said this was a program that would stand apart from anything that

Al Hamel, Howard the Turtle, and Michelle Finney in Razzle Dazzle.

had gone before. So Razzle Dazzle was chosen as the title which would best reflect the entertainment provided.

With the title established, the team next went to the drawing boards to give shape to the program's central characters. This was to be a program with genuine "stars" as its focal point. It was soon agreed upon that the "stars" would be a boy, a girl, and a big brother.

The boy was seen as a pesty young brother, the kind who loves puns and "corny" jokes; who always has something to say and says it. As the character began to evolve in his creators' minds, the reservation about actually having a boy play the role also grew. The question was asked: wouldn't something between Bugs Bunny and Charlie McCarthy have much more range for expression than a character built on a living boy? The answer was a resounding "Yes"!

Animals have for generations played starring roles in elements of our popular culture. A list of the most famous would have to include Winnie the Pooh, from the story-book world; Krazy Kat and Pogo (the possum), his spiritual descendant in today's comic strip; Rin-Tin-Tin and his latterday counterpart of the movies and TV, Lassie. No list would be complete, of course, without Mickey Mouse, who will celebrate his fiftieth birthday next year and who, with his friends Donald Duck, Bambi, and countless others, have made fame and fortune for their creator, Walt Disney. With this standard of success among his forebears in the "show biz" branch of the animal kingdom, it's no wonder that an animal character became a star in Canadian television.

Howard was the first name hit upon for what was seen as a puppet. Since they wanted a rather stationary character to balance the action of the two other personalities, Howard became a turtle. John Keogh created Howard's lively face and head and the special effects department built his shell. Keogh, of course, was the creator of Howard's voice and personality. A star was born.

For the girl and her older brother, Davidson turned to eleven-year-old actress and model Michele Finney, and Al Hamel, a handsome young announcer-performer recently arrived from CBC Windsor. Davidson had seen both perform on segments of Junior Roundup and felt they had the ability and vitality to maintain the pace of a daily live action show for kids. Michele's role was to be that of a bright and cheerful sister in her early teens. Al was to be an older brother giving freely and gently of his time, advice and leadership.

With the performing "stars" selected, the Davidson team turned to establishing a locale for Razzle Dazzle. The underlying idea here was that great things were going to happen on this show, and they needed a congenial environment. The "alley" became the place where the Razzle Dazzle characters and the kids of Canada were invited to meet every weekday at 5:00 p.m.

Then, like a chef mixing a great salad, the many and varied elements that have made Razzle Dazzle so outstanding were added to the show. Here Davidson wanted two major ingredients--entertaining action and audience involvement. The latter meant providing opportunities for young people to relate directly to what was done on the show. It was a bold experiment but it paid great dividends, even if the avalanche of mail it brought nearly threw the program staff off balance.

The children of Canada were asked to join the Razzle Dazzle Club. To keep the chain of membership going, if a boy or girl sent in the name of a friend, the latter was mailed a form letter which mentioned this fact. An application blank (with a request for a photograph) was enclosed along with a pin, a copy of the Razzle Dazzle Daily giving lots of detail about the cast and the program, a printed maze game and a decoder wheel. Twice a week, Howard gave coded messages which were to be decoded with the decoder wheel. The Trans-Canada Telequiz--always the first item after the opening --encouraged children in different parts of the country to compete by telephone. Two players were selected each week. Twelve questions were prepared: two questions for each player on Monday, Wednesday and Friday. The youngster was telephoned and, having been warned that he may not use help, was allowed to choose his question. A point was given for each question answered correctly and at the end of the week the participant was given a prize, usually a book, according to the number of points made. While the telephone exchange was taking place, the participant's picture was shown on the screen.

The audience was asked to contribute to the show by sending in riddles, "groaners" (corny jokes), stories, drawings, news items, comic sketches and plays. There was also a studio audience of about fifty with whom the cast interacted. As much as one-third of the program content was provided by the members of the Razzle Dazzle Club. In all these participatory activities, the individual worth of every contributing member was acknowledged. Mail response was high, often reaching as many as nine bags of letters each week.

Attempts are frequently made to use clubs and contests on television without notable success. Clubs emerge as a natural phenomenon in the 10-12 age group. They signify a desire for greater structure in relationships, a cognizance of differences in role (one plays halfback or lineman, not just football) and a realization that there are rules or codes to govern behavior which are not changeable at the whim of the player. So children create clubs, often short-lived but nevertheless momentarily functional. Clubs associated with TV programs are likely to fail because they serve no function in the child's life--they add nothing to his social relationships or interaction with his friends. Often their basic intent is exploitative rather than contributory. The Razzle Dazzle Club invited children to participate in, contribute to and appear on the program, all across the country. A viewer gained a feeling of membership with others, akin to adult membership in professional or trade organizations. More importantly, there was the opportunity to contribute, whether with jokes, skits, news items or something else, and the satisfaction to be derived from having something accepted for the program. In the contest, competence was rewarded--a prize was given for how well one did, not solely for winning.

As often as the budget would allow, the production staff produced on newsprint copies of the Razzle Dazzle News, labeled as a "Special Edition," which was sent out to members of the Razzle Dazzle Club. Examples of questions which might occur on the Trans-Canada Telequiz were presented, and members often wrote in with copies of their riddles, "groaners," stories, and drawings, which served as models for other members and encouraged wider participation. There is little doubt that the use of printed materials of this sort gave encouragement to participation and tended to increase the size of the audience for the show. Perhaps its most significant factor, as was the case with the Howdy Doody Show, was its daily occurrence with a cast of familiar characters to whom the children could relate. Great care was taken to make sure that relationships among the characters, as well as their invited responses from the audience, were of a positive and pro-social nature. This did not mean that the show was in any way preachy, its prominent feature being the fun and amusement it gave to young viewers and in which they themselves felt they were playing a significant part.

Children's games and contests frequently reflect a jumbled set of adult values in that they overlook the satisfaction to be had in making or doing something successfully. A contrasting situation prevailed in Razzle Dazzle. For example, a studio Christmas tree was decorated entirely with home-made decorations, permitting each child to perform at his best. A contest for the best ornament was considered to be unjust because of inequalities in age and skill. Adults persist in the illusion that adult life is competitive (it may still be for the salesman and the small shopkeeper) and they persistently use this as the appropriate model for children's activities. They fail to see that adults can at least choose their field of competition, which equalizes opportunity. Ample competition is provided for children every day in school. There is no reason to insist that it is a necessary element of fun, which is one thing television is trying to provide. Further, contests should be organized so that children are encouraged to try to do their best.

Ideally, also, studio contests should reward demonstrated competence, not chance, as is often the case. Chance can be reserved for Queen for a Day, where the disproportionate prizes provide viewers with joyous escape from the monotony of life. It is too often assumed that children's contests should parallel those of adults, with absurd contests or games such as wall-paper pasting and balloon popping chosen on the vague notion that excitement is essential, and jazzed up with expensive prizes adding nothing to a child's sense of values.

In addition, the production staff were passionately committed to the ideals of the show. The combination of meaningful audience participation along with the commitment of the staff gave great strength to the whole enterprise.

On the action side of the program, Davidson's team devised a wide range of characters whose activities covered puppetry, dance, magic, straight comedy from the regulars, slapstick skits by the Turtleshell Players, and other satirical skits involving stereotyped characters and parodies of adult behavior. The characters portrayed were executed by veteran performers: Mr. Sharpy (Paul Kligman); Ace Baker (Don Baker, who also wrote many of the shows later in the series); Sherlock House (Drew Thompson, who also played Mendel Meek, the milktoast neighbor who could unknowingly be quite heroic); Hiram Corntassel (Jack Mather); Mr. I-Got-It (Joe Austin); and Percy Kidpester (Ed McNamara), an exaggeration of the adult fault-finder! In addition, Michael Roth, with his magic and his impersonations, often contributed to the hijinks in the Razzle Dazzle Alley.

The production staff were always conscious of the need to sustain the continuity at a significant level of pace and interest. Recognizing the difficulty of achieving real humor, they often deliberately resorted to farce. "Groaners" were just that--corny jokes. Nutty Newsreels consisted of old newsreel excerpts taken from the stock-shot library and given a turn of the absurd.

Added to this were the puppets of John and Linda Keogh, cartoon stories with George Feyer, the Razzle Riddle, Turtleshell Theatre Players, Trans-Canada Telequiz, Ace Baker's Field Days and the daily adventures of The Terrible Ten. This last feature was a serial-type adventure made in Australia which used children in all the key roles. During one week an episode would be completed by screening about five minutes each day of the adventures of the horse-riding kids from "down under." Later, The Terrible Ten gave way to the Canadian adventures of The Forest Rangers. This series, produced by Associated Production Incorporated in association with the CBC, proved so successful in the Razzle Dazzle format that it was given an additional unsegmented run on Saturdays. Al Hamel introduced the Saturday show titled Razzle Dazzle with the Forest Rangers.

The Davidson group was also intent on giving satire a regular place in the show. They believed children could understand, enjoy and learn from satirical reflections on our daily world. Thus the Kooky Commercials found a regular place in the show. These take-offs on actual television commercials, voiced by Al, Michelle or Howard, were often bitingly funny. (Advertising copy writers could learn a good deal from these spoofs on their "important messages.") Howard's Hit Parade from his radio station COW offered another element of satire and this time the rock-and-roll pop tunes were the target.

Razzle Dazzle was on all counts a success. It had action, fun and adventure. It involved its audience; it entertained and indirectly it instructed. It gained widespread critical recognition and a sizable, loyal audience as well. And finally, the ideas of Davidson and his staff of 1961, later augmented by the efforts of producer Francis Chapman and writer Don Baker, found fruition in an enduring entertainment vehicle for children where many earlier attempts had failed.

The series reflected a conscious decision of the Children's Department to concentrate on satisfying a child audience and to use its reactions as guidelines for program planning and development, reducing adult response to a secondary position. After early criticism by adults, the show won wide community and national support. The "kids and turtles" of Canada knew that they would not be let down.

Razzle Dazzle ran for six years. The basic cast changed only once when Ray Bellew and Trudy Young took over from Al Hamel and Michelle Finney. Writers Cliff Braggins and Ron Krantz were ably assisted and later succeeded by Michael Spivak, Don "Ace" Baker and Jerry Ross. Neil Andrews and Brian O'Leary took over direction of the show under Bill Davidson. In the last few months of the show, Bill Glenn, with assistance from Ed Mercel, succeeded Andrews and O'Leary when Andrews moved on to produce and direct Through the Eyes of Tomorrow and Time of Your Life.

Drop In

The successor to Razzle Dazzle was designed by Ray Hazzan, who came to children's television from the News Department. To develop the series, Hazzan launched a pilot series entitled Dress Rehearsal during the summer of 1970. Rex Hagon and Susan Conway were chosen as hosts, with Lynn Griffen, Nina Keogh and Jeff Cohen as alternates. The program, which became known as Drop In, lasted for four years, featuring films of adventure and exotic places. The show "drops in" on such interesting places as the Ontario Science Centre or a Nova Scotia coal mine. Material was shot or procured from every region of Canada.

Music, aiming to appeal to a wide range of tastes, played a very important part in the development of the series. There were frequent appearances by young Canadian rock groups such as Ron Nigrini's Gentle Rock Band, Copper Penny, Milestone, The System, Perth County Conspiracy and Yours Truly. At the other extreme there was music to celebrate Beethoven's 200th birthday.

In addition to a wide range of information and music, Drop In provided glimpses of history, political assessment of the opening of the Canadian West with Don Harron and Tommy Tweed impersonating such figures as Sir William Van Horne of the Canadian Pacific Railway or Donald A. Smith, the chief factor of the Hudson's Bay Company during Confederation. In a lighter vein were a comic satire on the Hudson's Bay Company, a film by Chris Chapman on the fur trade, and Gordon Lightfoot's Canadian Railroad Trilogy performed by Ron Nigrini and the Gentle Rock Band. On another occasion Drop In dealt with the fad of comic book collecting to reveal some Canadian "oldies" such as Dixon of the Mounted valiantly risking his life in the pursuit of crime; Canada's leading wartime radio comedian/amateur detective, Dizzy Don and Friends; Johnny Canuck, Canada's answer to Nazi oppression and the destroyer of Hitler's war material factories in Germany.

During the four-year run of Drop In, the series often drew an audience of more than 800,000 viewers, three-quarters of whom were under 12 years of age, the remainder being in the 12-17 age range. This is a large audience for the 4:30 p.m. period. Although the show was produced with a relatively small budget, the production team was able to save money for special events such as a film showing the building of two yachts--the Mirage and the Merrythought--which were built for the Canada Cup sailing race. The Mirage was ultimately selected to compete against the American boat Dynamite in the Canada Cup sailing race in 1972.

Another time, Vancouver producer Keith Christie produced 13 programs in Europe to report on activities of young Canadians abroad in such diverse fields as astronomy, aeronautics, ballet, sculpture, painting, music, medicine, literature, haute cuisine, and swimming. The crew once took the viewer down the Rhine and visited four young Canadian musicians studying at the Beethoven Museum in Bonn. In the mood of tourists, the crew showed the changing of the guard at Buckingham Palace.

The information in the series was diverse, carefully researched and certainly interesting to young viewers. The crew not only featured the endeavors of young people themselves but also met with Prime Minister Trudeau.

Dr. Zonk and the Zunkins and Coming Up Rosie

Concerned about the diminishing audience for the afternoon period, Don Elder as executive producer worked with Gerry O'Flannigan and Trevor Evans to devise a plan for a daily show which would provide humor and fun. They conceived the idea of a robot, Dr. Zonk, and his two computerized robot companions. The host figure was a boy, Billy Meek, with a robot (Dr. Zonk) in his bedroom. Only Billy could see the robot, but with its help and that of the two computerized robots, he could take himself anywhere to realize whatever fantasy he chose. For example, he might say, "I wish I could print money," and promptly the viewer found himself at the mint, where he gained a lesson in economics. Twenty-nine episodes were produced in a well designed, fast-paced production, somewhat in the fashion of the Rowan and Martin Laugh-In.

With the success of this first series, Evans made episode #30 as a pilot for Coming Up Rosie, which had some of the same elements as Dr. Zonk, but more plot lines were introduced. Dr. Zonk had consisted mainly of short sketches held together with documentaries. The new show introduced live characters played by members of the Second City Revue.

Rosie Teacher, a freaky blonde who has just graduated from film school, applies for a LIP (Local Initiative Project sponsored by Government of Canada) grant and is determined to make great documentaries. She rented office space in the basement of a decrepit building at 99 Sumach Street, where she meets an incredible cast of characters, other tenants of the building, with whom she has various encounters resulting in improbable situations and very funny dialogue. Among her colorful associates are Barry Baldaro as her associate Dudley Nightshade. Together they produce documentaries under the corporate name of Zonk Productions for the school board. In the process of making low-budget films, she meets Ralph Oberding, the Neva-Rust Storm Door salesman; Catherine O'Hara as Myrna Wallbacky of the Ding-A-Ling Answering Service; John Candy as Wally Wypyzychuk of Sleep-Tite Burglar Alarms and John Stocker as the elevator operator and general man-about-the-building. While the show was scripted by Barbara Evans, David Mayerovitch, David Thomas and Stuart Northey, the cast of six never failed to make the most of the situations which were improvised, often providing unscripted, refreshing dialogue.

The title of the show was conceived by Evans' wife Barbara, one of the writers. The aim was to treat children as individuals and to work towards a high standard of production which children had come to expect in watching Hollywood adult sitcoms. In conceiving the series, Evans stated that "in any comedy vehicle, there is a base ... a premise founded on sociological events or crises which are currently in people's minds." In order to bridge the gap for young viewers who might not appreciate the satire, Evans would resort to slapstick presentation, sight gags and clowning to capture their attention; e.g., as Kiddo the Clown in earlier days on CFTO, "I used to do voices that had parallels to John Diefenbaker or Lester Pearson so that adults would get the subliminal message while the kids would get pleasure from the sight gag." There was a serious side to *Rosie* because the theme was how to cope with situations; whatever the outcome, you were not a failure just because you lost.

The group with which Evans worked was a repertory company--a group of players whose interaction with one another developed mutual loyalty and respect for one another while they shared laughter, tragedy, or warm feelings. Evans claimed that he and his audience were

> constantly rewarded by one or the other giving me something that made me laugh, made me think, made me experience an emotional mood or change. And yet, I could always relate to them because they were a homogeneous group of people who constantly were interesting. That's what made *M.A.S.H.* such a success, the *Mary Tyler Moore Show*, *Hill Street Blues* and the *Second City Revue*. We can have the same job functions or roles in life in any of these situations.

> All see the problem from different points of view but through interaction young viewers learn that they can have divergent views but still work together on the same team.

Evans experimented with production and writing techniques. Whereas in Dr. Zonk and the Zonkins he had relied upon stringing together short chunks of material using pixillation techniques, in Rosie he devised sub-plots, each of which kept coming to the surface, somewhat like Joyce's juxtaposition of images as a means of reflecting interrelated patterns of life. To facilitate this style and to quicken the pace of the show, he relied on post-production techniques, optical effects, squeeze zooms, etc. Since young people are quite sophisticated about such production skills, Evans saw the show as an opportunity to introduce an audience to new and more mature situations as they grew older. In his own words,

> If I could develop within the Children's Department a repertory company of players who could then spin off, each one!, into his own show, I would develop, over a period of ten years, a following ... for stars who would move into 7:30 p.m. to 8:00 p.m. spots in Canadian show business. Nine- to ten-year-olds would still be watching the same people at 20 and so on. This would be a 30-40 year job! But how else are you going to achieve a visual culture unless you train an audience? You can't expect them to read a bottom line "super" (that isn't there!) which says, "I'm sorry, folks, that the show doesn't look as good as M.A.S.H., but we didn't have the money and we didn't get the studio we needed." So the only way ... to prove to the Corporation that you can win an audience and a loyal following ... is to give them what they want to see and expect to see. They've been trained to watch American gloss.

At the end of two years, Evans discovered that the money needed to improve the show was not forthcoming and so decided to terminate the series. ("I was not happy with leaving--it was [a decision] that I literally sweated over. It was a tremendously stressful time for me, because, as I said, it was my Camelot--a dream that could not be fulfilled beyond this point. [For this reason] I preferred to do a mercy killing of the show, since I could not obtain more funds or more adequate studio space to top myself.")

Home-Made TV

Another significant endeavor of this period was Home-made TV which featured Fred and Larry Mollin, Barry Flatman, Phil Savath of Homemade Theatre and Jed MacKay as writer. The four performers had been working together as partners for some seven years in Homemade Theatre, an acting school for children in which they taught acting and improvisation. As well, they toured Ontario schools, conducted special workshops for groups interested in theatre, and mounted live extravaganza theatre productions such as Disasterland and Babes in Lotteryland.

Fred Mollin, the youngest member of the group, composed the songs and music. For three seasons, Homemade TV provided young viewers with comedy and fun in a program series which balanced pathos, satire, macabre jokes, slapstick and some serious talk. Each episode had a theme, such as problems at a school, fear and anxiety. The shows were loosely scripted, allowing for spontaneity and the opportunity for children to participate with the regular company.

Central to each episode was The Bit Story, with comic themes such as Zombie Teachers from Outer Space or Learning to Make Your Flesh Creep, Dum Dum School, Training Elephants as Paratroopers, Auto-leo-phobia (a fear of lions eating your car!). Viewers were invited to send their own ideas for the show. In this way, the writer and producer, along with the cast, were able to keep in tune with their audience, providing them with amusing sight gags and comedy sketches. Another feature was a segment entitled Sez Me, which provided kids with a forum for their opinions. They were not only able to work out some of their fantasies or common problems but, at the same time, they were learning about theatre and about television mainly through play and social intercourse with their peers on camera or vicariously as regular viewers.

After 1978, owing to budget cuts, no further attempt was made to develop comedy or variety entertainment for children. The biggest challenge to the present day is how to respond to the immensely popular sitcoms which currently attract young viewers on both U.S. and Canadian networks. Some argue that children take on adult attitudes at an earlier age than in previous years. Desperate for revenue, the CBC schedules sitcoms in the late afternoon because such programs bring in commercial revenue. In Quebec, it is against the law to advertise on children's programs. The English service Division of CBC has voluntarily subscribed to this policy. On the other hand, the immensely popular program *Switchback*, produced locally in Vancouver and in Halifax, draws very large audiences. The policy concerning this period is under review. Should an investment be made in the development of a daily half-hour which presents a mix of information and light entertainment? Should a new sitcom, in the fashion of *The King of Kensington*, be developed to focus on contemporary young people, e.g., *Happy Days*? If revenue is not readily available, should the policy on advertising be reconsidered? In what ways could a daily show be developed which would provide attractive viewing for both French and English young Canadians?

Chapter IV

MAGAZINE PROGRAMMING AND CONTINUITY IN CHILDREN'S PROGRAMMING

From the earliest days of television, access to a wide diversity of program material on film was in constant demand. To meet the daily requirement of a film segment for the Canadian Howdy Doody Show, a contract was made with Encyclopaedia Britannica Films for the use of their library of educational shorts. Since our contract permitted unlimited use of the films selected and since the library's range of subject matters was wide, we were able to use the films in other program formats.

Regardless of the source, we had to decide how to present and sequence the films used. At the outset, we recognized that simply to edit and run one film after another to the time permitted in the schedule would not make for a creative and dynamic experience for our viewers.

The development of magazine programming and the element of continuity was a significant change from the early days when the schedule was made up of an aggregate of often unrelated short programs, many of them 15 minutes in length. We discovered that the best way to hold a children's audience in a meaningful way was to schedule a daily magazine or a special magazine program such as Junior Magazine on Sundays, into which various elements, which formerly had constituted independent programs, could now be integrated. Shows like The Howdy Doody Show, Razzle Dazzle, and Junior Magazine all represented a kind of community of young people who were friends of the viewers. In many ways, the viewers felt themselves to be members of that community. They shared information presented by role models who would be attractive to them, young people who were meaningful to them as peers, presenting content in an experiential as well as an educational way. The various elements of the programs could be juxtaposed to add variety and color to the sequence of the information. As will be seen later, the programs afforded opportunities for the members of the daily presentation to pick up ideas, experiences and events which were meaningful to our young viewers. The same community afforded an opportunity to make fun of commercial messages, of aberrations in adult behavior which were in conflict with the injunctions parents frequently imposed on children. As well, we found the way to introduce and repeat program elements which had been much appreciated by audiences in the past. On one occasion per week a serialized drama could be scheduled. There was no necessity for the young viewer to remember that on a certain day he had to be present in order to see a particular episode, because frequently the presenters talked about the serialized drama and its relationship to other elements in the program.

The ultimate significant achievement of the creative use of continuity in magazine programming was achieved in several shows for different age groups, where visual organization and the sequence of images were refined to the point of a meaningful artistic unity. In short, our objective was to provide a pleasing visual experience at the highest aesthetic level while insuring that the information and human experience were authoritative and relevant to a child's experience.

Information programming itself presented artistic challenges and redefinitions of policy. Whereas in the early days programs had been built around the care of pets, inconsequential scientific information, etc., an attempt was now made to ensure that information was relevant to the patterns of play among children and of child growth and development.

As early as 1955 we scheduled a half-hour program entitled World Passport. David Clee, a geographer by training and an educator of teachers, was employed to select the films. At first he also appeared on the program to introduce the films. Later we added a personable young teacher such as Hetty Vickers or Ken Carghill to talk with selected guests who were familiar with the environment or content of the films to be presented. Clee looked for films with visual elements that would be attractive for young viewers, and for material pertinent to their lives or to those of children (of their own age) from a different culture. David Clee, along with producers Peggy Nairn Liptrot and Joanne Hughes Soloviov, were the first to recognize the immense importance of writing creative continuity to link the film sequences. The result was the creation of a well thought out program for children instead of a mere collection of films shown without a context.

It was through Ralph Ellis that we procured the Encyclopaedia Britannica Library. From the beginning Ralph took a great interest in our policy and worked hard to find material from international sources which we could use in serialized form for shows like *Razzle Dazzle*. (He provided *The Terrific Adventures of the Terrible Ten*, and *Skippy, the Bush Kangaroo* from Australia, along with a wide assortment of animated films from countries in Eastern Europe. From Western Europe, he procured the television rights to such valuable materials as those produced by the Children's Film Foundation in England and films like *White Mane* and *The Red Balloon* by the great French producer Albert Lamorisse.)

Because of the record we established for the use of procured films, the Children's Department of the CBC was the first broadcasting authority to procure the rights to use the library of film developed by the Disney Corporation for *The Mickey Mouse Club*. The material we procured was used in *Razzle Dazzle*, *Patti's Picture House* (with Donna Miller as hostess), Cliff Braggin's *Pictures with Woofer* and *Time for Adventure*.

In the agreement negotiated with the Disney Corporation, the CBC was permitted to choose some 200 hours of film which were edited and made an integral part of the aforementioned programs. Some of the Walt Disney features from which selections were permitted included *Beaver Valley*, *Wind in the Willows*, *Treasure Island*, *Nature's Half-Acre*, *Seal Island*, *Water Birds*, *Man and the Moon*, *Man in Space*, *The Legend of Sleepy Hollow*, *The Story of Robin Hood*, *When Knighthood Was in Flower* and *Stormy the Thoroughbred*.

At a time when CBC's effort in the Children's Department was only five years old, it was very reassuring to know that an experienced producer like Disney would permit such an unprecedented arrangement. Most of all, the Children's Department would gain greatly from the association. Since the CBC unit was made up of relatively young producers, it was a significant experience for them to talk to people at the Disney studios who had spent their whole careers making motion pictures. Consider, for example, William Park, who edited the children's newsreels in The Mickey Mouse Club. He was a 63-year-old grandfather who began his career as a silent news cameraman for Pathé newsreels.

In the music department there were musicians who had spent their entire careers writing and orchestrating music for Disney films. Program planners for children were chastened to see the primary value placed upon picture-making rather than upon philosophical ideas alone.

The climax of this persistent endeavor to build effective continuity in our television schedule was reached with Junior Magazine, which began with John Clark hosting a series of films selected by David Clee. On several occasions, Patrick Watson hosted the special for Junior Magazine. The show actually began as Children's Magazine at 5:00 p.m. on Sept. 25, 1955. By Dec. 4 we had moved the show to 2:00 p.m. and changed the title to Junior Magazine. After the experience with World Passport and the earlier version of Junior Magazine, we had become more confident in our ability to deal with devices for good program development and continuity. The term "continuity" is mostly used to describe the writing done in advertising agencies for commercial messages. In the early days of the Canadian Howdy Doody Show, we were concerned with such a definition as we exercised quality control over the content and presentation of these items. But we were also concerned that the flow of the daily show should not be radically disturbed by the introduction of commercials.

And so, over several years, we spent a great deal of time making our writers and producers aware of the importance of continuity. It was often as important or more so than some of the program content itself. In the words of one of the most gifted writers in the early days of children's television, Clifford Braggins, "a good continuity device is a method of providing logical, informative and involving introductions to and linkages between sometimes completely disparate islands of content."

In response to the challenge of presenting the film material from the Disney library, as well as from other sources,

Braggins devised a series entitled Patty's Picture House, with Donna Miller to sing original songs which Braggins composed. She interacted with Woofer, a large glove-puppet dog. Woofer was interested in everything. As Braggins describes him, he "devours the facts but always has some surprising interpretations of his own.... Woofer plays the part of the child's child." He is someone to love, to protect, to feel just a little superior to. And, in feeling that superiority, the child watching at home is often compelled to correct "a Woofer error" or to be amazed at Woofer's inability to understand some concept or other. Thus the child is drawn towards creative thought and activity of his own. Joanne Soloviov later demonstrated her skills in the art of continuity with Sing Ring Around and Time of Your Life, as she had done with Hidden Pages and Junior Magazine.

Another example of continuity in the use of film in television was Passport to Adventure, produced by Doug Davidson and John Twomey, with Elwy Yost presenting great films of the past. Each day a segment of the movie would be presented with information about the background of the film and the artistry of its direction. Elwy Yost moved on to TV Ontario where he modified the format into Magic Shadows and Saturday Night at the Movies.

The late Bruce Attridge* gave the show its shape and it eventually became the centerpiece of our achievement. Concerning his role in the development of the show, he says:

> The only studio available was a small two-camera studio. It had restricted lighting facilities; no on-camera rehearsal could be provided before the day of the show. Dry rehearsal could be arranged for Saturday afternoon and technical crews could be scheduled for 7 o'clock on Sunday morning. What this meant was that a live hour program sent to the network would have to be put on camera in slightly fewer than five hours.

---

*This excerpt from the interview with Bruce Attridge took place in Coquitlam, B.C. on Dec. 5, 1982. Attridge died on Dec. 19, 1982. The quotation reflects and commemorates his sensitive genius.

I then asked the Supervising Producer for departmental meetings to consider the information we had. The first question to be answered was whether an hour's show could be produced live under the known limitations of space, cameras and rehearsal time. There was a consensus that a calculated risk should be taken in view of the opportunity to program for a national audience at the time when many families could be assumed to be at home.

At this stage of the planning the Department, acting as a group, was most effective. Up to this point, the Children's Department in Toronto had been programming for younger children, but not specifically for a youth audience. This was an audience that seemed to me to have a potential to grow from the center out, attracting other family members. The vital question, of course, was whether the middle years of childhood was a sufficiently homogeneous and important an audience to demand an independent format and special production techniques.

Some early research which had been done in the United States, plus information supplied by the CBC's research and statistics group, indicated that there was a core of such an audience. American networks had, however, scheduled only action/motion stylized drama--for example, the western. There was agreement in the Department that stylized adventure was not a sufficient basis for our audience. A root cause for rejecting such formats was that they provided a disastrously narrow range of information and emotional experience. Priority should be given, it was thought, to a variety of emotional and informational experiences, in the performing arts and in the sciences, as basic human and democratic values.

My summary of the policy objectives involved (a) to create some significant understanding and regard for the world community of the young and their various ways of life; (b) to create a balanced hospitality in the young for the impact of science and technology on our society; and (c) to bring to our cameras young people who had already developed demonstrable skills in science and in the performing arts, and who could demonstrate enthusiasm and zest for life's experiences.

Planning then moved to specifics. The production decisions taken at that time are now well understood;

they were not standard at that time. Information specialists with telecast experience were contracted to prepare research and presentation materials in the natural and physical sciences, athletics, music and dance. The tight on-camera rehearsal time dictated that three segments of the show at least be on film. Some film production was begun within the CBC film unit. In addition, an independent commercial Toronto film company (Chetwynd Films, Ltd.) was contracted to begin the first of several series of six- to seven-minute open-ended films for insertion into the program itself.

Young people were used as performers in these films. They were shown in a variety of situations at work and at play, to fit in with our policy. A film researcher was contracted to screen from existing commercial film libraries high quality film that could be cleared for television. The focus in these films was the lifestyle of young people around the world.

The type of studio design chosen should perhaps be called studio background, as opposed to set design. The basic intention was to use virtually all of the studio space for camera movement. The stylized studio background was intended to look like a studio, rather than a room or place. The design organized and defined space for camera shooting and achieved atmosphere with textural and lighting interest.

Permission was sought and obtained from the Musicians' Union to use commercially recorded music as background for choreographed segments. A choreographer was contracted to create two or three dances or other choreographed movement for each show, using young professional dancers. These segments were normally 3-1/2 to 4 minutes in length. They were attractive in themselves, but they were also useful in providing a change of pace and mood. They also cut down on verbal communication.

The scripts were kept to a minimum; their chief purpose was to bridge segments where visual cues needed support. The moderator was encouraged to be relaxed, to speak the King's English, and to show genuine interest in the events and people of the show.

As the program went into its second year, it moved into a three-camera studio. Plans were then begun for specials. The first was scheduled on United

> Nations Day and was built upon Hindemith's opera *Let's Build a Town*. The symbolism of building a town from the ground up was extended to building and mutual caring purposes of the United Nations. Shortly after, with a related purpose in mind, I produced a 20-minute film observing the anniversary of the International Declaration of the Rights of Man. The visual material was taken from the famous collection of photographs, *The Family of Man*. Film/camera/ movement supported only by music focused on the twin rhythms of work and play, a strong theme in the collection. This film is now on file with UNESCO in New York and Paris.
>
> Further developments in music specials came with the formation of the CBC Youth Choir, directed by Elmer Iseler. Mario Bernardi brought together and conducted the small but balanced orchestra.
>
> The program ran for several years. At intervals the CBC Division of Research and Statistics confirmed that the audience was indeed composite and had kept its core audiences of youth and family viewers. (Interview with author, 05/12/82.)

The production team included the host John Clark, a film director, Patricia Latham, research, Rose Wilcox, continuity writer Joanne Soloviov, Hank Hedges as science editor, and Doug Maxwell for sports and recreation. In cooperation with Hank Hedges, Fred Sullivan, the well-known senior Special Effects man, adapted a prism for the television camera lens which made it possible--for the first time in the history of television technology--to project the image of a tiny organism through a microscope onto the screen. Other specialists were called in for special information segments. David Clee continued to select the films. His careful research into procurement of film was matched by Patricia Latham, who not only prepared documentary films for the production but also used her skills as a writer to devise original dramas and to do her stint as a continuity writer. We had the benefit of her many years of training and experience under the late Mary Field, Director of the Children's Film Foundation of Great Britain.

Junior Magazine became a medium of presentation for artists who achieved fame in their own right. Roberta Maxwell served as a co-host with John Clark from time to time and performed the dance shot in silhouette at the opening of the show. Teresa Stratas made her debut on *Junior Magazine*. Louis Applebaum was our music consultant; Fred Rogers and Bob Homme both made their first appearances at CBC on *Junior Magazine*.

By 1962, there was a general feeling that a Sunday show for youth should be more topical. The format of *Junior Magazine* was changed to *Time of Your Life*. This new show was to reflect the ideas and interests of young people in their early teens. Based on modified formative research (full facilities were not available to us at that time), the show dealt with young achievers, young people's social problems, physical activities and cultural interests. Dramas written by teenagers were staged every third week; e.g., Norman Skolnick's *The Sewer* and *Ants Don't Leave Footprints*. Bill Davidson designed the format with Sandy Stewart as director. The show was hosted by Peter Kastner and Michelle Finney.

Upon the departure of Bill Davidson, Perry Rosemond was given responsibility for the youth show. He modified the show to a more visionary concept embodied in the title *Through the Eyes of Tomorrow*. Perry was producer, with Neil Andrews and Herb Roland as directors. Joanne Soloviov served as continuity writer and worked with the young people on the show. The hosts for the show were teen-agers Brant Frayne, Carol Hunter, Wayne Thompson and Paul Saltzman. The format shifted from a somewhat self-centered, confrontational approach to a more inquiring and investigative thrust--e.g., a behind-the-scenes look at the recording industry, an interview with Buckminster Fuller, etc. In planning the show, Rosemond was always motivated by the conviction that young people really are interested in information when it is meaningfully presented. A good programmer "is always waiting for the world to tell its story." Since he had chosen them carefully, he would let the young people on the show decide who should appear; by trusting them he was able to bring out the best in them. In this spirit, the team once asked Chester Ronning, the great Canadian specialist in Oriental history, to comment on film footage of the Vietnam War as seen from the North and some from the South. They tackled problems such as the use of LSD, the razing of Africkville (the black ghetto in Halifax), and the Separatiste movement in Quebec. Visually, *Through the Eyes of Tomorrow* differed radically from *Time of Your Life* in the latter was situated in a "place" whereas Through the Eyes of Tomorrow took place in a "pit" arranged for face-to-face discussion.

Throughout the development of these shows, the issue of continuity remained. The production teams learned more and more as they were confronted with new situations. The climax of the whole endeavor came in 1967 with the plans to celebrate Canada's Centennial. Three major documentaries were produced on film: The Restless Years by Perry Rosemond, A Working Summer by Neil Andrews, and Countdown to Gold Medal by Denis Hargrave. In The Restless Years, Rosemond worked with Gordon Pinsent to shape the dialogue and record the patterns of life among young people in the Yorkville area of Toronto. A Working Summer was a record of the adventures of the National Youth Orchestra as they toured Europe. Countdown to a Gold Medal was a documentary about Canadian participation in the Pan-American games.

The highest achievement of any of these shows was the visual organization and sequence of the images which told the story. Bruce Attridge sums up the philosophy of this endeavor as follows:

> I think I could almost say that if one started with the idea of no words at all and then added words as they became essential, that would have been a good point of view to have from the beginning. Of course, in a program that is carrying information you're going to have to have some words spoken, but I think the most effective continuity is visual in itself. In other words, when you want to move from a science to a dance segment, I don't think it's necessary to use words, but the visual flow must be there; the visual cues and the words used, I think, should be very minimal. This was a constant area of discussion among the people with whom I worked and it would be true to say that we began with many more words than we ended up with at the end of a season. (Attridge, 05/12/82)

In 1970, Don Elder returned to CBC to be executive producer of a replacement for Through the Eyes of Tomorrow which was to be known as The New Majority. The shift in emphasis was towards the increasing population of young adults who were streaming into adulthood from the baby boom after the Second World War, and who now constituted more than half the population of Canada. Most of the material was shot on film but was packaged in studios. The host of the series was Ian McCutcheon. The show focused on information of interest to youth and combined investigative reporting and documentary analysis. It dealt with fresh approaches to areas of interest, ranging from unusual theatre to radical politics, leavened with entertainment of various kinds. The series of 1971 was re-worked and re-packaged for a half-hour presentation entitled Video I on Wednesdays at 4:30 p.m. during the first and second quarters of the same season. The program dealt with project "D.A.R.E." (Development through Adventure, Responsibility and Education), a project of the Rehabilitation Centre of the Department of Correctional Services of the Province of Ontario) and it won the Prix Jeunesse International in Munich in 1972. Video I was presented by Rainer Schwartz, assisted by John Kastner as alternate presenter and story editor and producer Bob Gibbons.

The series was replaced by Youth Confrontation in 1973 and later changed to Speaking Out. The program was an edited record of a meeting or confrontation between a group of young people, mainly senior high school students, and an adult. The series was issue-oriented rather than personality centered. The guest adults were chosen because of their power and influence in the areas of controversy, and not necessarily in the public eye. About twenty young people were selected well in advance of the show and chosen from drop-in centers, Y's and community organizations rather than from particular schools.

The participants were approached individually by mail. The concept of the show was outlined in the letter, along with some information about the subject to be discussed and some references to books or articles which would provide background for the issues to be discussed. Emphasis was placed on the importance of their involvement and responsibility as the audience; the success or failure of the show would rest with them. It was pointed out that within the parameters of this studio situation they could accomplish something if their arguments were strong and sound enough to communicate their position to the guest and so to cause a change in his thinking as well as that of the viewing audience. Over the season, the program dealt with such subjects as Arctic oil, professional sport (a form of modern serfdom?), drug use, sex education and abortion, religion and morality. The show originated in several regions of Canada, and consisted of 26 episodes.

Other approaches to magazine programming have been attempted more recently, such as Galaxie, a cooperative venture between the cable companies and TVOntario, discussed in Chapter II.

During the '70s, the CBC produced several packages of film in various sample formats to fill spaces in the summer and other schedules. In almost every case the budgets were very small, thus eliminating the possibility of creative continuity, regardless of the quality of the film. Whatever would we have done without the films from the Children's Film Foundation in England? Just after the Second World War, the J. Arthur Rank Organization cooperated with the theatre owners to establish the Children's Film Foundation to produce children's films for Saturday Morning Cinema Clubs which were sponsored by theatre owners throughout Great Britain. With the advent of television, these films were made available for distribution to broadcasting corporations across the English-speaking world. More films of high quality, made especially for a young audience, were produced by the Foundation than by any other agency in the world. Revenue from the sale to broadcasting organizations was turned over to make more films for children.

The CBC was one of the first to benefit from the use of these films, which were distributed first by Ralph Ellis Enterprises. Indeed, Mr. Ellis was responsible for supplying the CBC Children's Department with more films of good quality for children than any other distribution company. CBC's Children's Magazine on Sundays at 5:00 p.m. featured the Foundation's films and was the beginning of Junior Magazine in 1958. In the late '70s, W.O.W., the children's weekly special on Saturdays, included some of the Foundation's latest films for children. For the summer seasons (a time of low budgets for children's programs) from 1963 to 1966, Time for Adventure presented hour-long adventure films from the Foundation. In the summer of 1966 some of the shorter serialized films were shown in a half-hour period under the general title Summer Camp at 5:00 p.m.

Another combination of films in a half-hour series was Along the Way (1974). The first 15 minutes featured nature study "Along the river and the seashore," produced in Great Britain with Mark and Bella and their very knowledgeable uncle. These segments also contained material featuring two young Canadians, Len and Bruce, accompanying a forest ranger along the trail.

The second half of the show presented the talents of young Canadian film makers. Mark Irwin, a York University student in film arts, made a film entitled "For the Love of Horse" featuring 13-year-old Anne Lawson practicing for equestrian trials on her horse, Firewater. She was being coached by Olympic medal winner Jim Elder. Most of the remainder of the films dealt with Canadian subjects.

Other variations included Vacation Time as a summer replacement, enabling the presentation of films produced by CBC stations across Canada. During Canada's centennial year a series of films was presented covering action, adventure and documentary subjects, all for and about Canada. The program material included a 16-part outdoor series called "Survival in the Wilderness," a two-part action-adventure story entitled "Three Plus One," a look at the R.C.M.P. Musical Ride, the "Story of the St. Lawrence Seaway" and "Bonjour Montreal."

Peanuts and Popcorn (1976) was presented in the spirit of the old Saturday morning (10:30 a.m.) movie house to exhibit serialized adventures, cartoons and feature films including the first-ever all-Canadian animated cartoon serial, The Undersea Adventures of Captain Nemo (by Rainbow Animated Limited). Feature films included a Swedish production, The White Stone, and an American-made film entitled Rookie of the Year, about a "rookie" who turns out to be a girl playing on an all-boy baseball team. At 9:30 a.m., Parade was scheduled for younger viewers; it included repeats of The Friendly Giant, Mr. Dressup and Mon Ami.

In 1978, For Kids Only was devised as a magazine show on Wednesdays at 4:30 p.m. with specials to be shown on Fridays. The Children's Television Department organized a panel of 30 children under age 12 to plan the elements of the show. By choosing "average" kids they hoped to find out their real interests and then have kids on the air who could do interviews and pursue topics in a way that would interest viewers. A real effort was made to select subjects which represented the various regions of Canada. The Friday specials focused on drama. Unfortunately, the pilot for a series entitled The Stowaway was never fulfilled as a series because money was not made available.

A new upbeat magazine series entitled Going Great is hosted by Chris Makepeace. Makepeace is an accomplished 19-year-old actor who puts his talent, energy, and curiosity to work in interviews with young people across Canada. Each half-hour show contains up to six items where viewers have the opportunity to meet talented and creative young people across Canada. To date the series has featured interviews with a teenaged disc jockey, white-water rafting in northern Alberta, a visit to a Sioux Indian powwow in Manitoba, and a figure-skating champion from Quebec. The series is produced in cooperation with the children's television department by Michael McLear of Cineworld Incorporated. Here is a good example of the kind of cooperation which is being encouraged by Telefilm Canada between broadcasting agencies like the CBC and independent film producers. The show has won awards with the Children's Broadcast Institute and has been sold to Nickelodeon Incorporated of the United States. In its latest innovation, Chris Makepeace is joined by 17-year-old Darcelle Chan of Burnaby, B.C. and Keanu Reeves of Toronto. All three hosts cover items shot in Montreal, Calgary, Vancouver, Winnipeg, Toronto, Los Angeles, and New York.

Welcome to My World, a magazine program for 6-12-year-olds, produced by CFTO-TV in Toronto, is an ongoing production of more than 52 episodes. The series covers such topics as science, nature, recreation and "The Things We See," presented in both field and studio segments.

Chapter V

INFORMATION PROGRAMMING FOR CHILDREN

From the earliest days of television many programs were presented, both for adults and children, dealing with a wide range of information. Close-ups enabled the presenter to demonstrate intricate steps in such crafts as carpentry, auto mechanics, or cooking for adults, or simpler handicrafts for children. Information about the education and play of children from other lands was a natural source of entertainment. It was also quickly realized that effective communication with audiences, young or old, depended very much on the presenter's ability to engage his audience and to inspire the viewer to follow up on instructions.

For over thirty years, information programming has been at the center of the debate about the value of information as entertainment or education. During the late '50s and early '60s, much emphasis was placed on the "master teacher," frequently in combination with specially produced segments demonstrating information which could best be understood visually. These segments were designed to make information accessible in classrooms where facilities for demonstration in science or vocational courses were limited. A further distinction was made with "educational" television, which was intended for general enrichment of the curriculum rather than for direct instruction. In both ITV and ETV for children there was a curricular thrust designed to help in the sequencing of information for effective teaching and learning.

In comparison with these dimensions of information programming, there was "entertainment," which entailed the presentation of facts, human experience and new worlds to explore in an informal, non-sequential way. In the early days of the development of program policy at the BBC they used to classify their programs as "information, education, and entertainment." To this day they have steadfastly kept separate their departments of Schools Broadcasts and Children's Programmes. Current information programs such as John Craven's Newsround or Think Again certainly capture children's interest but can scarcely be called "educational" because there is no specific instructional or curricular aim intended.

For many years during the radio era the same policy prevailed at the CBC--largely because the first supervisor, R. S. (Rex) Lambert came from the BBC and held the post for over 20 years. I succeeded him on his retirement and the two departments remained separate. Bruce Attridge undertook the supervision of the Children's Department. Most of the programs for both departments were produced at the network center in Toronto. Provincial school television was mostly of the "instructional" (ITV) genre, produced mainly for the province of Nova Scotia by CBC production personnel. Occasional provincial programs were produced for Manitoba and Newfoundland at the respective CBC studios. The provinces mostly depended on the national school telecasts, the majority of which were produced at Toronto and were of the ETV genre. After about 18 months, the two departments at CBC were combined under my direction and the Department became known as Schools and Youth. Bruce Attridge returned to program planning and production as Executive Producer.

With the advent of the Council of Ministers of Education and the development of educational television in the more affluent provinces of Ontario, Quebec and Alberta, the CBC gradually withdrew from production of schools programs. Ontario became the leader in production of educational television in English Canada.

Most of the educational programs produced were of the enrichment variety, i.e., "Educational," designed to complement the curriculum in science, mathematics, reading, etc. At the same time, TVOntario originated Polka Dot Door, Today's Special, Cucumber and Monkey Bars, which combined information or entertainment for informal, out-of-school viewing. Instead of making a distinction between "schools'" and "children's" programming, they elected to group their programs under the heading of "the children's market." A mix of both educational and entertainment programs was prepared for a four-hour stretch of informal viewing under the general title Galaxie.

A publication of TVOntario, "The TVOntario Method: Nine Steps to Superior Children's Programs," describes the planning of a typical school's broadcast--as the British would have it. Based on a case study of the first series of Readalong, the booklet shows the progress of planning and development of the series from the conception of the idea from a series of meetings with teachers, parents, education officials, and the staff of TVOntario. Step 1 entailed the assignment of a writer to prepare six pilot scripts in three stages: an outline of the general idea for the program; a first draft of the format with the concrete ideas carefully mapped out; and the final draft of the finished program. At this point, Step 3, pre-production is undertaken by the team of producer, director, and educator to plan the art work, graphics, and special effects required to ensure effective visual continuity in the program. After the six programs are produced, they are tested with young viewers to see how well the program works. Do the children learn what is expected? Is the program entertaining? Resource materials are prepared for use by students as well as teachers. Because TVOntario's funding comes mainly from provincial government ministries and because their mandate is primarily "educational," their program schedule must meet the needs of their clientele. Now that they are raising public funds by subscription, they will be able to broaden their mandate in an even more diverse program schedule.

While "educational" and "entertainment" programs are not mutually exclusive, there is a hazard in promoting both as equally valid means of entertainment. Although an educational program can--and should--be interesting, it is unlikely that a large segment of today's young audience would choose to view a school's broadcast when given the choice of any number of adult sitcoms or detective stories available at the same time.

Regardless of these issues, there remains an audience for well-presented information. As an attempt at diversity in scheduling and the provision of alternative programming for children, the Galaxie package, which includes all of the aforementioned types of informational programming, gained a considerable audience. Such a package included programs which provided information about people who were famous in history or young achievers, as well as factual or scientific knowledge. During the time that the Lively Arts Market Builders (LAMB) "C"ulture channel was on the air, information programming was sequenced with various graphics which identified program transitions. In addition, there was a series of characters associated with magic, and with artists whose work might interest children. There were short segments on "how things work," as well as Mr. Fixit, who made simple repairs to toys. These "wrap around" items facilitated the organization and sequencing of widely diverse programs under the general name of Odyssey.

From the earliest days of television until the present, parents, educators, and television producers have had a constant preoccupation with the interface between reading and television viewing. The CBC's Hidden Pages (1954), TV Ontario's Reading series (1975) and Read All About It (1980-82), The Magic Lie (1978, CBC), Bookstop (1984, CKY-TV, Winnipeg), and Library Storytime (1980, CKBI-TV) are varied examples of the use of television to advocate reading. A current series of six programs for parents produced by TV Ontario is entitled Hooked on Reading, produced by Linda Rainsberry and directed by Ted Follows, with an attractive viewers' guide written by the well-known critic of children's books, Michele Landsberg. Viewers are invited to join the adventures of Todd, Cassie, and Robbie as they share with their father his enthusiasm for the world of books. In a dramatic format, the children come to understand their father's concern about too much television viewing. With a combination of knowledge about how to motivate a child to read and sessions of story-telling, the program dissolves into dramatized scenes from books carefully selected to capture the imagination of children. The format is designed to engage both parent and child in a pleasurable but informative viewing experience.

Information about Hobbies and Crafts

At the very beginning of television, Tom Martin, the assistant supervisor of art for the Toronto Board of Education, was the presenter of Hobby Workshop. The aim of the program was to encourage children to participate in arts and crafts activities using materials likely to be available in most households. Always mindful of the need for simple and direct presentation, Martin used young people to execute the projects on camera.

In selecting the host for this show, the producer was concerned with competence in the field of art education. What was missing was a certain dynamism in personality. He tended to be somewhat structured in his approach, and as a result the youngsters on camera responded in a disciplined but rarely spontaneous manner.

Later an attempt was made to lighten the seriousness of the approach in *Hobby Workshop*. To this end, a younger but equally skilled teacher, Ross Snetsinger, was chosen. Segments of craft activities were alternated with Ed McCurdy's folk songs. Both men had interesting and engaging personalities which allowed for "ad lib" dialogue, providing some wit, humor and byplay. The creativity of the two performers in *The Ed and Ross Show* proved to be an interesting experiment, especially as a means of personalizing as well as expressing the performers' creative instincts.

Later, Snetsinger appeared in his own shows, *Ross the Builder* and *See for Yourself*, and as the handyman in the Firehall of the *Whistletown* series. Ross shared each of these shows with characters who appeared regularly, such as the puppet Polly the Parrot or Foster. Michael Roth, the magician, regularly appeared on *Ross the Builder*. The major part of the show was devoted to crafts for children who visited Ross's studios. *See for Yourself*, another version of the show with Ross Snetsinger, dealt with the romance of transportation, featuring Ross's intricate set of electric trains. Stephen Barringer shared the show with Ross as they demonstrated the operation of a railroad. The show also featured crafts and children often sent in ideas of their own.

While not exactly a hobby or craft show, *Harriet's Magic Hats*, produced by ACCESS Alberta, is an information program to help young viewers explore future vocations. In a series of thirteen 15-minute shows, a seven-year-old girl, Susan, uses a variety of hats from her Aunt Harriet's curious collection to introduce pre-school, primary and upper elementary school viewers to a variety of occupations. Susan chooses a hat appropriate for the occupation and the viewers are transported by various electronic devices and technical wizardry to the job's location. Susan has a foil in the puppet character Ralph, the parrot who challenges her to meet his needs. For example, Ralph urges Susan to visit a grain elevator in order to provide him with ample birdseed, or to take him to the veterinarian when he doesn't feel well.

Information about Animals

The most elaborate show in this area of information was *This Living World*, produced in both French (*La Vie Qui Bât*) and English from Montreal and discussed in detail elsewhere in this report (see pp. 195-97). The remainder of the programs were mostly procured for general audiences--e.g., Jacques Cousteau--or produced by other departments. *The Nature of Things*, produced by the Public Affairs Department of CBC, was extensively viewed by young people.

In the earliest days, Rick Campbell, a TV staff announcer in Toronto, did a weekly show called *Pet Corner*, which comprised tips on the care of pets and visits from the keeper of the Riverdale Zoo.

A more recent format, *News from Zoos*, was designed by Michael Spivak in association with the CBC. Each show is hosted by a chimpanzee (Charley Chim), voiced by Carol Banas. Each episode shows unusual events involving birds and animals from all over the world. The Chimp cheerfully introduces Rosie, an eight-thousand-pound Indian elephant, who has been pregnant for two years. As the cameras roll, Rosie gives birth to a baby boy. The infant elephant can be seen thrashing his way out of the birth sac and struggling to stand up.

Each show contains three or four segments showing unusual features in the lives of exotic animals. Enormous grizzly bears are transported to a marvelous new home. They play in a waterfall, climb rock ledges, and swim in their own pools, as they explore their new habitation for the very first time, or "extraordinary equipment allows the camera to look right *inside* a living bird during an important test to determine the sex of members of a fine flock of White Ibis."

These half-hour shows are written by Jill MacFarlane with music by Michael Spivak.

The series Klahanie originated from Vancouver. The word "Klahanie" came from the Chinook Indian trading language and, translated literally, means the great outdoors. The object of the program was to take viewers to see some of the flora and fauna of some of the most beautiful and inaccessible parts of the world. While many sites in the wilds of British Columbia are presented--The Forbidden Plateau wilderness of Vancouver Island, Vaseny Lake in the Okanagan Valley and Wells Gray Provincial Park in eastern B.C.--the producers ranged as far as Death Valley in the U.S.A. and the north German coast to study birds. Attention was given to conservation and protection of the environment as well as to skills required for survival in some of the more rugged realms of nature in the world.

The Kangazoo Club is a series of 26 episodes, each 24 minutes in length, produced by Quadramedia Management, Inc. in association with the Global Television Network. Kangazoo is a big cuddly kangaroo with a pouch full of animals found in zoos. Two young hosts, Melissa Glavota and Russell Chong, guide young viewers on expeditions to the Metropolitan Toronto Zoo, Marineland and the Game Farm at Niagara Falls, and the African Lion Safari in Rockton, Ontario. The hosts interview animal handlers, asking questions that children would like to have answered. The studio audience is also given an opportunity to ask questions. As well, each episode features original songs relating to the animals by composer Nancy Ryan. The show ends with a meeting of the Kangazoo Club to share letters, drawings and jokes from the viewing audience.

Programming in Science

The first science show for children was hosted by Percy Saltzman and was entitled How About That? (1953). Saltzman was an alert, disarming, urbane and attentive host. He had an intimate manner of presentation which made viewers of all ages feel at home with him. The simplicity of his language complemented the simplicity of his carefully planned experiments. Upon reflection, we noted at the time that the essential impact of the program was demonstration rather than exploration and discovery. The program's title seemed to convey the idea that scientific phenomena were unusual. More emphasis was needed on stimulating a sense of wonder, providing opportunities for children to share in the enterprise of exploration and discovery; e.g., the aim of a program on heat conduction should not be "to prove that iron expands when heated" but rather "to see what happens when iron is heated."

In the fall of 1959 another series was introduced from Ottawa. Science All Around Us featured Lorne McLachlin, a master at the Ottawa Teachers' College. Much of the material was planned jointly with Dr. Henry Hedges, who was the science consultant for Junior Magazine and a personal friend of McLachlin's. Saltzman placed more emphasis on entertainment, while Hedges and McLachlin focused on stimulating the viewer's curiosity about his physical and natural environment.

Two decades later, in 1980, the Children's Department initiated Just Ask Incorporated with Dr. David Suzuki and his robot assistant, Rastra (played by Joan Stuart). The series began with a popular thrust, answering questions about such mysteries as why people snore, and why some cats are "left-handed," why penguins don't get frost-bitten feet, etc. Suzuki stated, "My idea is that kids should understand how the world around them works. But a lot of kids' shows tend to say, 'Look, it's magic!' They mystify science rather than make it accessible to the public." And so, instead of playing the role of the omniscient host, he acts as a popular master of ceremonies, answering questions from a "Star Wars" set which features a blinking computer, a friendly robot and dozens of flying saucer probes that float off to find the kids who ask the questions. Of course, a simple problem might raise a complicated answer; but when it's reduced to its simplest components and leavened with a cartoon (animation by Neil McInnis), a song (music by Bill Taveniuk), or a film clip, it becomes clear.

> Often, questions are answered by having children demonstrate experiments on the set; young viewers are then encouraged to try the experiments at home. Thus, a query about the eye leads to experiments that can be done with lenses; a question about ants gives way to tips on building an ant farm; one project even has young experimenters reconstructing a skeleton--a chicken's.

> "To me," says Suzuki, "the exciting thing about the show is that it leaves kids with ideas they can pursue. If they want to make paper or set up their own hydroponic gardens, they'll know how to start. I think it's important not to alienate them by showing experts explaining. After all, it may look incredible but it's not magic. It's only science."
>
> [Gerald Levitch, "It's Not Magic for David Suzuki," TV Guide, February 21, 1981, p. 18.]

Of course, quite young children watched Dr. Suzuki on The Nature of Things and enjoyed Jacques Cousteau and the National Geographic specials. The essential value of well-produced science shows for children is to stimulate a child's natural curiosity about the complex world around him and to help him ask the right questions to find answers and to develop a theoretical sense of inquiry.

The Amateur Naturalist, with the famed naturalist Gerald Durrell, is produced by Primedia Ltd. with Paterson Ferns and Paula Quigley in association with the CBC. The series features unusual dimensions from the world of nature filmed on location around the world. A principle of inquiry motivates the viewer in all that he sees. At the same time, ecological and environmental factors are introduced. Each episode includes a field trip, showing what can be discovered in remote corners of the world, or in the viewer's own environment. Through the most advanced techniques of time-lapse and microphotography, the series explores the hidden world--one that is invisible to the naked eye. Durrell makes the home experiment segment as illuminating as it is fun. He shows how materials found in the average home can be used to study a bird's nest, make a wormery, or create a herbarium.

This is the third nature series presented by CBC television with Gerald Durrell, the former series being The Stationary Ark, in which Durrell presents his famous animal sanctuary dedicated to the protection and preservation of endangered species.

The series The Stationary Ark was followed by a 13-part adventure series revolving around the rescue and breeding of endangered animal species across the world. The show, entitled Ark on the Move, illustrates the work being done in captive breeding at Durrell's unusual zoo, the Jersey Wildlife

Preservation Trust on the channel island of Jersey. In areas such as Mauritius, Madagascar, and a number of the world's outer islands, Durrell and his wife Leigh, along with wildlife expert John Hartley, study the behavior patterns of such exotic animals as ring-tailed lemurs, Gunther geckoes, and pink pigeons in their natural environment--an environment fraught with danger from cyclones, predators, and erosion. In monitoring the wildlife population, an attempt is made to decide which species are endangered and which need to be taken back to the island of Jersey for captive breeding purposes.

As was the case with Ark on the Move, the series Durrell's Russia was co-produced with the CBC and Pat Ferns of Primedia. The Durrells in this series examine endangered species and programs for their breeding and reproduction across the vast and diverse terrain of the USSR, from the Arctic to the desert regions, from mountains and rivers to seas and lakes. In this case, CBC and Canada's Primedia were joined by Prime Time Television in the United Kingdom and Gostelradio in the USSR. TVOntario and Channel 4 in the UK cooperated with CBC and Primedia in the production of this series.

Another new series, entitled Wonderstruck, hosted by Bob McDonald, attempts to present good science information based on questions which invite the curiosity and investigative skills of young viewers. It recognizes the need for young people to know about science and technology, but recognizes that kids need to see the funny, surprising, mystifying, and challenging areas of science as well. The young audience is introduced to physics, astronomy, genetics, paleontology, and numerous other subjects which would capture the interest of young viewers. Each half-hour program in the series contains a detailed look at one or other of these interesting aspects of science, linking them to snappy quizzes, "what-ifs," and theories. The program is aimed at children of 9-13 years of age.

An interesting comparison can be made between Just Ask Inc. and a new TVOntario educational series entitled The Science Alliance, presently scheduled for Sunday morning viewing on TVO at 11:15 a.m. As described by TVO,

> The Science Alliance encourages kids to re-create

Wonderstruck, with Bob McDonald. (Courtesy of CBC)

landmark discoveries of early science in simple experiments they can do themselves.

Each 15-minute program in TVOntario's award-winning ten-part series features easy-to-duplicate experiments that introduce children to the basic principles of physics and chemistry.

Hosts Judy Haliday and Rex Hagon begin the fast-paced shows with five quick clues to soon-to-be-explained scientific riddles based on questions posed by children.

While the young members of the Science Alliance carry out many of the experiments on camera, film clips show real-life applications of the principles involved.

Each program features an invisible entertaining announcer who brings kids "Bryant's Giants of Science."

At the end of each show, viewers are given several problems to solve and are encouraged to learn more about the subject on their own.

The Science Alliance was produced by Milton van der Veen.

Patrick Rose provides the authoritative voice for Bryant, and the science consultant is Eustace Mendis, the chief scientist of the Ontario Science Centre.

Know Your World is produced by ACCESS (Alberta Educational Communications Corporation) for nine- to eleven-year-old viewers. The intent of this series of eight 15-minute programs is to stimulate problem-solving ability and scientific inquiry in activities in the natural environment. As the producer says, "the schoolyard becomes a laboratory for discovery and everyday materials are transformed into scientific apparatus as the characters in each mini-drama seek answers to queries such as 'Why do kites fly?' 'Why do I forget things?' 'What makes plants grow?' and 'What good are mosquitoes anyway?'"

The Four Seasons, five 15-minute episodes produced by Backing Productions of Toronto for the National Geographic Society of Washington, D.C., takes a look at life on a dairy farm through the seasons, showing how seasons can affect what farmers do from seeding until harvest. The effect of the seasons on life in the pond, woodlot, and fields is also examined.

The Way I See is a series of ten half-hour programs produced by ACCESS for young viewers aged 9-11. The format combines an exploration of the world of nature with art and drawing. Host Al Stuart helps in the exploration of the natural environment while he demonstrates how man has represented nature in art and sculpture throughout human history. Viewers are stimulated to make creative responses to their discoveries and their perceptions of nature.

In the effort to serve all age groups with respect to science programming, a new series entitled Owl TV has been introduced for children ages 7-12. The program originates from the Young Naturalist Foundation (the publisher of Canada's leading children's magazine, OWL) and the national Audubon Society. In this case an effort is made to involve children in the shaping of their world. To achieve the maximum degree of identity between the show and the young viewers, it was decided that stars should be real children and not professional actors. The children were chosen for their curiosity and interest in the world. The young people on Owl TV share their ideas, their humor, and their questions, making the series fresh with the spontaneity of kids enjoying themselves. The format includes not only information about nature, science, and the environment, but the content is linked by fast-paced games and puzzles which are designed to delight and challenge young viewers. In aiming to communicate the spirit of the show, the writers have provided the following description of three of the programs:

> "Animals close up" focuses on the fascinating owl through a visit with a most remarkable rehabilitator--Kay McKeever of Canada's Niagara Peninsula. In this award-winning segment, Sara Elliot, 13, visits Kay in her home, the world's largest rehabilitation centre for owls, where she and her husband have devoted their lives to rescuing and rehabilitating injured and orphaned owls. Introduced to several of the 150 birds in residence, Sara learns how injured owls must be cared for in captivity, how those that become "imprinted" and think they are people cannot be released to the wild, and how the owls take care of their young. Most importantly, through Sara, viewers get insight into the innovative work of one of the world's outstanding naturalists.
>
> "The mighty mites" are three kids who possess

The Mighty Mites, in Owl TV. (Courtesy of CBC)

the magical ability to shrink in size to explore microscopic environments. In the first "hair-raising" adventure, Sophie, Mark and Nicky Mite explore the ecosystem of a pond, discovering the many creatures that live beneath the murky waters. The Mighty Mites shrink to have a closer look at tadpoles and diving beetles, one of which comes to Sophie's rescue when she finds herself in a dangerous situation.

Bonaparte, the wise-cracking skeleton whose regular appearances on Owl TV help viewers to understand the workings of their bodies, makes his debut in the first segment of "You and Your Body." Kyla discovers the skeleton "hanging around" in the room of her brother, a medical student, and quickly learns there is more to this skeleton than meets the eye. In developing a reluctant friendship with the skeleton, she shakes his hand and triggers his total collapse.

> Kyla, ever inventive, takes the skeleton (whom she soon coins Bonaparte) to a doctor and learns about the structure of the human anatomy.

These examples give some idea of how the writers and producers of the program Owl TV strive to reach their audience in a creative and responsible way.

Mr. Microchip is CBC's first formal venture into programming about computers for children. A show to be shared by parents with children, its aim is to demystify computers and their functions. With Skip Lumley, a computer business consultant, neighbors Dayna Simon and Steve Grosfield learn about and work with computers in Lumley's garage. Each program is devoted to one aspect of computer functions. An attempt is made to put computers in their proper social and human context. As the series progresses, "the audience learns, along with the kids, how computers work, how to tell them what to do, how computers' brains compare with people's, where computers are used, and how they can help us" (CBC program notes).

The series is designed as an information program for general viewing. Like the programs from TVOntario, it has educational usefulness while it serves the interests of the informal viewer.

The series was created by Skip Lumley and Michael Hirsh, Nelvana and Ventura Pictures, produced by Michael Hirsh and directed by Peter Jennings.

Computer Literacy, produced by ACCESS, consists of three 10-minute animated programs to demonstrate how computers work, how they are programmed, how they are used and how they affect society.

Nibbles, a series of five programs of varying lengths (1-40:10, 2-41, 3-72.30, 4-12:35, 5-30) introduces viewers to the fundamentals of computers, using animation and documentary elements from TVOntario's basic series Bits and Bytes. The themes includes programming and languages, the computer's impact on society, information processing and specifics about electronics and technology. The series aims to help young viewers (ages 13-17) to become computer literate and to explore basic concepts.

Healthwise is a series of twelve 15-minute programs produced by Take III Productions of Ottawa for Coronet Instructional Media, Ltd. The series is designed to introduce children to the importance of health care. A variety of physical and mental health issues are presented.

The World's Children, a series of thirteen programs, each 15 minutes in length, produced by David Springbett and Heather MacAndrew of ACCESS Alberta, presents aspects of the daily life of children in developing countries. The series aims to present a positive look at life in developing countries where, in the absence of affluence, there are many compensations in rich tribal traditions, skills and family ties.

Fabulous Festival consists of thirteen half-hour programs done on location at the Vancouver Children's Festival. Al Simmons, as a warm, innovative and funny clown, acts as host to take the audience on an eventful series of tours. They meet many of the performers in the Festival; they take in the music and variety acts, and join in with the audiences in the big red and white tents found throughout the Festival park.

News and Documentary Programming for Children

The first "newsreel" for children on the CBC network was *Children's International Newsreel*, originating in Montreal. The 15-minute show was made up of segments procured from the news service of the European Broadcasting Union and presented without a host.

The central feature of news for children has been the feature *What's New?* which began when Ray Hazzan joined the Children's Department in 1970, having spent many years in the News Department. To enliven interest in the news items, Noreen Young's political puppets were used. As the show has developed over the past ten years, it has become the major current affairs show for young viewers. In addition to the news, there are special items on working kids, science, and other items which are given in-depth treatment. Because the production team used the news service for its source of program material, the News Department at first felt some resentment; but now, because of demonstrated quality in writing and editing, the *What's New?* team are invited along to share in investigative reporting.

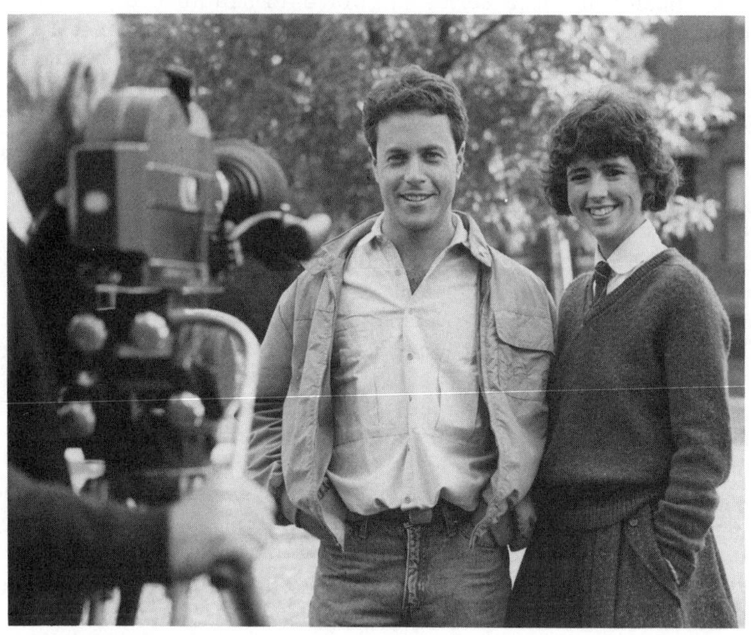

Howard Green and Jennifer Gibson host What's New? (Courtesy of CBC)

On the Global TV Network, Ron Krantz edits a weekly program called Kidsbeat. Stories are carefully edited to encourage interest in the important changes in contemporary society. A key objective is to provide insight into the lives of extraordinary people and acknowledge colorful, unusual events. The result is a weekly video magazine with contemporary music, pictures and stories that invite curiosity about the world of today and tomorrow.

Kidsworld, a show produced jointly by TVOntario, Astral Television Films and Global Television, consists of an anchor group of three young people. The concept for the show originated in the United States. The Canadian production still includes items by junior correspondents in the U.S.A. The anchor group provides continuity for reports by their peers from all across Canada with updating by child correspondents in different cities, very much in the fashion of adult reporters. Some stories are informative: an inspection of a submarine in drydock at the Halifax naval yards; an eight-year-old girl who organized a protest march on behalf of animal protection; boys and girls who act as pages at the Ontario Legislature. Other stories are just plain fun: a dog who drives a cow; kids who dance on rollerskates; and even a fish that walks. Also on Kidsworld, children interview famous personalities of interest to kids: René Simard, Henry "The Fonz" Winkler, Cindy Nicholas, Veronica Tennant, Kristy McNichol, Maria Pallegrini and Stevie Wonder.

In an even more popular vein, CFTO introduced After Four (1964). The show was conceived to retain some of the elements which young people enjoyed in rock bands and "dance party" shows, while the young people were also presented as intelligent individuals, confident in their personalities and capable of a wide range of talent. In the beginning the show was hosted by Ted Curl (formerly of His Time) and Carol Goss. The first show featured a folksinger, a hot-rodder, Pete Roberts, who took four years to build his hot-rod at a cost of $2,500. The machine was able to reach a speed of 100 miles an hour. There was a simple film review and a film of a fashion show.

In the following year a young singer, Jerry Martin, took over the role of male host with Carol Goss. A news segment was introduced and the rock group The Big Town Boys was presented. Carol Goss did a historic interview with Gregory Peck. In 1967 a further change was made when Carol Goss married and moved to the CFTO's Toronto Today show. Four hostesses of different backgrounds and talents took over. There was Linda Louie, a gifted Chinese Canadian, Virginia McEwan, an aspiring actress, Susan Taylor, a singer, and Trudy Young, known for her role in CBC's Time of Your Life, Razzle Dazzle, and the Barney Boomer series.

When the CBC acquired library film rights to Walt Disney's Mickey Mouse Club Show, items of news about children of the world were often integrated into several CBC shows, e.g., Razzle Dazzle, Pictures with Woofer, Patti's Picture House and Howard Presents. In some ways, the model established by William Park of Disney Studios for news reporting for children was exemplary for many years to come.

Documentary Programs

There were several outstanding documentary series, such as Children of the World which was produced jointly by UNICEF, National Educational Television (now the Public Broadcasting Corporation of the U.S.A.), and the CBC. Some film teams visited countries like Dahomey, Brazil, Guatemala, Somalia, Thailand and Nepal, where UNICEF located young people who talked about their culture and their way of life--for example, 11-year-old Nicholas Mignanwande, a member of the Fons tribe, lived in the village of Ganuie in Dahomey beside a large lagoon on a house built over the water on long stilts. He tells the story of life spent going to school in the morning and helping his father fish during the afternoon. In Guatemala two girls, Norberta (12) and Herlinda (10), tell about the colorful religious ceremonies and of their ancient Central American civilization and pay a visit to the thousand-year-old Mayan city of Iximache. In each program some emphasis is placed on the social problems, to make viewers more aware of the need for support from more affluent countries. The Guatemalan girls take the viewers on a visit to their father's farm which produces corn, beans, and coffee. On the way, Herlinda finds a sick baby lying in rags in a peasant's hut. The next day she and her father arrange to take the baby to a health clinic in a nearby village. These films were produced by Perry Rosemond and Denis Hargrave and written by Jim Carney.

In another series, Spread Your Wings, produced by Paul and Deepa Saltzman of Sunrise Films Inc. for the CBC, young people from many different countries reflect their varied traditions, culture and lifestyle. Frequent attention is given to the skills and talents of young people with stories such as those of a teenaged violin maker in Germany, a girl learning to carve gourds in Peru, a young girl who makes hand-made paper in Japan, an American girl who is an award-winning photographer, and a teenager in France who makes stained glass windows.

Closer to home but in the same vein was Travellin' Time, which was designed to salute a Canadian province each week in song, dialogue, folk tales and film. To provide continuity for each show, Valerie Siren, Brian Beaton and Teddi Moore appeared on camera. The show was written by Charles Winter and Arthur House, and produced by Dan McCarthy.

Locally, the first carefully planned documentary, A Walk with Kirk (1954), for the Toronto area was produced on film for the Children's Department by Chetwynd Films. The 15-minute program was designed to emphasize the recreational aspect of a child's education. The writer and performer was Professor Kirk Wipper of the Physical and Health Education Department of the University of Toronto. The program was developed in consultation with Mr. Gordon Wright, the Director of Physical and Health Education for the Ontario Ministry of Education. The purpose of the show was to stimulate enthusiasm and interest in the community and its facilities for recreation, as well as an interest in civic responsibility. For example, a football game was associated with the need for funds for the Red Feather campaign (later the United Community Fund); hiking was related to conservation; and camping to individual skills and leadership. A close relationship was maintained with schools so that interest in the school's extra-curricular activities would be maintained. Care was taken to see that the program complemented the curriculum which was being developed in-school.

In a similar vein, two shows originated from Vancouver, Barney's Gang (1958) and Follow Me (1960). Barney's Gang included filmed visits by a small group of youngsters to places of interest in and around Vancouver--a riding academy, the airport, a tugboat with a deep-sea diver. From time to time the pattern was diversified; West Coast Indian legends would be told, with drawings to illustrate them. On other occasions, the host comedian-singer Barney Potts would introduce young people with unusual hobbies. Follow Me (1960) was a simplified, 15-minute version of Barney's Gang.

Alphabet Soup is an information show for children in the 7-10 age group. Each week a guest introduces a new topic based on a letter of the alphabet: A is for Abracadabra, B is for Beer, C for Clay, D for Detective, etc. The show was hosted variously by Trudy Young, Mavis Kerr, and Lynn Griffin. The guests were well known personalities and authorities in their respective fields who discussed the various subjects in detail, answering questions put to them by the host. The show was produced by Bruce Raymond Ltd. for the CBC. It was produced by Dennis Coles and written by Pat Patterson.

Sports Programs for Children

The CBC's first serious attempt at sports programming for children was Sportstime (1957), produced by John Kennedy and hosted by Doug Maxwell. The program was designed for children aged 8-12 to develop their interest in creative play both in school and in their own back yards. In the first season, there was a greater emphasis on individual sports. Expert demonstration in studio and on film allowed young viewers to learn the fundamentals of the game. Film footage of Olympic champions was also shown, to demonstrate what can be accomplished by good instruction and good practice. Doug Maxwell often invited coaches and players to the studio to demonstrate special skills. On other occasions, attention was given to younger children when grade 3 pupils were brought to the studio to illustrate "warm-up" games with hoops, benches and ropes. Simple games which can easily be organized by young children were enthusiastically demonstrated.

The Fit Stop (1973) revived themes of Sportstime, but this time the emphasis was on fitness. Host Jan Tennant and Clarke Wallace, along with fitness expert Dr. Bryce Taylor of York University, aimed to involve young people in games like tennis, badminton, skiing and other sports which they can continue to play as adults. Guests discussed various aspects of sports and fitness. In another segment of the show, young guests were given the chance to test themselves to see how fit they really were. Each show contained a puppet segment with Noreen Young's puppets, including a hockey helmet, a football helmet, a bottle of liniment, an old shoe, and a knapsack. The knapsack complained that he was getting no exercise because people just weren't walking any more.

Yes, You Can (1980), produced by Michael Lansbury of CBC with Kevin Gillis, Tammy Bourne, Trevor Bruneau and Patrick Ford, and written by Jack Hutchinson with Jamie Waynes, aimed to represent the issues of fitness and sport. Creator and producer of the series Michael Lansbury had had previous experience as a lead singer in a rock band, and as a producer and director of major sports events such as the Commonwealth Games, the Olympic Games and the Grey Cup. He was also noted for his imaginative use of variety and other non-sports elements. The host, Kevin Gillis, is a well-known writer of music and lyrics for major TV shows (Celebrity

Cooks, The Diefenbaker Years, This Country in the Morning, etc.). Writer Jack Hutchinson had written Countdown to a Gold Medal for the Children's Department in 1967. He has written for Front Page Challenge, Marketplace, and Sports Weekend.

The show had several components: (1) Sports Spoofs--animated elements making puns on sports jargon ("fly ball," "foul ball," "stolen bases," etc.); (2) Fitness Tips, featuring animated Pete the Skate-Boarder showing appropriate goals of achievement for youngsters--e.g., how many push-ups, sit-ups or leg lifts they should be able to do; (3) Food Hints, under the buffoon Coach Cuddles Ford, a relation of calories to energy; (4) Inquiry clinic, for diagnosing common sports injuries; (5) great moments in sport; (6) profiles of current athletes; (7) mini-instruction with the athletes profiled; and (8) vignettes from the history of sports.

Another half-hour series produced by Sunrise Films Ltd. under the direction of Paul and Deepa Saltzman, entitled Spread Your Wings, focuses on the special relationship between young apprentices and master craftsmen in countries around the world. Paul Saltzman, the son of the distinguished performer Percy Saltzman, who for many years did the weather on television at Toronto, also made his mark in children's programming with the early program How About That, referred to in the first chapter of this book. Paul made his mark with children's television as a host on Junior Magazine. He later took up a long-term interest in film production and produced films about the Third World. He has an innate respect for youngsters regardless of their origins, racially or nationally, and was fascinated by their interest in elder craftsmen who could pass on to them knowledge and skills about crafts and the cultural tradition of the nation from which they came. For example, in one show there is a visit to a teenaged violin maker in Germany learning his craft from a master; another young girl who makes hand-made paper in Japan; an American girl who is an award-winning photographer; and a teenager in France who makes stained glass windows. In addition, the series focuses on such countries as Bali, Zanzibar, Guatemala, Hong Kong, Sweden, Iran, and Yugoslavia, and on the home ground two of the programs in the series present Canadian artists--a totem-pole carver in British Columbia and a young Inuit from Quebec who is learning to create soapstone carvings. The policy behind the show entails a common spirit of respect for family, tradition, religion, and nature, showing that, while the world changes, the value of the heritage of the past can be preserved by concerned, creative young people.

Information Programs from Museums

The first museum show on CBC used remote equipment to do a series of shows from the National Museum of Ottawa entitled Let's Go to the Museum (1954), produced by Marion Dunn and hosted by Robin McNeil. The show featured the work of National Museum artists on full-scale models of nature, people in their own settings, folklore including Christmas festivities among the Huron Indians, and the story of meteorites. The series also included a film record of a nature study outing with the Macoun Field Club of Ottawa, a club for junior field naturalists sponsored by the National Museum and the Ottawa Field Naturalists Club.

Let's Look (1958) originated in Halifax with Donald Crowdis, the Director of the Nova Scotia Museum of Science. His workshop was crowded with interesting objects such as live lobsters, seeds, Indian tomahawks, etc. The object of the program was to demonstrate to children that not only unusual objects but everyday commonplace phenomena can be extremely interesting if looked at just a little more closely. The program was aimed at children aged 8 to 12 and his subjects ranged from questions about smoke and how it makes the sky blue to the history of musical pipes, including the bagpipes, how sails are made and how they work, the movement of tides, and the tradition of Hallowe'en and the animals associated with it. The producer was Sandy Lumsden.

The Secret of the Samurai (1977), produced by TVOntario in cooperation with the Royal Ontario Museum, was designed to increase awareness and to develop interest in museums among the 8-12 age group. The specific purpose of the program was to study the samurai model of the Japanese soldier. To capture interest, an adventure/ghost story was devised with two young people, Brian and Jenny, hiding from a mysterious spirit in the museum. Tension and excitement were created by having exhibits come alive. They enjoyed the tension between the protagonist samurai and the antagonistic hunter, and especially they seemed to enjoy the Japanese game of "stone, paper, scissors" which Brian and Jenny played with the samurai. The research study done with 350 children confirmed that this was a good way to interest children in museums and there is good potential in such a format to make information a significant experience for children.

Information Programs About Art

In 1957, Alan Jarvis, then the Director of the National Gallery of Ottawa, undertook with CBC the production of a series entitled The Things We See (1957), based on a series of small art volumes published in England by Penguin Books ten years before. The TV series proved to be the first real venture into visual education, today considered to be so essential in the evaluation of film and television programming. As Jarvis explained, "Fundamentally, art is a way of seeing rather than of doing or making, and the first telecasts will be programs about seeing with fresh eyes.... My idea is still, rather than 'elevating' public taste, to increase people's enjoyment in looking at everything around them; landscapes, houses, everything embodying industrial design, and finally the fine arts--painting, drawings, sculptures" (CBC Times, June 30-July 6, 1957). And so the first program dealt with how the camera can teach us to look more closely, to bring things into focus, to "concentrate vision into a heightened awareness of some aspect of an otherwise chaotic environment."

The series also focused on how the artist transferred this heightened awareness to paper, canvas, or clay. Jarvis, an artist himself, demonstrated the process by doing some drawing, cartooning and clay modeling on camera. He also strove to show the wide range of artistic endeavor, explaining that it is not all concerned with things of beauty. He showed war art and other "ugly" dimensions of painting where the artist's preoccupation was with visual accuracy rather than esthetic expression.

For many years Betty Nickerson produced a series of art programs for the Department of Education in Manitoba. Busy Fingers was a visual extension of the art curriculum, but one of Betty's abiding concerns was with the variety of artistic expression among children of all ages in many countries of the world. In a special, Through Children's Eyes, she demonstrated some one hundred paintings from 30 nations by children ranging in age from five to the late teens.

Art in Action (1959), with Professor George Swinton of the University of Manitoba Faculty of Art, presented a series of programs to explain the basic principles of design, the artist's method of creating interest and excitement with his paint brush, and the development of art over the centuries. He had a special interest in landscape painting, and gave his views on such subjects as the traditional perspective on space, the use of color as light among the impressionists and as a means of expressing emotion among the expressionists. Since Swinton was a painter himself, he could convey both the experiential and the informational aspects of the theory of art and design.

In a curricular vein, TVOntario seeks to combine elements of education and entertainment in a series, Artscape, designed for pre-teens. The following description of the program demonstrates the move from dependence on an authority figure (such as Professor Swinton or, in the case of music, David Ouchterlony or Eugene Kash). It also demonstrates a creative shift from didactic modes of direct instruction to enrichment of the curriculum in art with inventive forms of presentation.

> Artscape carries viewers to a wondrous fantasy land where visual arts reign supreme.
>
> This TVOntario series for preteens promotes the discovery of the joys of artistic self-expression through perception, understanding, and creation of art at home and at school. Artscape demystifies art concepts such as line, shape, form, pattern, texture, color, and perspective.
>
> The series' protagonists--Craig and Tracy--are swept into Artscape through a painting in an art gallery, at the urging of an audio guide that soon proves to have a mind of its own. Tracy and Craig must use their wits, senses, and talent--in short, think art--to find their way back to the gallery.
>
> On their magical, musical journey back home, Craig and Tracy develop their senses of artistic expression through numerous adventures and encounters with the fantastic, and often humorous, residents of Artscape. These characters introduce the children to works by Canadian and international artists, as well as the work of children and native artisans.

Information Programs about Dance

The first children's program devoted to dance originated in Montreal with In the Story Book (1956), with Steve Woodman as narrator-host and choreography by Heino Heiden. As the title indicates, the emphasis was on fantasy and fairy tales of Andersen, the Brothers Grimm, Lewis Carroll and J. M. Barrie. Ann Fafoutikas prepared the scripts.

The following season a more formal attempt was made when Toes in Tempo (1957-1958) originated from Winnipeg with the Royal Winnipeg Ballet. Shirley Knight served as host for the first series and J. Harkany, choreographer and ballet teacher, hosted the second. Part of the show was devoted to demonstrating basic principles of ballet to the audience, while the remainder of the show presented excerpts from popular ballets performed by young dancers and "story" ballets, such as "The Emperor's New Clothes" and "Hansel and Gretel."

In 1959, CBC Winnipeg picked up the story theme from Toes in Tempo to present a new production of the Royal Winnipeg Ballet in Dancing Storybook (1959). Producer Neil Harris said that "our purpose in this show is to entertain our young audience by dancing and acting out the adventures of two young people as they search for a patch that is missing from a magic coat left to them by their father." The show was written by Marion Waldman with choreography by Brian MacDonald. As the series of adventures progressed, the young searchers meet with curious performers, pirates, gypsies, brave knights, dark and evil villains. In these early attempts to present ballet effectively on television, producers were struggling to achieve the energy and visual depth of the stage presentations. In Junior Magazine, Alan and Blanche Lund worked closely with the production team to achieve the highest esthetic style. Bruce Attridge as executive producer observed that Norman Campbell was doing outstanding work with ballet. "I think his shooting gets the energy of dance on the screen. He rarely, if ever, truncates the body and the illusion and mystery of the dance is preserved."

Information Programs About Music

Like dance, art, and storytelling, music on television enlightens the viewer's mind about facts, events, phenomena, theories, history, etc. But such presentations are also experiential for the viewer. The facts become meaningful only when they become a part of the viewer's emotional or esthetic experience. The role of the producer is to blend these elements into a meaningful and artistic presentation. Too often, because of low budgets or because of the expert's lack of understanding of the television medium, the presentations consist of "talking faces" or ill-conceived camera-work, leaving the viewers with an experience which is flat and uninspired. Let's Make Music (discussed in Chapter II) was accompanied in the schedule with Ed McCurdy singing folksongs on Ed's Place. A blend of humor in the situations lightened the presentation while at the same time the essential aesthetic quality of McCurdy's singing was preserved. Folk Songs (1954) from Montreal were presented by the well-known Canadian folksinger Alan Mills. Later, Grace Bartholomew acted as host for a variety of folk singers (1955). No special effort was made to develop a unique television presentation. The shows were mainly a sequence of songs presented by the singers themselves.

Another series, The Song Shop (1958), featured folksinger Tom Kines. In this case a visual dimension was added, with Kines in the character of a shopkeeper of a curiosity shop. The objects which decorated the set became the occasion for singing songs evoked by their memories. From time to time guests were introduced; e.g., Janet Jamieson played the violin while Kines "remembered" the Bard of Armagh with Irish melodies.

In another genre of folksongs, Stu Davis first introduced a series, Swing Your Partner (1957) from Winnipeg with songs and stories of the Alberta plains. Along with the songs and stories were interviews with some early settlers, who described their experiences in the old west when they were young. Also, a group of eight Winnipeg teenagers performed square dances as they were done in pioneer days.

A further variation with Stu Davis came with Rope Around the Sun (1958). More cowboy songs were combined, this time with descriptions of a prairie cowhand's daily life, the work he does, his traveling, and his relations with his friends with whom he works. Kerry Wood of Red Deer, Alberta, wrote the scripts.

Shifting from folk songs to grand opera, the CBC in collaboration with Alan Wargon produced 39 episodes of Mister Piper (1963), starring Alan Crofoot. Weighing in at about 300 pounds, Crofoot had a fine tenor voice and an engaging manner which made children want to play with him. Each program consisted of four segments. The first was "Take Time," a story with graphics with Crofoot's voice over film as narration. "Port of Call" was the second segment, with film about children of other lands. The third segment enabled Crofoot to perform magic from his bag of tricks, and the fourth segment used miniature sets and voice effects to show a rabbit, a cat, and a rat on adventure trips. In each of these segments Mister Piper continued to express himself in robust song.

An interesting comparison in the presentation of music information can be made between The Magic of Music (1958) with Eugene Kash from Ottawa CBC and the series Music Inc. (1979) from TVOntario. In one program by Kash, he demonstrated specifically and directly how many horn instruments made of brass evolved from ancient instruments made of animal horn. Guest musicians played compositions for horn showing the many ways in which composers have utilized the horn-shaped musical instrument, during the course of its development from the cremonial ram's horn of biblical times to the modern brass instruments and the French horn.

Music Box is a series developed by Heather Conkie for TVOntario to guide young viewers through the world of music from medieval to Baroque to romantic to pop. The 15-minute programs feature "a magical musical friend who can talk, sing, and make things appear and disappear at the drop of a B flat." The program is scheduled at 10:45 a.m. and repeated at 2:00 p.m. for school use. The educational content introduces children to such musical concepts as tone, color, tempo, meter and melody. Musical guests, familiar songs, and musical instruments are presented facilitating comprehension of many dimensions of music.

While this show is a school broadcast very similar in "content" to former CBC shows like Let's Make Music with David Ouchterlony and The Magic of Music with Eugene Kash, the curricular design of the series makes it useful both for in-school and out-of-school use, especially in the context of a well-conceived magazine show.

Tune Up Time, produced by ACCESS, is a series of ten 15-minute programs based on the creative ideas of Zoltan Kodaly and Carl Orff in the field of music education. With host Mr. Tune Up, the programs show the evolution of music from the discovery of rhythm in everyday sounds to the sophistication of the pentatonic scale. In an innovative and entertaining way, musical concepts of rhythm, pitch, tempo, beat, and patterns of melody are presented in an experiential mode for young viewers and listeners.

The highest achievement in music at CBC was the youth concerts that became a monthly feature of *Junior Magazine*. The quality of this endeavor was later briefly matched in three specials of the 1979 series *W.O.W.*, which will be discussed later. The first musical special, scheduled on United Nations Day, was built upon Paul Hindemith's opera *Let's Build a Town*. Bruce Attridge conceived this project and the other major specials. He described his experience as follows:

> The symbolism of building a town from the ground up was extended to the building and mutual caring purposes of the United Nations. With a related purpose in mind, I produced, shortly after, a 20-minute film observing the anniversary of the International Declaration of the Rights of Man. The visual material was taken from the famous collection of photographs, *The Family of Man*.
>
> Film/camera/movement supported only by the music from Vivaldi's The Four Seasons focused on the twin rhythms of work and play--a strong theme in the collection.... With the help of a distinguished editor, Michael Foytenyi, an early decision was made on the music.... Two alternating sections of the Four Seasons--the adagio and the allegretto--contrasted very sharply; the adagio for the meditative part of the film and the presto allegretto for the work section.

Care was taken to consider the experiential needs of a young audience and so, Attridge continued, "the number of cuts for that audience, I thought, should be limited and should be based on the music plus the amount of time that we felt young people should need in studying a portrait."

Other youth specials entailed the formation of the CBC Youth Choir under Elmer Iseler and a seventy-piece orchestra under Mario Bernardi. Speaking of the legitimacy of presenting a large orchestra on camera, Attridge says,

> ...But as long as orchestras are put on camera, the director with his own natural preoccupation to achieve visual results, interest, will be fighting against the quite legitimate demand, the need to hear music without broken attention. A type of shooting which is sometimes called analytic shooting is widely used now--you see it everywhere on screens: the director will block his shots using the score as his guide and in cutting from a cover shot to, say, a close-up of a cello or an oboe or timpani or whatever, the intention surely is to assist the audience in identifying hidden voices in the orchestration. I think that's quite legitimate. Anticipatory shots of a single instrument on the first brief sounding of an important theme would also be a visual cue to an attentive listener. For example, in the Beethoven 9th, several intimations of the melody which becomes so overwhelming in the Ode to Joy were given earlier in that movement; but I think to cue the audience that something is about to begin is sufficient reason to make use of camera cuts. To alert the audience to important things to come would be, in my view, appropriate and what I think is _not_ appropriate is to disturb a normal shooting pattern, that is overhead shot, long shot, medium shot, incessantly to catch flying hands and fingers and feet just because it's interesting to see how fast they go or to catch the solo singer--really getting what she should show only to her dentist!

Harry Somers, the distinguished Canadian composer, served as host for the youth concerts in 1962. An example of the range and experience of music can be seen in the following line-up for the first concert of the 1962 season:

1. Gordon Delamont's Allegro and Blues, under Jerry Toth and the Jazz Group

2. Finale, Concerto for Violin and Orchestra, Op. 35, Peter Ilych Tschaikowsky with Jaime Laredo and Mario Bernardi with the CBC Symphony Orchestra

3. Henry Purcell, _Songs from King Arthur_: "Come

if you dare," "How Blessed are Shepherds," "'Tis love 'tis love." The CBC Youth Choir with Elmer Iseler.

4. Clermont Pepin, Toccato for Piano premiere played by John McKay

5. Maurice Ravel, Elborada Del Gracioso, CBC Symphony Orchestra under Mario Bernardi.

6. Bela Bartok, Six Roumanian Dances, with Jaime Laredo, violin, and Mario Bernardi at the piano.

7. Dankworth and Leiber, Improvisation for Jazz Band and Orchestra, under Mario Bernardi.

One can readily see that care that went into the planning of this concert which was typical of the other concerts, some of which included ballet, some stories for young children, e.g., a musical version of Leonard Weisgard's _Mr. Peaceable Paints_ with Fred Rogers or Mary Grannan's story of the _Jewels of Fermanagh_. As often as possible young people were chosen as artists, e.g., Jaime Laredo was 21, having won the Queen Elizabeth of Belgium International Music competition at age 17. Clermont Pepin's Toccata was especially commissioned for this concert and John MacKay played it at Pepin's special request.

It was not until nearly 20 years later that music specials on such a scale were presented as part of the weekly series on Saturdays at 12:30 p.m. in the 1980 season. Four such specials were included in the series _W.O.W._ (Wonderful One-of-a-kind Weekend). The first was _Pirate's Gold_, shot at Newfoundland's historic site Ferryland, with the well-known Canadian Irish folk artists Called Ryan's Fancy. It was written by Pat Patterson about the ghost of Captain Kidd which continued to haunt Kidd's Island in Ferryland Harbour. With the help of singer Beth Harrington, the treasure is found, but not without much joyful singing by Ryan's Fancy and Beth. The show was produced and directed in Newfoundland by Jack Kellum.

Another music special was the production of Gian Carlo Menotti's _Chip and His Dog_ with the Canadian Children's Opera Chorus and performed by children. The story is best described by Menotti himself:

> Chip and His Dog grew out of my own experience with my adopted son, Chip, who has a dog which is entirely his. I was influenced by the fact that dogs are very important to children. Sometimes when they have problems, only the dog can understand, and talking to it seems to help.

Ruby Mercer commissioned the opera for the Guelph Spring Festival and Stan Swan was the director.

A special for the series was produced with the folksinging trio Sharon, Lois and Bram in Toronto's Kensington Market. With Bill Usher, the Kensington Kids and a friendly elephant, they explore the area, play in the playground, and of course provide rhythm and song.

The final musical special featured the Canadian Brass in Ottawa, performing for children at various sites, such as Parliament Hill, the National Gallery, the Museum of Modern Science, on the Rideau Canal and at Ottawa Airport.

Classification of music programs for children is problematical because of a distinction sometimes made between factual information about music and music programs designed primarily for direct esthetic experience. Because of the nature of the presentation, popular, rock band music is included under variety programs.

Quiz and Game Shows

When Marce Munro came from Vancouver to take over the post of Director of Television at Toronto, he proposed that Reach for the Top, a popular game-quiz show for high-school students, should be launched in the Toronto area. A meeting was held with superintendents of the area school boards to show a sample of the program and to arrange for their cooperation. It was made clear that the show was essentially entertainment, but everyone acknowledged the value of intelligent young teenagers learning the poise and self-confidence required to appear on camera and to become familiar with the production of a television show. Neil Andrews was the first producer with Warren Davis as host. Dr. Charles Booth, who had recently retired from the post of assistant deputy minister of education for Ontario, took on the duties of referee. The show has been on the air continuously since 1965 and has become a national institution. In 1967, the CBC bought the rights to the show from Richard St. John and, from this point on, the show was developed in each CBC-owned and -operated station with play-offs arranged to culminate in a national prize-winning school.

Recently, after some 22 years, it was discovered that only 12 percent of the show's audience was teenagers, while 57 percent was 55 years of age or older. The sample was a total audience of 400,000. On this basis, a decision was made to take the show off the air and to replace it with a show more relevant to the needs of entertainment for teenagers. There was a national reaction; many people wrote to report how meaningful an experience it had been for them to participate in the show. For the time being the show will continue, but a national committee has been set to make recommendations about its continuation or replacement. The committee, chaired by Nada Harcourt, includes Leo Rampen, Program Director, CBMT; Ross McLean, TV producer and instructor at Ryerson Polytechnical Institute; and Kathy Chilco, independent producer in Vancouver.

In 1968, Swingaround was developed as a spin-off from Reach for the Top for children in grade 7. The show was introduced by host and quizmaster Lloyd Robertson and competition took place among four students, two from the two schools which made up the audience. In addition, a "telephone quiz" was added. Two students were chosen in advance from schools anywhere in Canada. They were informed that they were members of the two participating Toronto teams and they were asked to deal with four questions. In addition to questions, some skill games were used to entertain an audience of younger viewers both in studio and among the television audience.

Just for Fun (1975), a so-called "un-quiz" show for grade 7 students, with Margaret Pascu, was undertaken. The show gained its reputation for fun rather than competition when it turned out that the hostess did not always know the answers. Occasionally when she did not know the answer she would look sideways to the technicians and the floor director, who frequently participated in the fun. As well as a quiz, the kids were asked to participate in such contests as hula-hoop twirling and broom-balancing. Another example of the humor arising from non-competition was the boy who, when asked

foil, "El Nurdo." Then there are "straight" information segments, e.g., a visit to an advertising agency to learn how signs and advertisements are designed and executed. George Henderson of the B.C. Lions Club provides some humorous interaction with El Nurdo while he has more serious exchanges with Captain Cool (Bill Reiter). The show is produced by B.C.T.V. of Vancouver.

The theme of safety for children is common among children's TV from the very beginning. Howdy Doody had placed great emphasis on safety. A cartoon booklet was made available on request for its many viewers. Many local commercial shows emphasized safety among other cautionary elements. This season, TVOntario has taken a more systematic approach to the problem of teaching children about safety and has turned out an entertaining program which will meet the needs of the informal viewer as well. TVO describes the program as follows:

> Children who think ahead and think of others can become safety scouts like Henrietta, the main character in TVOntario's Calling All Safety Scouts.
>
> Safety scouts prevent accidents, and Henrietta helps children to stay safe at home, in school, and in the neighborhood. In fast-moving 15-minute programs, Henrietta adopts disguises to facilitate her search for people who deserve to receive a safety scout badge.
>
> Calling All Safety Scouts alerts children to accident prevention and the risks of everyday life through songs, riddles, quizzes, and limericks. Each program has three major segments: "Guess the Accident"; a soap opera, "Better Safe Than Sorry"; and the Safety Awards Show.
>
> Children will recognize some of the award winners from another TVO series, We Live Next Door. They're joined in Calling All Safety Scouts by delightful characters like Tangles the Dog and Eeny, Meeny, and Miny mouse.

Funtown, produced by CKY-TV Winnipeg, was an hour-long variety show for younger children with Bob Swartz acting as Mayor and host. The show is made up of interviews with interesting people from the Winnipeg area, e.g., one show featured Indonesia and some Indonesians who had settled in

Winnipeg and opened an Indonesian restaurant. National dances were performed and some songs were sung. Intermittently the Mayor asks questions about customs of the people and the geography of the many islands, large and small, which make up the republic. Stories are read and skits performed by the puppets. The show runs for one hour and is produced and directed by Aaron K. Johnston.

Adventure of Snelgrove Snail takes place in an underwater village of Snailsville. Some dramatic story action takes place among the various puppets representing undersea creatures. An educational theme runs through the program: episodes about pioneers and a homily about a little knowledge being a dangerous thing. The characters also demonstrate their performing talents in events like the gastropod follies.

The Wonderful Stories of Professor Kitzel is seen weekly on CFTO-TV Toronto. The show is made up of a series of stories about history, inventions, or any other subject matter which might interest children (e.g., the Wright brothers, Robin Hood, etc.), visualized with stills and some animation, especially created by Geoff Loynes under the production of Shamus Culhane of MG Film Productions. Several short stories are included in each half-hour program. Continuity is provided by Professor Kitzel, an animated figure who uses puns and other word plays to maintain viewers' interest. Credits for each filmed story are run at the end of each episode, which tends to fracture the continuity. Presumably the productions were originally conceived as short films to be sold on the international market. Professor Kitzel is a simple device to provide continuity for a half-hour program.

Chapter VI

DRAMA AND STORYTELLING

From the beginning, dramatic presentations have been a central concern for producers of children's TV programs. Following the precedent of the BBC, the CBC undertook the dramatization of both classic novels and novel/stories by Canadian authors. Within the opening week of 1952, the CBC presented Jules Verne's *Twenty Thousand Leagues Under the Sea*, followed by Wilkie Collins' *The Moonstone* and Canadian author Thomas Raddall's *Roger Sudden*. The first original dramatic series was *Space Command*, produced and directed by Murray Chercover for family viewing. With Alfie Harris as scriptwriter and John Lowry's ingenious special effects, Chercover developed a pro-social action show full of tension, drama and jeopardy. The element of violence was tempered by careful development of the characters and meaningful justification for the physical action. The brilliant cast included William Shatner and James Doohan, both of whom went on to star in *Star Trek*; Robert Barclay, Cec Linder and Eileen Taylor Smith. With Lowry's help they were able to simulate weightlessness by "flying" the characters. They also created the effect of rockets flying in space. In Murray's home workshop they devised models which they then took to the Hand Fireworks Company to procure the right mixture of chemicals for propulsion. The models were flown against limbo, so that the cameras could create the illusion of rockets flying in space. Many of the techniques employed would not be acceptable to present-day audiences but at the time the show was the most popular dramatic series on the air.

Back in 1953, Alfred Harris, the writer of *Space Command*, set forth his philosophy of science ficiton in the *CBC Times*.

> Science fiction has passed through its period of carefree adolescence and has attained a sincere and self-searching young maturity. But the term itself is greatly in need of definition. Science fiction is _not_ concerned with wild flights of the imagination. Weird, fantastic tales of space-monsters, moon-maidens, space-pirates and space-spies are not science-fiction--even though they often do, unfortunately, masquerade under that name.
>
> Science fiction deals with recognized scientific principles and theories, projected logically into the future and developed according to accepted hypotheses to some scientifically plausible conclusion. It deals not only with the technological, but with the human element involved. In its early days science-fiction considered only the machine. Today, good science fiction considers the machine, but also its effect on man, on man's relation to man and to the expanding universe. Good science-fiction today still has its gadgetry, but the emphasis is no longer on it. The emphasis rests squarely on the basic scientific theme and human relations involved. When gadgets are introduced, they are explained and proven theoretically plausible.

Thirty years ago, Harris wrote that "mature science fiction has an important part to play in our 20th-century world. Space flight is no longer impossible." Quoting Dr. Wernher von Braun as his authority he argued that "Practically it will be attained ... within the next 25 or 30 years." But, Harris continued,

> its purpose and its goal must be recognized and made clear. Good science-fiction can, and does, prepare the way, suggesting possibilities, exciting enthusiasm, forecasting results. It assumes that change is the constant and natural order of things, and prepares the way for that change by anticipating it.
>
> The series _Space Command_, starting March 13th on CBLT, is designed primarily for the younger members of the TV audience. It will follow closely the known facts and plausible hypotheses. The first few scripts will deal with sun spots and their possible effect on space flight and space stations. Later in the series such themes as evolution, space-medicine, the meteorite danger, the origin of the astroid belt, and

> many others will be projected into the future and developed.
>
> Of course, in a series such as this, adventure is a _must_--but all adventure will be firmly rooted in motivations and causes that could occur _only_ in space, born of space-conditions. Stories of space-spies, space-romances, and space bandits will be avoided, since they are nearly always ordinary spy, bandit or love stories with a "space" background dragged in arbitrarily.
>
> "Space Command" will be an earth-wide organization which directs, maintains and carries out Earth's conquest of Space. In the series, we will follow the "space-education" of one young man--Frank Anderson --as he gains experience in some of the many divisions of "Space Command"--the transport division, the satellite division, the investigation (scientific) division, the exploration division, and others--and in each he will learn something new about the conditions our scientists today know to exist in space.
>
> --Alfred Harris, "Science Fiction TV," _CBC Times_, Mar. 8-14, 1953.

Over 150 weekly episodes of _Space Command_ were produced for the general evening television schedule--7:30 p.m. in the first year and 6:30 p.m. in the second season.

The first regular dramatic presentation for children produced in CBC studios was _Hidden Pages_, with Beth Gillanders as hostess. The details of this series are discussed in Chapter II.

Because of high costs for dramatic production and because Toronto became the major center for production of adult television drama, much of the effort of the Children's Department was confined to simpler formats for storytelling. For pre-school children, puppets were mixed with live characters, as in _Maggie Muggins_, _Planet Tolex_ and _Old Testament Tales_, originating from Toronto, with _Timothy T_ and _Man from Tomorrow_ from Vancouver. _Storybook_ featured Beth Gillanders and _Story Seat_, Lillian Carlson and Norman Young. _Albert's Place_ had Nonie Stewart, Robert Clothier as the handyman and John Chappell as the singing guitarist, and Vancouver's _Peppermint Prince_ featured John Chappell. Kitty Marcuse was the writer for _Timothy T_, _Man from Tomorrow_ and _The Peppermint Prince_.

Another 15-minute story-telling show, Pieces of Eight (1959), came from Halifax. Tales of pirates featured H. Leslie Picot as Rango, the captain of the pirate ship, The Black Avenger. The stories, written by the famed specialist in Maritime folk songs, Edith Fowke, included pirate songs sung by Leonard Mayoh's shantymen accompanied by accordionist Jimmy Nas.

The Fables of Lafontaine (1958), made by the French film producer Marc Gaudart, used live animals from the Mount Albert farm of Miss Lorna Jackson.

"Animals are real actors," Gaudart is quoted as saying. "If you see them at the zoo or the circus, you see them acting all the time, and the children are strongly attracted to them. If you want them to act well you must show them kindness and warmth, and not approach them as if you want to display them to ridicule. Then they will act by their own instinct. The art lies in being ready with your camera when they are."

As a film maker in this situation, Gaudart shows great patience. His director of photography, Fritz Spiess, spent many hours studying the behavior of the animals he used, to find out what problems he might face; e.g., the mouse who refused to ride in a canoe, the bored monkey who became fascinated by the studio wires and rafters, the rabbit who became so fond of sitting in a jeep that he refused to get out to race with the tortoise. The stories included other animals such as parrots, frogs, cats and pigeons.

Tales of the Riverbank, privately produced by Dave Ellison and Ray Billings, also features live animals as characters in original stories. In this case, a hamster, a white rat and a tame skunk are photographed in poses which make them credible as actors. As with puppets, the animals are "voiced" and a narrator picks up the action as the various transitions are made from one situation to another. The show runs on Global TV in a re-edited 30-minute version as Hammy Hamster.

These 15-minute programs were matched with 15-minute information programs to make up a half-hour in the late afternoon. This half-hour was preceded or followed by a regular daily show such as the Canadian Howdy Doody Show or Razzle Dazzle, making a daily hour package from 4:30 p.m. to 5:30 p.m. The period 5:30 p.m. to 6:00 p.m. was taken up with procured syndicated adventure film series.

After *Hidden Pages* completed its three-year run in Vancouver, Ray Whitehouse proposed a weekly series, *Tidewater Tramp*, featuring life in a tramp steamer sailing up and down the coast of British Columbia. The original writer, Captain Tom Gilchrist, had been a steward for the old Union Steamship Company and was thoroughly familiar with the long B.C. coastline. He conceived the idea of a "tramp" ship which could go anywhere. The success of this series, which was produced electronically in the studio with filmed segments, led to the development of a more enduring series on film.

The Beachcombers, written by Mark and Susan Strange, has been on the air continually for 11 consecutive years with two originals, Bruno Gerussi as Nick, and Robert Clothier as Relic. The plots center on a family: Molly and Nick, along with Jessie, Sarah, and Relic; Pat O'Gorman, Jack and Constable John are on the fringe of the family. As in many families, there are quarrels, usually centered on Relic.

Paul Grescoe, writing about Clothier in *TV Guide*, reports that on his return home in 1954 from a sojourn overseas he "agreed to supervise diamond drilling on one of his father's mining properties on the northern B.C. coast. It was here that Clothier met a couple of the raunchy old characters who, years later, would help him in his interpretation of Relic: Porcupine Bill, a laconic prospector who delivered mail by sled; and Steve, a deaf hermit who slept with a rifle." In the earlier stages of the show, Relic "was a rather one-dimensional, miserable creature," according to Clothier, but "over the years, he has fleshed Relic out to make him a solitary old rascal who must hide his vulnerability. And his defence is bristles and bad manners." (*TV Guide*, July 23, 1983, pp. 2-7.)

In the seventies, the idea of *Hidden Pages* was revived by John Kennedy in a totally different format in *The Magic Lie*, a weekly half-hour series featuring adaptations of Canadian novels and stories from the different regions of Canada, hosted by W. O. Mitchell. Such children's classics as Roderick Haig-Brown's *Starbuck Valley Winter*, L. M. Montgomery's *Emily of New Moon*, *A Horse for Running Buffalo* by Madeleine Freeman, and Margaret Laurence's *A Bird in the House* were presented.

It was during Kennedy's tenure as Head of Children's Television that Noreen Young, the talented puppeteer and writer of Hi Diddle Day, devised the format for Pencil Box produced by Rod Holmes from Ottawa. Children were encouraged to write stories, some of which were selected and edited for production. The show ran three years, winning an ACTRA award in its first year. In the same vein, Homemade TV was introduced in 1977 with young people doing "take-offs" on currently popular TV shows and commercial messages. Young people were also encouraged to submit short film subjects (about three minutes on 8mm, Super 8 or 16mm film). The mainstay of the show was the Homemade Theatre Company led by Fred and Larry Mollin, Barry Flatman and Phil Savath.

Throughout the years, dramas for special occasions such as Christmas would be undertaken, e.g., Mary Grannan's The Rustler and the Reindeer or The Princess of Tomboso. On several occasions a combination of music and drama was featured on Junior Magazine. Time of Your Life, a successor of Junior Magazine, presented a drama every third week of its run (1962-64). The dramas for this series emphasized action and the adventures of young achievers.

Two other attempts were made to provide a regular dramatic series for children with the presentation of the Golden Age Players of Montreal under Valentine Boss in 1957. Fairy tales such as The Snow Queen and other titles by Hans Christian Andersen were presented with a limited budget. The presentations remained essentially theatrical; not enough attention was paid to the artistic and technical demands of television production. In contrast, Bill Glenn undertook a series from Toronto ten years later entitled The Mystery Maker The 13-week series was written especially for TV by Lyn Cook and filmed on location in Stratford featuring leading members of the Canadian acting community--Frances Hyland, Joseph Shaw, Ruth Springford and others. The series ended for lack of funds.

In 1968 a weekly sitcom was designed. Barney Boomer, produced by Stuart Gilchrist, was set in the Oakville harbor, where a houseboat arrives with a charming young man in the person of Heath Lamberts. In this imaginary community a set of relationships developed which made up the plots of each episode. Since it was an ambitious undertaking for the limited budget and facilities provided, the series gave way to a simple game show, Swingaround. Within a few months Gloria White launched a new series, Toby, about the Mitchell family.

Toby is a highly intelligent 16-year-old girl described as having "the I.Q. of an Einstein and the imagination of Salvador Dali." Toby, played by Susan Petrie, had a younger brother Mark, played by Peter Young. Her father Leonard was a lawyer (Arch McDonnell) and her mother Jennifer was played by Micki Moore. Jean Jacques (Joy-Joy) Roberge (Robert Duparc) played the role of a young French Canadian exchange student from Montreal. The series was written by David Mayer and Bill Lynn. Again, just as the potential of such a series began to be realized, budget cuts forced its withdrawal from the schedule.

The major thrust for children's drama has been made most recently by the former Head of Children's Television, Nada Harcourt. Recognizing the enormous success of children's theatre companies like Theatre Direct and Young People's Theatre, and the astonishing success of Steven Spielberg's _E.T._, Harcourt concluded,

> if you can make a film that truly expresses the child's world with talent and genius, you are obviously going to have first class material. People, in hard times, want to be reminded of the way they were and to expand the awe and wonder that a child has. At its best, that is really the best theatre, the best television, namely--to have the experience of being transported out of oneself.

The security which the viewer gains from such experience is rooted in values cherished by North American families. Since the lives of children are dominantly absorbed in family concerns and issues, drama for children should arise from this milieu and be seen by both adults and children. In this way, children will be presented on the screen as the complex, intelligent and competent people they are, interacting with responsible adults.

To realize this general goal, Nada Harcourt has worked patiently with a number of private film producers. For younger children, funds have been deployed to Linda Schuyler and Kit Hood of Playing With Time Inc. to produce the series _The Kids of Degrassi Street_. "The world of Degrassi Street ... offers a slice of life that is instantly recognizable." Following the adventures of a group of neighborhood kids in east-end Toronto, the films explore some of the personal and ethical choices children face as they grow and learn about themselves and others. "The lively variety of situations, together with the themes examined, make these half-hour dramas both entertaining and educational" (Linda Schuyler and Kit Hood).

Just Down the Street is a collection of dramatic films for and about children scheduled at 4:30 p.m. beginning on October 18, 1982. Each of the films in this series has the distinction of being made from a child's point of view, giving the audience an understanding of how children grow and learn in a variety of situations.

The series led off with The World According to Nicholas, about an eight-year-old's struggle to understand the complex world around him. The four-part film has young Nicholas dealing with the harsh reality of a family break-up, the comedy and adventure of friendship, the laughter and thrills of things scary, and the charm of magic. The episodes were produced and directed by Bruce Pitman, starring such distinguished Canadian actors as Michael Fletcher, Don Francks, Barbara Hamilton, Jane Mallett, Barry Morse, Kate Parr, and Fiona Reed.

Other films in the series included Jenny Cuckoo, a story from Halifax about two young girls from different ethnic backgrounds who are momentarily united through one common but unforgettable experience. Other programs were repeats from the series The Kids of Degrassi Street produced by Linda Schuyler and Kit Hood, e.g., "Noel Buys a Suit," "Lisa Makes Headlines," and "Sophie Minds the Store."

The series was continued the following year, and included "Pete Takes a Chance," in which young Pete embarks on a get-rich-quick scheme which backfires; "Chuck Makes a Choice," in which Chuck develops a crush on a new girl at school, but doesn't want her to know that his father is in jail; "Billy Breaks the Chain," in which the curse of a chain letter falls on Billy as he anxiously awaits acceptance at summer hockey camp; "Casey Draws the Line," in which, through a difficult experience, Lisa and Casey learn a lesson about sharing and trust; "The Young Juggler," a Christmas episode set in the last century, telling the story of a blind boy who finds friendship, self-respect and happiness through his association with a young street performer.

Glen Salzman and Rebecca Yates (Cineflics Ltd.) have produced such outstanding hour-long dramas as Reaching Out and Jen's Place the former with Robert Kennedy playing the role of a young paraplegic and the latter with Megan Follows as a teenager coping with the unpredicted separation of her parents.

In addition to the above, Cineflics Limited produced a tense family drama entitled Corletto and Son. Mike Corletto is 17 and dreams of becoming an iron worker like his father and uncle. He thinks higher education is a waste of time, and has failed a course in high school. His father Nick, on the other hand, is determined that his son will attend university and become an engineer. Nick is furious about the failed course and threatens Mike with the loss of his summer job on the construction site unless he goes to summer night school. Mike reluctantly agrees, but the tension between father and son continues to grow as each stubbornly sticks to his own ideas.

Another drama, entitled Introducing Janet, deals with an overweight 16-year-old girl who hides her loneliness and insecurity behind a steady stream of wisecracks. While researching a school paper on humor, Janet meets up with Tony, a stage-struck waiter who is preparing for his debut at a comedy club. Janet helps Tony polish his comic material, while Tony helps Janet get to like herself.

Another special drama, produced by Ariadne Ochrymovich, entitled The Juggler, is a story of two young boys living in Quebec City in 1825. André Delisle is a wealthy aristocrat, and Barnaby is a street urchin. André lived in a large, beautiful house with his parents and many servants, apparently lacking nothing in the way of material goods. However, André was born with very little vision, and was constantly doted on by his mother and somewhat ignored by his father, who could not accept André's handicap. Most of the time he was left in the care of his nurse, who loved him, but he found her math lessons boring and the fairy tales ridiculous. He was lonely, and had no friends. Hearing music in the street, he seeks to investigate its source. Eventually, wandering in the village square, he once again hears the music and relates it to a juggler performing his act. The juggler, of course, is Barnaby, and André and Barnaby quickly strike up a friendship. The drama develops as Barnaby and André decide to write a routine which includes André as a clown and Barnaby as the juggler. While the parents object strenuously, he does manage to escape and eventually is found with Barnaby, dressed as the clown; so redeeming is their performance that his parents recognize his talent and the drama ends happily.

In keeping with the vein of using drama to reveal and to resolve problems which teenagers have in growing up, the CBC itself produced a play called _On My Own_, which is the story of Kim, a bright, pretty, and popular high school student who suddenly finds her life changed when she is diagnosed as an epileptic. Frightened and embarrassed after suffering a grand mal seizure at a school dance, Kim is further depressed when she is ostracized by her friends and rejected by her boyfriend Tony. Things seem at an all-time low when she fails to qualify for the school swim meet and then suffers from an unsightly rash, a side effect of her medication. Through the support of her best friend Susan, and Steve, a new boy in her class, she gradually struggles with her own self-doubt and fragile self-image to convince herself of her own personal strength. The play was written by Gordon Ruttan with help and advice from John Ellis; it was produced and directed by Dennis Hargreave.

At the same time, Playing With Time produced a special program entitled _Growing Up with Sandy Offenheim_. The theme of the program has to do with the feelings of a young person who feels deserted when left at home by her older brother or sister who have gone to a party. The author, Sandy Offenheim, has built the script around lyrics and music which she had developed over several years. A beautifully animated sequence about a family of butterflies serves as a thematic link between the vignettes. Additional animation is based on the drawings of Patty Stren, a popular writer and illustrator of children's books. "Plasticine people" illustrate what it's like to "swallow your tooth for lunch," and how it feels to be "high to tummy," a child's-eye view. Children join the Offenheim family with short vignettes of their experiences, and exemplify how ridiculous grownups sound when they talk to babies.

Concurrently, Harcourt has worked with Evergreen Raccoons Productions in Ottawa to produce a sequence of animated specials such as _The Christmas Raccoons_, _The_

Raccoons on Ice, The Raccoons and the Lost Star and The Raccoons--Let's Dance. Most recently, a series of eleven half-hours has been completed for presentation in the current schedule of the CBC. Kevin Gillis, producer-director as well as creator of the Raccoons characters, also composes the music for the productions. He was host of Yes You Can, the sports program referred to elsewhere in this history. He began his career as a songwriter and performer, and has toured with such celebrities as Mary Travers of Peter, Paul and Mary.

The Raccoons specials have received high ratings in Canada and the U.S.A. as well as in the international market. The full animation is done in Canada (with the facilities of Atkinson Film Arts in Ottawa) with four drawings per 35 film foot without high re-use repeating backgrounds and animated cycles (repeat drawings) so common in less artistic animation.

More recently, Harcourt concluded a series of six dramatizations of Canadian short stories with six more currently in production, all to be scheduled for showing in prime time. The series of 12 half-hour dramas, titled Sons and Daughters, all deal with believable young people facing issues and problems of common concern. All 12 of these dramas are based on well-known Canadian stories by writers such as Alice Munro, Earle Birney and L. M. Montgomery. The stories selected focus on young people in search of themselves and the joys and sorrows associated with that search common to all mankind. Set in the forties, Munro's "Boys and Girls" explores the frustrating period in a young girl's life when she discovers that her parents expect and demand that she follow the traditional woman's role. L. M. Montgomery's "I Know a Secret" is a tale of a young girl new in town and desperately trying to belong. Taunted by village children, she courageously confronts the local ne'er-do-well and learns the best secret of them all.

Harcourt pursues the development of drama for children over seven because she believes that from that age on they are almost totally absorbed in adult entertainment. It is therefore immensely important to provide the best dramatic entertainment possible in order to increase the young viewer's sense of selfhood as a competent Canadian individual. Harcourt says, "What's wrong is that children are under-represented on television. Having to deal with this problem every day,

I think of them as the last minority.... Children like to see themselves depicted honestly and in a complex way on television.... They don't like false situations of any kind.... They do like to see other ordinary children in extraordinary situations," but they demand sincerity and reality as the certain means to build self-confidence and to help them realize maturity.

From the earliest days, attempts were made to provide Canadian serialized dramas for children. The first abortive attempt was a joint project between the English network and Radio Canada to produce a series based upon the explorations of Pierre Radisson. With bilingual actors, the series was shot on location in both French and English. These were the days when cost accounting for television programs was very simplistic. In this case, most of the budget was used up after six or seven shows had been completed. Fernand Doré, the head of children's TV in Radio Canada, then took over the production, revising the budget and predictably, scaling down the size and extent of the enterprise. Today, better planning eliminates the possibility of such disasters.

In spite of the fiscal problems, the scripts by John Lucarotti, based on Radisson's journal, were carefully researched. The producer, Jean Yves Bigras, and director Pierre Gauvreau for the CBC worked with Omega Productions of Montreal to make the production as authentic as possible. The title role was played by Jacques Godin, with René Caron as his fellow explorer, De Grosseilliers.

Many years later, with some support and commitment from the CBC, Maxine Samuels undertook production of The Forest Rangers, an outdoor adventure series about the exploits of a group of boys and girls (Junior Forest Rangers) and their adventures involving the local adult forest rangers and the Royal Canadian Mounted Police. The stories ranged from scenes of actual forest fire fighting to gold prospecting to slapstick comedy.

The leading role of Chub Stanley, the young city boy who goes to live with his foster parents in the fictional town of Indian River, was played by Ralph Endersby. The Chief Ranger, George Keeley, was played by Graydon Gould and his younger brother, Peter Keeley, by Rex Hagon. Others in the cast included Sergeant Brian Scott of the RCMP, played by

Gordon Pinsent, and Junior Forest Rangers included Mike Forbes (Peter Tully), Gaby LaRoche (Syme Jago and Susan Conway), Zeke (Ron Cohoon), Joe Two Rivers (Michael Zenon), Ted (George Allan), a comic character McLeod (Joe Austin). The producer of the first two seasons was Ted Holliday; Bill Davidson took over in the third year.

Ralph Ellis of Manitou Productions developed Matt and Jenny in the late seventies with cooperation from Société Radio Canada and the Global TV Network. The series of 26 half-hour programs centres on the adventures of Matt and Jenny Tanner, brother and sister aged about 14. Ellis provides the following description of the series:

> Matt and Jenny on the Wilderness Trail, 1850
>
> A colourful and exciting, early prime time, outdoor action-adventure television series set in Canada and the bordering United States during the middle of the nineteenth century.
>
> The story of Matt and Jenny Tanner, brother and sister, aged about fourteen, working class, street-wise children from Bristol, England, who emigrate to Canada with their mother in 1850, about a year after their father's death. They are leaving the world of Charles Dickens for the world of Mark Twain, Fenimore Cooper, Hawthorne and Thoreau translated into Canadian experience. Their objective is to join their uncle and his family, who emigrated to a farm near Halifax, Nova Scotia, a few years earlier.
>
> However, on board ship, tragedy strikes. An epidemic of typhoid fever breaks out, and the children's mother dies. Her dying wish is for the children to continue the journey and join their uncle in the new world. But Matt and Jenny fear that the Captain or some official will return them to England, or place them in an orphans' home in Montreal. They plot to escape when the ship docks at Halifax to unload cargo.
>
> While attempting to escape they are falsely accused of theft and must flee the city and the police. In this situation they are helped by Adam Cardston, a tall, mysterious man in his forties, who had been a passenger on board the ship. All we know of him is that, after spending many years travelling throughout the world, he is returning home to Canada. He

is on his way to the West, for reasons known only to himself.

The young Tanners have a rough, hand-printed map that gives the location of their uncle's farm. Adam Cardston offers to help them elude the police and reach the farm safely. They set out by coach, then by foot through the bush, where they encounter their first North American wilderness adventure on a wild ride through the rapids on a runaway raft. During this exciting action they meet Kit, another unique wilderness character. He is about twenty-five, a young Daniel Boone, knowledgeable about life in the bush, expert with animals, strong and agile.

When the young Tanners reach the farm they discover that it is abandoned. They learn from an old Indian woman that their uncle and his family left for the West by wagon three months ago, planning to work their way across Canada and the northern United States, through the camps and settlements along the wilderness trail. The children are determined to catch up with them and join the family. Adam Cardston and Kit, who will be travelling west on the same trail, agree to keep an eye on them ... and try to help them find their relatives.

With that story established in program number one ... our series of wilderness adventures gets under way.

The latest foray into serialized drama for children is The Edison Twins, produced by Ian McDougal for Nelvana Ltd. in association with CBC Children's Television and the Disney Cable Channel in the U.S. The series is an innovative drama adventure series about Tom and Annie Edison (played by Andrew Sabiston and Marnie McPhail) as teenagers who solve life's little problems and mysteries through an exceptional knowledge of science.

Their younger brother Paul (Sunny Thrasher) possesses an extraordinarily entrepreneurial skill. His enthusiasm to be involved with his older brother and sister puts him right in the thick of things--like the time he went monster hunting and fell down the bluffs only to be rescued by Tom and Annie.

Most recently the CBC has launched a new television series entitled Spirit Bay under the supervision of Dennis Hargrave. The six new half-hour shows in this series deal

The Spirit Bay Braves, in Spirit Bay. (Courtesy of CBC)

with life in a native community in northern Ontario. The series is produced by Eric Jordan and Paul Stephens in association with CBC and Telefilm Canada. The films are shot in the remote area of McDermid, a northern Ontario community in the Rocky Bay reserve where a fictional Ojibway community exists. The residents of Spirit Bay have adapted to white society while retaining traditional links to the land through trapping, fishing, and hunting. The episodes will focus on the spiritual kinship between Spirit Bay families, nature, and modern life on the reserve, from a child's viewpoint.

Babar and Father Christmas is a fully animated half-hour special produced by Atkinson Film Arts and MTR Ottawa Productions Ltd. in association with the Canadian Broadcasting Corporation. The program was scheduled at 7:30 p.m. on December 15 as family viewing. The story, Jean de Brunhoff's last book, published in 1940, is narrated by his son Laurent de Brunhoff, with Alison Clayton as producer.

The productive culmination of cooperation between the CBC and independent producers was most fully realized in the 120-minute production of Louisa Maude Montgomery's Anne of Green Gables, presented as a mini-series in December of 1985 in two one-hour episodes. The role of Anne, performed by Megan Follows, was outstanding. The show was the highest rated drama in CBC's history and won an Emmy for the "outstanding children's program of the year." A sequel based on other stories about Anne written by L. M. Montgomery, such as Anne of Avonlea, Anne of Windy Poplars and Anne of the Island, is scheduled for presentation in 1987-88.

Nada Harcourt, executive producer of independent productions, along with producer Kevin Sullivan, worked with a team of technical people who had had previous experience with independent productions for children. The experience accumulated among a community of concerned artists and technicians gave Megan Follows the support she needed to give her dynamic portrayal of Anne of Green Gables.

Danger Bay is a dramatic series of 26 half hours about a trouble-shooting veterinarian, Grant "Doc" Roberts, who is also curator of marine animals at the Vancouver Aquarium, and his two children, Jonah (14) and Nicole (12). They live on Danger Bay on a small island just off the beautiful and rugged coast of the Pacific Northwest. Dr. Roberts fights against toxic waste dumpers, poachers and ecological disasters while he raises his two children as a single parent. He is often helped by his two children as well as by family friend Joyce Carter, an expert helicopter and seaplane pilot. The stories are about hair-raising rescue missions when people and animals are in conflict.

Trapper Jack is a series of 30-minute dramas for children which present problems of young people and their families trying to meet the hostile challenges of the environment of northern British Columbia. Trapper Jack, who usually comes to the rescue in critical situations, is a mythical old man of the mountains who can be seen only by children. The series is produced by Peter Reynolds-Long and Walter Liimatainen of CFTK TV Skeena Broadcasters Ltd. of Terrace, B.C.

Another series by the same team, is entitled Young Offenders. Two half-hour dramatic episodes focus on the problems of young teenagers in confrontation with the remote

[Top:] Megan Follows and Richard Farnsworth in Anne of Green Gables.
[Below:] Megan Follows and Dame Wendy Hiller in Anne of Green Gables--The Sequel.

environment of northern British Columbia. In one episode, a teenager seeks to vent his anger and hostility in drinking and reckless driving. He ends up in a high-speed chase with the law in which a tragic accident occurs. The viewer follows the juvenile through a trial in which the Royal Canadian Mounted Police, the lawyers, and ambulance personnel all play their real-life roles. An another episode the subject of peer pressure on teenagers is the theme. A young man becomes involved with two other teenagers who coerce him into being the "lookout" during a break/enter theft. Again the viewer witnesses the trial.

Rocket Boy, a pilot series of five half-hour episodes, also produced by Nelvana, Limited as a live-action drama series, tells the story of how Slip Stevens, a simple electronics clerk, is summoned by Palemon, "The Wise One", to his luminary spaceship. Here, Slip is transformed into Rocket Boy, a Guardian of Good, a man of unnerving wit and awe-inspiring intelligence. It is Rocket Boy who endangers himself and fights against the evil clutches and hair-raising schemes of the legendary "Hawkhead," so that our children might live in a galaxy where honor, truth, freedom, justice and common decency prevail.

Inspector Gadget is a series of half-hour dramas with animation by Nelvana Limited, produced by Michael Hirsch, Patrick Laubert and Clive A. Smith. From humble beginnings as Police Inspector in a small provincial town and a near-fatal slip on a banana peel, Gadget is propelled into a world of international crime and intrigue after a sophisticated, top-secret operation transforms him into a mechanical miracle. Each episode pits Inspector Gadget, and his trusty assistants Penny and Brain, against a colorful and unique adversary of the International Order of Crime, M.A.D., and its maniacal master, Dr. Claw.

Adventures in Rainbow Country (1968), a popular family adventure series, features the life and adventures of a 14-year-old boy growing up in Canada's rugged north. Betty Williams, whose father disappeared in mysterious circumstances, helps his mother and sister operate a year-round resort lodge on a beautiful bay near Whitefish Falls.

Betty's closest friend and confidant is a teenage Indian boy, Pete, who is wise in the ways of the wilderness. Other

Chapter VII

VARIETY PROGRAMMING FOR CHILDREN

In many ways, programs under this heading are extensions of either magazine programming (Coming Up Rosie, Homemade TV or For Kids Only). The difference is that either they deal with a single subject like "rock music" or they occur once a week rather than daily as was the case with Coming Up Rosie, which also had something of a plot to each episode. A show like You Can't Do That On Television, produced by Roger Price for Standard Broadcasting Company in Ottawa and carried on both CTV and the Nickelodeon Pay-TV system in the U.S.A., is pure light entertainment. Michele Landsberg of the Toronto Star observed that show had

> the goofball charm of a Second City apprentice who's stumbled onto the set of a Monty Python film. 'Television, like teachers, should be on the side of kids' ... and his young performers, ages 10 to 18, respond to the unpretentious mood and wacky scripts with marvellously laid-back, wry comedy performances. [May 11, 1982]

The kids set out to ridicule everything from politics to television commercials. There is much contrived confrontation with adults about issues of common concern. Many of the themes deal with the plight of the underdog, who frequently finds a way to put down his tormentor. The show appreciates contemporary teenage humor and rewards sincerity. Price, born in the United Kingdom, received his early training in the Children's Television Department of the BBC. By his own admission, he is influenced by A. S. Neill, the headmaster of Summerhill School who spent his life trying to develop a curriculum which would help adults to see the world from a child's point of view.

As early as 1954, the show *Youth Takes a Stand* was presented as a panel organized around contemporary issues of concern to teenagers. Messrs. Vern Trott and Gordon Blackford of Forest Hill Collegiate Institute, Toronto were the organizers. In contrast to the leadership given by Price to *You Can't Do That On Television*, the young people selected often tended to deal with issues as they expected adults might. We later learned ways to win more sincere and immediate responses from the participants in the show.

Concurrently, from Montreal, *Small Fry Frolics* (1952), with Frank and Dorothy Heron, was produced for younger teens to respond to some of the problems of growing up, like keeping a bank account or baby-sitting. This part of the show took the form of a "press conference" with a panel of youngsters aiming questions at a guest. In another section of the show, the participants engaged in a quiz. The winners appeared on the next show and if they won a second time, they went to a third program where the winner was given a briefcase. The show continued for three years, after which it was transferred to radio.

As a summer replacement for *Hidden Pages*, Vancouver provided the *Junior Television Club*: five children as hosts interviewed other children with interesting hobbies. Gregory Helem undertook the hobby section, which dealt with the care and feeding of pets including some unusual ones such as a year-old bear cub. Averil Campbell acted as emcee for discussions about pocket money, the use of make-up, etc., while Bobby Olson interviewed athletes and experts on crafts and camping. Margaret Stott undertook the job of introducing young musicians and the group hosted performances by talented young people.

Clubhouse 8 (1964), from St. John's, Newfoundland, was scheduled on Saturdays at noon as a local show with Barbara Crosbie and Sean O'Leary hosting young people who demonstrated their hobbies and pets. Free beanies in the show's colors, badges with the name of the show and free ice cream were given out. In addition, there was a swap shop where boys and girls could show viewers the articles they would like to trade. To add a light touch of variety, there was a rousing singalong with some of St. John's best piano players.

Youth '60 (1959-60), produced in Toronto, was first hosted by two young people who had met at the U.N. Model Assembly--Penny Williams and Dorothy Crothall. The show was a shop window for young talent including a 14-year-old singer, Richard Prew from Hull, an instrumental group from Edmonton, The Harmony Kids, and Valery Siren, a talented folksinger from Toronto. They also talked about art with a young sculptor, Brian Salter, and a fashion artist. The show also included adults such as physicist Dr. Donald Ivey from the University of Toronto, wrestler Whipper Billy Watson and forensic scientist Dr. H. Ward Smith. Tommy Hunter later served as host on the show introducing Joey Hollingsworth as a dancer.

Club 6 was a local variety show for teenagers produced in Toronto by Paddy Sampson with Mike Darow as host. The show was a spin-off from Dick Clark's American Bandstand--a compromise between teenagers' dancing and a public affairs show. Each show featured one school giving some attention to the achievements of its pupils while the hosts in general, including the studio audience of some 200 young people, enjoyed rock music. Mike Darow, known for his regular rock show on CHUM radio, was the host.

A variation on program formats for teenagers was Tween Set (1966), produced by Denyse Adam from Montreal. As the title indicated, the content was aimed at the "in-between" set--the 10-12-year-olds. The format comprised a weekly quiz, a panel discussion, word games such as "rain or shine" and "spell-o-rama," and special guests such as hobbyists, gym teams, folkdancers, musical groups or choirs. Junior hosts were chosen from the Tween Set to introduce the show and provide continuity between the segments. The junior host and hostess changed every six weeks to provide more opportunities for participation. A senior host acted as quizmaster and a senior hostess served as moderator of the panel discussions. Tweens at home were invited to join in by sending their answers to a Weekly Home Challenge. Three winners would be selected from Montreal, Ottawa, Winnipeg, St. John's or Halifax, wherever the program was seen. Winners received a gift certificate for a long-playing record of their choice. They were also invited to become members of the Tween Set and receive membership pins. Mail response indicated that the show had a steady loyal audience: they received about 1000 letters a week.

Music Hop (1963) originated with the Variety or Light Entertainment Department as a half-hour showcase for aspiring folksingers, pop vocalists, rhythm and blues singers and rock and roll performers. Stan Jacobson was the producer and Alex Trebek the host. They auditioned teenage performers to select a vocal trio to be a regular part of the cast with the orchestrated group headed by Jazzman Norm Amadio. Guests were brought in to give the show a professional air but there were regular auditions for young dancers, singers and performers who would contribute to the show.

After a successful year, Music Hop was expanded to five days a week with editions from CBC regional centers. Co-hosts presented a show like Music Hop, subtitled Let's Go, from Vancouver, Montreal (Jeunesse Oblige), Winnipeg, Toronto (Music Hop), and Halifax. In 1965, Dave Michie, a "deejay" with rapid-fire delivery, took over from Trebek as host. The nature of the show is best summed up by writer Sandy Stern, who wrote the following in response to Ralph Thomas's critique of the show in the Toronto Daily Star in 1967. The show is

> a reflection of the hit parade and that can be anything from rock to R&B to bossa nova, etc.... The musicians happen to be studio musicians and the fact that they are top jazz musicians is coincidental. They are on the show because budget and time requires our musicians to be expert readers. Unfortunately, the majority of your so-called crack musicians can't read a note! [Toronto Daily Star, Oct. 7, 1967; quoted from a column by TV commentator Ralph Thomas.]

As she says, the show is "pop," not "pop-rock."

In keeping with the professional tone of Club 6, Music Hop and Let's Go, the Light Entertainment Department continued the tradition with The Music Machine (1970), featuring Moe Koffman's Orchestra and highlighting outstanding pop and rock musicians with hits of the day along with flashbacks to the past. Also, in keeping with Music Hop, new, young performers were introduced, including The Machinery, a pop-singing group, and Steve Kennedy of the Motherlode rock group. Fans of rock music will remember Brian Russell and Rhonda Silver, Laurie Hood (of the Sugar Shoppe), Terry Black from the Toronto company of Hair, Tranquility Base

Alex Trebek, original host of Music Hop.

from Hamilton. There were interviews with these "celebrities" plus commentary on new records. Big band singer Bob Francis was the host, the director/writer was Ron Meraska and the producer, Jack Budgell.

As the series continued over some three or four years, The Rolling Stones were among their guests. Keith Hampshire, the young singer-actor-comedian, took over as host, backed up by a nine-member Canadian group, Dr. Music. Comedy segments were provided by members of the team The Zoo Factory (Dan Hennessy, John Stocker and others). A spoof of Ann Landers with advice to teenagers came from Lorraine Precious; a "good news" routine was done vaudeville style, to offset some of the day's gloomy headlines; a variety of stand-up jokes was provided by members of the Keith Hampshire Fan Club, whose members included a woman roller derby skater with the name Wanda Crusher.

After Four (on CBC) became a generic title for the daily children's half-hour programs Monday to Friday during the 1977-78 season. Among these programs was a pilot program entitled After Four which featured Christopher Ward and his band. In 1979 the pilot was developed into a full series known as Catch Up, starring Christopher Ward and his band with Margot Pinvidic featuring new songs written by young Canadians. The theme song, "Catch Up," was written by lead guitarist David Whipper. Along with repeats of songs written for After Four, excerpts from Ward's album "Spark of Desire" were performed. In addition, Ward and Margot Pinvidic conducted a lyrics contest among the viewers. The prize-winner's lyrics were then set to music by Ward and played by his band.

The New Music (1979) was presented by CITY TV Toronto as

> an innovative, street-wise video equivalent of Rolling Stone magazine. The New Music uses port-a-packs instead of typewriters, capturing the raw energy of today's and tomorrow's headlining rock'n'roll stars with concert clips, news, reviews, and exclusive interviews. Rock veterans J. D. Roberts and Jeanne Beker take to the streets to talk with the fans, the musicians and the artists who have made rock'n'roll their life.

CITY TV scheduled the program daily at 10:40 p.m. Monday through Friday, featuring rock and reggae groups. At the same time, the hosts under John Martin's direction tried to achieve a personal approach. "We try to get the performers out of context and bring them down to a one-to-one level." They tried to keep the show timely, as when they interviewed audience members the night after the Who concert tragedy in Cincinnati.

> We try to promote Canadian talent and cover groups like Rish and Triumph who wouldn't originally get TV exposure. It's hard to keep a finger on the pulse of what is happening because new bands are popping up each day. But we're running into so many musicians with something to say. [J. D. Roberts]

Music programs are always likely to be part of the children's schedule. It was appropriate that the programs described above should have originated with the light entertainment department rather than with Schools and Youth, because of their ready and available knowledge of the talent required. The policy of encouraging new Canadian talent was consistent with that of Schools and Youth.

Rod Coneybeare described his experimental series, The Bananas (1969), as "sensible nonsense for anyone who's hip." Bob Gibbons, the producer, said it's "sane madness for kids 9 to 14." In keeping with Rod Coneybeare's philosophy as a writer, he avoided patronage of kids and gratuitous violence. Instead, he blended humor, satire, and slapstick to make a fun-filled half-hour with a serious intellectual quality behind it. "I wanted a free-flowing, fantastical, way-in show, neither namby-pamby nor full of cartoon violence, a kind of Godard or Fellini film for kids, but with enough understated slapstick to draw adults too."

To realize their intentions, Coneybeare searched through the CBC's Props Department to find a mad mixture of costumes and special effects to fill the set of Bananaland. The Pet Mouth was a huge mobile rubber mouth which, when fed a wheelbarrow of food by the Bananas, would regurgitate educational information. But whenever the pet got out of hand, its lips could always be buttoned.

Another dramatic device employed was The Reverse: a

running skit in which children act like adults and vice versa. For example, a son arrives home after a hard day's work in the sandbox, all set for a quiet evening with soft drinks and comics, only to find that he must punish his father for riding his bike.

The cast comprised The Bananas--Melody Greer (22), Bonnie Carol Case (21), John Davies (32), and Francois Klanfer (27)--and Alan Maitland, the Great Announcer (an off-camera guide through Bananaland and a foil for the Bananas, providing the only semblance of logic and continuity to the show--even though he does betray from time to time that "deep down" he is a Banana too).

Ed Hausmann summed up the spirit of the show in the Toronto Star as follows:

> The Bananas run around in different costumes in nearly every sketch, and there are about a dozen sketches in each show. It could be called a Laugh-In for kids, but Coneybeare's idea is to go beyond that--to be, through some strange chemistry that he's only beginning to understand, a catalyst for making kids think. You may argue that the theme song, for example, is downright inane--but when it's performed by the Bananas it could just be a subliminal satire on all commercials and musical comedies you hear these days:
>
> When a Banana wakes up in the morning
> It knows the day has a peel!
> It's all toast and jam-ah
> When you're a Banana!!

The show was a trial series which, by all accounts, was a success. Unfortunately, there were not sufficient funds to allow for further development of the series and it was replaced two or three days in the week by The Banana Splits, an inferior but popular syndicated film show of cartoons, music, comedy and serials--enthusiastically sponsored by Kellogg.

The Marbles (1970) was another attempt at comedy-variety for children, devised by producer Gloria White. Like

Bananas, the show had a team of regulars selected from a panel of some 80 candidates. The final six who were selected included Harriet Cohen and her husband Graham Teear, Mary Bellours, Gail Malenfant, Rudy Lavalle and Stephen Katz. The show consisted of a series of fast-paced comedy sketches and blackouts with as many as ten costume changes on each show.

As in the case of The Bananas, an attempt was made to see humor and satire through a young person's eyes. In choosing the subjects, the writers (David Mayer, William Lynn, Gary Gray and Fred Hallett) kept in mind good taste and "kookiness"--anything a kid might enjoy. For example, in bidding Sir Francis Drake good-bye as he goes off to meet the Spanish Armada, Queen Elizabeth warns him in a "mother-like" tone to button up warmly, wear his mittens, and if he gets the sniffles to go right to bed and drink plenty of hot tea. When Drake is out of sight the Queen turns to her lady-in-waiting (not smiling) and says, "I do hope the dear boy smashes the Spanish; otherwise, I will have to cut off his head."

> No attempt is made to cover any of the subjects in depth ... nor do we adhere strictly to the facts, but if the mere mention of a subject can entertain, then our purpose is achieved.
>
> We also present contemporary manners and mores in a satirical way, social advice for the young, their questions and some answers. In short, we take a look at most everything that affects our youngsters today --parents, schools, sports, current issues, dating and fashion. Sometimes our sketches have a message, sometimes they are strictly for fun.

Heard regularly throughout the shows are Mr. and Mrs. Announcer--two off-camera voices supplied by Alan Maitland and Maggie Morris. They announce the sketches, talk to the Marbles and to each other. Appearing frequently throughout the series are two comical cavemen, Conklin and Fogbert.

The Marbles was replaced by Drop-In, described elsewhere as a magazine program.

In Marc's Grab Bag (1973), a young musician, Marc Stone, sought to share his show with young musicians like himself as well as creative people in other media. Besides songs written and sung by himself, he presented a rising young pop star, Shirley Eikhard of Oshawa, and actor/comedian Eugene Levy. In later shows, the Grab Bag included comic Valri Bromfield, sketch artist Geraldine Johnson, violinist John Robinson, animator Helen Morency, singer Tony Kosinec, puppeteer Nina Keogh, singer/composer Lisa dal Bello, dancer Vera Beloshisky and filmmaker Mark Shel. The show was backed up by a trio, sidemen Lorne Grossman, Richard Fruchtman and Alan Shiner on piano.

From Newfoundland came Skipper and Company (1980), with Ray Bellew playing the role of an old retired sea captain around whom most of the action takes place. He is often joined by his friends, the postman, Vincent Vagabond, a weary "magical" friend of the captain, Charlie Lee, the captain's cook, who is often heard screaming and yelling from his kitchen, and Corky, an old companion.

The setting is the Captain's living room where he meets and introduces young and old talented entertainers of Newfoundland--folksingers, dancers, composers, instrumentalists, dramatists and guests with interesting hobbies, such as model boat builder Bill Noseworthy with his model of a Lunenberg banker, sailing by remote control on the waters of Quidi Vidi Lake. The show also included information segments, with a sergeant of the Newfoundland constabulary, Premier Joseph Smallwood, a carpenter, and an anthropologist. The show was produced by Jack Kellman and was seen across the English network of CBC.

A unique variety show entitled Just Kidding (1982) was produced for cable TV in Whitehorse, the Yukon, where Virginia Gibberd persuaded the business community to provide $1000 for videotape to record the show for broadcast. With volunteers whom she had to train, and with technicians and performers trained by Jean Stanton of the local children's theatre, they developed themes ranging from rock and roll to ventriloquism, interviews with biologists about the fragile environment of the Arctic, and covered an anti-cruise missile demonstration in Whitehorse.

Switchback (1980) was originally developed by Nijole Kuzmikas in Toronto as a show uniquely conceived for local station production on Sunday mornings.

> It is a 90-minute live magazine variety show for 10-14 year olds. It is a combination of cartoons, serials, videotapes of rock groups (these are procured materials), along with our own live phone-ins, in which the audience is able to participate in a weekly traded newsletter. Once a week, Switchboard publishes a traded newsletter which kids, who have contacted us during the week have listed items which they have to trade, e.g., a person who has a skateboard and is wanting to trade it for a soccerball. In addition we have our own produced items be they little comedy skits or interviews with rock stars, sports celebrities, etc.

The show, presented from Vancouver with host Rick Scott, won the ACTRA award for its freshness and its relevance for a teen audience. The idea was picked up in Halifax where Stan Johnson as host and producer John Nowlan have had equal success.

The success of the show rest on its local live presentation and the opportunity it affords for immediate interaction between the audience and the set. The show offers potential for the use of computers, of Telidon and other new technologies --especially if game shows can be effectively adapted for interactive TV.

Let's Go (1979), produced by Gary Robson at CKY-TV, Winnipeg, with Janis Dunning as hostess, provides both entertainment and learning experiences for viewers aged three to 12. With a minimum of props and musical instruments, the children who participate in the show are left free to create ideas and implement them. With the help of Janis Dunning, the children propose new hobbies or turn a simple song into a musical drama. Ms. Dunning uses her skills in music and choreography to help the children express their ideas more fully and more meaningfully.

Hobbledehoy is a magazine show for CBC Montreal produced by Denyse Adam with host Ian Finlay for children of the middle years. The show, written by Arnie Greenberg, is a combination of short items ranging from crafts to take-offs on gourmet cooking to "kid-jokes and limericks," interesting out-of-the-way news items, and guessing games. The sequences are well designed, leaving the viewer with a clear sense of comprehension. At the same time the show moves along at a fast but rhythmic pace.

An elephant and Eric Nagler join Sharon, Lois and Bram, and children on The Elephant Show. (Courtesy of CBC)

The latest innovation for young children is The Elephant Show, featuring Sharon, Lois, and Bram, who have developed a national reputation for their skills of communication with children through music. They play games, sing songs, tell jokes, exchange stories, and visit new and wonderful places. Elephant plans to spend the day at the National Ballet School of Canada and join an aerobics class. The whole group visits Black Creek Pioneer Village, or attends the September apple-pickers' festival, or spends an exciting afternoon at the colorful Kensington Market in Toronto. Each program revolves around a theme and features music videos, animation, live concert performers and a special guest each week.

Another new series, entitled Vid Kids, features the internationally known and loved chidlren's performer Bob Schneider, whose singing, dancing, and acting out of the lyrics of two of his original songs occurs in every episode. The program will provide a showcase for 13 guest performers who in true music-video style bring their unique songs to life. More than 500 dancing kids, swirl and whirl in the spectacular Vid Kids' disco to well-known tunes from the Beatles to Wham.

A new Canadian series, Vid Kids. (Courtesy of CBC)

The series is a co-production of M&M Productions and Avenue Television Incorporated, with the participation of Telefilm Canada, the CBC, and Carlton Productions Ltd. The producer and director is John Muller, with co-producer Tom Reynolds and co-director Chris Terry. Janis Nosbakken served as the senior story editor.

Tiny Talent Time, produced by CHCH-TV in Hamilton with Bill Lawrence as the host, realizes the traditional formula of young performers demonstrating their skills in instrumental music, song and dance. The host introduces them and asks questions about family and school along with questions about their interest in performance. A variation of this format is to be seen in Stardate, a production of CHSJ in Saint John, New Brunswick, providing talented children with the opportunity to entertain other children.

Willy and Floyd, a weekly half-hour program produced for Carlton Productions and CJOH-TV Ottawa by Bob Swaffield, attempts to combine humor with "entertaining information." It is difficult to know the age group for which the show is intended. At what age can one expect children to be interested in disco dancing? Willy and Floyd have a kind of "Laurel and Hardy" relationship, more "verbal" than "situational." They share "corny" jokes, sometimes in reference to the informational segment being presented.

The Dale Harney Show features Dale Harney (who also stars in Dale Harney's Magic Palace and Lynsky and Co.) with a magazine of magic tricks, social games, riddles and a segment, "It's a Fact," presenting unusual information from sources such as Ripley's Believe It Or Not or the Guinness Book of Records. The segment is without visuals--simply a graphic card with voice-over. The riddles are presented by Harney and the answer given after the commercial or public service message. A studio audience of children participates in the magic tricks and in the games for which prizes are given.

Dale Harney's Magic Palace is a variation on the original show, entailing the introduciton of other magicians who team up with Harney, focusing especially on card tricks or sleight-of-hand. They team up on more spectacular tricks, such as disappearing acts.

Lynsky and Co. is another variation of the team of Harney and his wife Sheila to provide a variety show for a younger audience. Ralph, an oversize "hound dog" (a man dressed in a hound dog costume borrowed from a local shopping center), acts as a foil to frustrate Harney's magic tricks or Lynsky's songs. Sheila Harney plays Lynsky but takes on various roles, as a comic Roxy who presents interesting information, or Jivin' Jackie the disc jockey who sings popular music. Much of the continuity depends on word play and some slapstick with Ralph providing many of the comic or absurd situations.

The Treehouse Club (1971) with Danny Coughlan is a standby of children's programming from Kitchener's CKCO-TV. Each week a group of children "climb the ladder" to the Treehouse to be greeted by Danny and his puppet friends JoJo and Frank. The show is built around Coughlan's ability as a singer and his skill in drawing. The content is based on Ted Rooney's five textbooks which deal with reading, mathematics, spelling, grammar and sensory-motor body balance exercises. The script contains many elements of cautionary wisdom and exhortations for conventional manners. Visitors include regulars such as Lisa, the mailgirl who arrives with letters to Danny. She then stays on to demonstrate, with the children's participation, some useful physical exercises. This year, on-location segments have been added, e.g., Danny's interviews with Wayne Gretzky, a feature on the Blue Jays, and how to become a good baseball player. The drawing segments now include the use of computers. The show is produced by Ted Roony and directed by Calvin Shaver, while Betty Thompson serves as consultant for the series.

Oopsy the Clown (CKCO-TV Kitchener) is written and produced by Robert J. McNea, who has had a career as a professional clown for nearly 40 years. With the help of his family, Ooopsy the circus clown has taken up residence at the hill place in the imaginary town of Daisyville where several of his puppet friends also live. Frances Kay McNea portrays Dairy Dora, the Daisyville milk lady who delivers her dairy products "in metric format." She is also featured in "Crafty Fun" and acts as the main puppeteer.

Michael McNea plays Mr. Pouch, the Daisyville mailman. He does his job with a variety of exasperating comic routines. Michael also plays Billy Baker the doughnut maker, whose doughnuts all have square holes. Like his father, he has taken up clowning and occasionally appears as Punky the Clown.

Kathy Lynn McNea, a professional pianist and singer, performs popular songs as well as her own compositions designed for children of all ages. She assists as a puppeteer and plays Willhamena, the Baker's Wife and Birdy Featherwing, a naturalist and bird lover.

The Buckshot Show is a half-hour show from CFCN-TV with host and creator Ron Barge (Buckshot) who has entertained children in the Calgary area daily from 12:30 to 1:00 p.m., Monday through Saturday, for the past 17 years. With a group of puppet characters led by Benny the Bear, Heathcliffe the Dragon, Dafney the Dragon, Foghorn the Firefly, Rodney the Rodent and Farley Frick from Maple Crik, Buckshot "strives to be fun for children in the pre-school and elementary school age group and, at the same time, recognizes the opportunity to provide important quasi-educational elements. This responsive mix of program elements includes fire safety, water safety and bicycle safety, information on community events the children would want to be aware of, and music and song selected and performed in a fashion directly for children."

The show is presented live for the most part. From time to time, mini-dramas are produced with the characters from the regular Buckshot Show. More attention is given to production values. One comedy/drama, "The Missing Caper," won the annual Children's Broadcast Institute Award in the independent station category. In keeping with the policy of attracting a local audience, the theme was on developing awareness of the planning for Calgary's 1988 Winter Olympics.

Video Hits: in response to the current craze for rock videos among young people, a personable hostess, Samantha Taylor, presents a sequence of current rock video hits on the CBC network.

Archie and His Friends, produced by CKY-TV Winnipeg, is an on-going half-hour series for pre-school children in which ventriloquist Uncle Bob and Archie entertain children with crafts, animals and birthday telephone calls. Guests of interest to children are introduced frequently.

All for Fun, CKY-TV Winnipeg: Al Simmons and Barbara Freundl portray a variety of characters as they entertain and educate young viewers with skits, jokes, songs, experiments, crafts and visits to interesting places. The series consists of 26 episodes, each running for 58 minutes and 50 seconds.

Paul Hann and Friends, produced by CFRN Edmonton and carried on the CTV network, is a 30-minute variety program for children hosted by folksinger Paul Hann. This is a fast-paced entertainment show presenting a variety of guests including clowns, mime artists and puppeteers. The host, originally from England, makes the most of his accent to create humor in his rendition of country and western music (the Cockney Cowboy). The show aims to encourage audience participation.

Telecultura: over 100 50-minute episodes produced by the Graham Cable Corporation to entertain children of 6-12 years of age. The program is a magazine of stories, games, letters of the alphabet and numbers spoken in Italian. The host, Angelo Delapia, is a teacher with the Toronto Board of Education.

shows of this kind for children who like to take information in at their own pace.

In the mid-seventies, TVOntario attempted to meet the challenge of entertainment television for children on Saturday morning with two magazine shows, Cucumber (an acronym for Children's Underground Club of the United Moose and Beaver for Enthusiastic Reporters) and Monkey Bars. Cucumber was presented as a variety and write-in show carefully designed to stimulate and engage the child's active participation in an entertaining and educational situation. The series was hosted by two characters, "Moose" and "Beaver," who encourage the young viewers to participate in the program by becoming members of the "Cucumber Club." The target audience was the 6-9 age group. The show was developed by Clive Vanderburgh and the roles of Moose and Beaver were performed by Nikki Tilroe and Alex Laurier respectively.

A research report on Cucumber indicated preferences for Moose over Beaver, possibly because Moose was the vehicle for movement from the world of reality to the realm of fantasy. While there was great enthusiasm for membership in the Cucumber Club, few if any knew what the acronym represented.

Another series produced by TVOntario, entitled Monkey Bars, was a 50-minute variety/magazine show created for children 7-12 years of age. The show was undertaken as a challenge to the highly commercial fare available on Saturday mornings for children on most networks. Each program incorporated a variety of entertaining and educational elements of particular interest to this age group. The purpose was to stimulate them with ideas and to cultivate a sense of wonder about their environment. The objective was to increase their familiarity with career opportunities, recreation, and fitness activities. Language and communications skills, as well as information about the world of careers, was introduced. The format was based on two characters named Hassle B. DeMille and Dingbat, who keep popping up to confuse the musical group of kids who are called the Monkey Bars. The children sing, dance and act their way through the program with the assistance of Hassle, "a theatrical impresario and junk dealer" who is not very fond of children and who is determined to put a stop to all the fun that they are having. The confrontation between the Monkey Bar kids and Hassle and Dingbat provides the framework for a number of weekly situations, each intended to accommodate educational objectives. The shows included various elements of audience participation, comedy sketches, and over 60 original songs. The basic dramatic devices of jeopardy and adventure, fantasy and lots of music, are used to weave together the educational elements of each program.

When TVOntario diverted the money for these programs to extended adult programming in the evening (Night Music), the production unit moved over to CTV to develop Kidstuff (see Chapter IX).

Since its establishment TVOntario has developed four series which were designed primarily for out-of-school viewing --Polka Dot Door, Cucumber, Monkey Bars and Today's Special Under the umbrella of Galaxie, some four hours of programs including the aforementioned along with selected educational programs and others procured from outside sources were assembled for daily presentation. Galaxie began in 1980 when Rogers Cable TV, the Canadian Satellite Network and TVOntario pooled their resources and talents to develop the program package. The agreement, now about to enter its fourth year, required the cable companies who took the package to pay six cents per household. The agreement entailed annual payment to OECA of $450,000 which went to the development of Today's Special. At its peak of distribution some 25 cable outlets carried the package from coast to coast from 12 noon until 4 p.m. Depending upon people, promotion, access to stations, the viewership varied, but it is estimated that across Canada some 1.5 million homes receive the package. During this time, Galaxie has been laboriously delivered to participating cable companies by means of videotape packages. The CRTC has so far not approved delivery by satellite. Currently the cable companies have been paying eight cents per subscriber per month and offering Galaxie as part of their basic cable service. Costs are absorbed.

The creation of the Ontario Communications Authority came at a time in the 'seventies when the value of instructional TV (ITV) had been thoroughly tested in North America, especially the National Program for the Use of Television in the Public Schools of the United States, sponsored by the Ford Foundation. The only extensive application of televised instruction took place in Nova Scotia, where Grade XI physics and chemistry (and later instruction in oral French) was tried. Teams of teachers worked with those teachers who made the television presentations and the experts in the subject to present a sequenced curriculum in daily 20-minute programs which enabled classroom teachers to do follow-up work in the remaining 25 minutes of a 45-minute period. Under these circumstances the use of television for instructional purposes was reasonably successful. Less successful was the attempt to give instruction via television at Scarborough College in the University of Toronto--a project which was abandoned after only a few years.

From the beginning, TVOntario provided a short series of programs designed to enrich the curriculum. As the production teams gained experience, the quality rose and, in the fashion of Sesame Street, considerable attention was given to artistic presentation of the subject matter in order to capture the interest of young viewers. The success of these techniques observed in classroom situations encouraged TVO programmers to offer the same programs for informal viewing in each package as Galaxie. Should TVO's application for a children's channel be successful, these same programs will most likely be further used for informal viewing.

This portion of the story of children's TV has been confined to the TVO programs which were intended from the beginning to be recreational programs for out-of-school viewing. Schools programs which contain original production techniques and have been used for informal viewing out of school are referred to elsewhere in this report.

Complementary to TVO's endeavor in pre-school programming is Come With Me, produced by ACCESS for children aged 3-5 and designed to help children sort out the realms of fantasy and reality. The action entails visits of two curious youngsters, Kim and Noel, to both rural and urban settings in the company of a wise and friendly old gentleman, Mr. Peach, and a dog, Kelly, who speaks only to kids. Mr. Peach is a great storyteller. At critical points in each show the company is transported by a magic ring to a farm, the Dinosaur Park, a live theatre performance, or sometimes such ordinary activities as helping Mr. Peach give Kelly a bath. The series consists of thirteen 30-minute episodes.

Chapter VIII

PRE-SCHOOL PROGRAMMING

Another area of great concern was pre-school programming. The formats for these programs fall basically into two groups; those which feature a strong personality suitable to evoke meaningful responses from children, and those which are based on the principles of early childhood education. Much has been learned over the years about the responses of young children to television. While this increasing knowledge does affect the content of the programs, the basic formats remain relatively unchanged.

Perhaps the most obvious fault of many programs designed for early childhood viewing is the condescending or patronizing adult. Such personalities frequently appear both in educational programs and in those produced purely for entertainment. Often, program planners are anxious to impose upon children some conventional or conformist tradition which adults expect children to obey. When morality is confused with the "goodness" entailed in brushing one's teeth and going to Sunday school, then one knows that the presenter or writer is confused about the process of education. Essentially there is a lack of concern for the young viewer's individuality.

Bernard Slade remarked that sentimentality was unearned emotion. He argued that there was nothing wrong with sentiment; sentimentality was something different. In short, when feelings are genuinely expressed through the adult's concern for the child, then quality in performance and response is likely to result. Programs for this age group tend to be enduring. The CBC has produced The Friendly Giant for 25 years and Mr. Dressup for 18 years; the attention of young audiences to these distinguished performers is well-deserved.

From the earliest days of television, acute observers noticed that young children achieved a wider vocabulary more rapidly as a result of watching television. No evidence has been provided to explain exactly why this phenomenon took place, but I would venture one or two observations.

At the outset, children are exposed to a wide number of commercial messages, especially when they are watching television unsupervised. We are all familiar with the fact that television commercials rely heavily upon single concepts matched with pictures; to drive the point home, repetition is a common experience. Young children pick up these messages and can imitate them fairly quickly, albeit in large part without comprehending what they are saying. At the same time, while they seem not to fully appreciate the content of the commercial message, some transfer takes place which enables them to use the vocabulary they acquire. In a more positive vein, a number of good children's programs assist the child in learning to speak and perhaps to read, by the manner in which they unify the experience of both vision and sound in such a way as to integrate learning for the children as they grow and develop over the years.

Another factor in the development of pre-school programming for children arose from the distinction necessarily made between play and the didactic element. We learned, early in the game, to choose personalities for children's programs who were capable of inviting playful responses from their young viewers. At the same time, these carefully selected hosts had the natural gift of making children feel that they were important as individuals. The development of such self-confidence was of significant importance to them as they grew towards maturity. The factor of play is an important element in that it entails imitation of gestures which are meaningful to children on the one hand, while at the same time it captures the element of spontaneous imagination and an attempt to organize the world into a meaningful context for themselves. On the other hand, the didactic element is more inclined toward direct teaching. No one will deny the importance of the didactic in the education of growing children: teaching them how to cross the street safely, how to avoid hazards which otherwise they would learn by bitter experience, the arts of reading, writing, and arithmetic all are skills which have to be presented directly and formally to some extent. Nevertheless, underlying all of these must be the more fundamental element of creative play, so that the child can internalize for himself the importance of reading and the meaning of reading; the importance of writing as an instrument for controlling his environment and carrying on effective communication; and of course, numeration itself, enabling them to quantify in a meaningful way the elements in their environment which are so necessary for the ordering of their experience.

Continually throughout the development of policy in this area, we were anxious to allow the playful element to be the dominant factor, avoiding the sharp separation of entertainment in the home from the formal experience of education itself. At the same time, nothing that was presented for children for informal viewing should be inconsistent with the experience they were having in school.

The Friendly Giant

In reviewing his long tenure as a performer on television, Bob Homme insists on simplicity of production, using only those techniques which he believes children can figure out for themselves. He depends heavily upon dialogue with the puppets, Jerome the Giraffe and Rusty the Rooster. Rod Coneybeare, who has been his associate for many years, has a great gift for ad-libbing and is immensely playful. During rehearsals, the ad-libbing between the two men is quite adult, but nevertheless playful. However, once the show hits the air they seem to be able to retain the playfulness at a level which children both appreciate and understand. Bob assumes that the children enjoy "listening." He doesn't try to make either the puppets or the children into performers. He just assumes that his own relationship with the children will enthrall them and keep their attention. He talks to children as he would to adults and maintains a meaningful, yet playful relationship with them. He keeps in mind that children need to know older people as friends and as people who respect them while they provide support.

Whenever the dialogue presents any kind of problem arising from the relationship between the puppets and the Friendly Giant, Homme always involves the children in solving the problem. For example, when Rusty can't close the stage curtains because the drawstring doesn't work, he offers assistance, but also involves the children. Children are involved

Bob Homme in The Friendly Giant.

immediately rather than observing a planned strategy. On one occasion the book was not available--somehow the props man had mislaid it--and Coneybeare from behind the scenes was unable to put his hands on it. Coneybeare and Homme contrived a situation which involved the children in a desperate hunt for the story. They demonstrated effectively that relationships, to be meaningful, cannot be manipulated; they always entail sharing.

Homme is aware that children thrive on repetition, because it presents a familiar experience. Over 25 years he has been able to select the best books available and repeat them for each new crop of young viewers. To establish the honesty of the situation, he will even occasionally use a tattered book to show that it has been used before.

Homme is basically a musician and is anxious to communicate the experience of music to children. He does not seek to find what they like, but rather to think in terms of what they might like. He chose the recorder as an instrument for the theme song because it suited the Giant's castle and did not have the heaviness of a saxophone. He maintains a high standard in programming the music for his concert and the music itself constitutes a good part of the show's continuity. Periodically he brings in other puppets and establishes a concert emphasizing rhythm, continuity and play, to which children naturally respond. Indirectly, such an experience contributes to the child's growth and development in creative terms.

Homme has a sense of rightness about children's response to his performances. He is indeed a "friendly" giant who loves children, and they in turn respond to him as the warm, concerned human being that he is. In commenting on the success of The Friendly Giant, Rod Coneybeare refers to it as an island of literacy. It is a quiet program in which each of the characters listens carefully and respectfully to the other. It is a secure area for the young viewer; the characters are reasonable and believable. He acknowledges Homme's knack for combining fantasy and reality with broadcasting. There is no condescension, pandering or sentimentality. The genuineness of the relationship between Coneybeare and Homme is immediately transmitted to young viewers and, in large part, contributes to the unending success of the show.

The show originated at WHA-TV in Madison, Wisconsin in 1954 and was telecast daily in the early evening as the final program for young viewers aged 2-6 just before sign-off. While the program was never designed to be educational or didactic, indirectly The Friendly Giant was always preoccupied with the child's growth and development. When asked to undertake specific instructional programming, Homme would still insist on his indirect mode of intuitive communication. Let the Friendly Giant speak for himself:

> A typical program found Friendly, as teacher, talking to Rusty and Jerome abut noisy words, words like crash, bang, smash, wham. All three of the characters expanded on this theme, eventually coming up with some new noisy words of their own invention. We dealt with the concepts of echoic words and onomatopoeia without encumbering anyone with those especially clumsy terms. This part of the program was made as entertaining and amusing as possible. The final few minutes were devoted to Rusty and Jerome's assignment for the next day. It was understood from what the teacher had said before the viewing began that this assignment was also intended for the classroom students. Now, to avoid the pitfall of stimulating mere imitation, the subject we'd been talking about was changed from noisy words to quiet words and Friendly would say, "words like...." At this point Rusty and Jerome quickly stopped him, saying "Shh! Don't say a word--we want to think of them." So not a hint of any kind went out to the students in the classroom. Friendly suggested that they might make up a little story or a bit of verse using quiet words or perhaps a long list of quiet words--some old and some new--and at this point the program closed in the traditional manner.

Homme summarizes the philosophy of his program as follows:

> What we're getting at with our program is simply the encouragement of respect for the words and music of life, a love of listening, of reading, of talking things over, of absorbing as much of what is all around us as we can possibly hold and then sharing it. We firmly believe that listening and reading are not

> passive experiences. That is why our emphasis is on instrumental music and books.... Remember they're hand-picked--left-handed, in the dark, catch as catch can.

The Friendly Giant as a series has been on the air for over 25 years. Homme's efforts have been recognized by the award of the Ryerson Fellowship, the principal honorary award of the Ryerson Polytechnical Institute of Canada. Over many years the program has won recognition from agencies concerned with the welfare of children and leaders in the field of broadcasting to children. The awards have included the Children's Broadcast Institute of Canada, the Ohio State Award, Liberty Magazine Award, and an Emmy as well. The spirit of Homme's achievement in this regard is best summed up by the citation of the Academic Awards and Ceremonials Committee for the Ryerson Polytechnical Institute. The committee stated that the award was "rooted in our conviction that The Friendly Giant program's elegance, gentleness, and its uncompromising commitment to its audience of pre-school children reflect the highest possible standard of integrity in children's television programming. It is your work as creator, writer, and principal performer that we wish to recognize."

Mr. Dressup

Mr. Dressup emerged from an earlier attempt to devise a regular daily show for children entitled Butternut Square. This show was to be a combination of entertainment and educational elements under the supervision of executive producer Bruce Attridge. Stuart Gilchrist was the producer and it had a successful early run with Sandy Cohen and Ernie Coombs as the main characters. Because of an increasing shortage of studio space, the show was cancelled, but protests from an enthusiastic audience were sufficient to effect a compromise, resulting in Ernie Coombs becoming Mr. Dress-Up in a simplified format reduced from 30 to 15 minutes.

Judith Lawrence was the puppeteer who devised Casey and Finnegan as the main characters in relation to Mr. Dress-Up. Once again, we have the triple relationship between a single main live character and two puppets. Judith learned about puppetry from an Australian show called The Children's Session. Casey simulates a child of about four or five, always

Ernie Coombs and friends, in Mr. Dressup. (Courtesy of CBC)

behaving in a childlike way. Finnegan, on the other hand, is a bit of a trouble-maker; he doesn't speak but usually whispers messages into Casey's ear. From time to time Aunt Bird is introduced as an older person to whom the children can also relate in a meaningful way.

The show is scripted so as to establish a one-to-one relationship. It is always low-key, but demands full attention from the young viewer. The pace of the show enables the child to think about the experience he is having. Repetition is built into the show: each program plays three times over a two-year period. Judith Lawrence believes that children have much longer attention spans than many adults believe. When she deals with the kinds of problems that Coombs does, she tends to dramatize them rather than to give more verbal or didactic explanations in the fashion of Mister Rogers. She interacts a great deal with Ernie Coombs and between the two of them they work the situations through their own imaginations, capturing the possibility of a child's attention to both reality and fantasy.

Mister Rogers' Neighborhood

Mister Rogers, performed by Fred Rogers for many years, provides an interesting comparison with The Friendly Giant and Mr. Dressup. Fred Rogers began his TV career with Josie Carey in a show entitled Children's Corner on station WQED Pittsburgh. Fred was the puppeteer while Josie did song and dance routines for children. The basic format of the show was to provide a realm of reality and one of fantasy, interconnected by a toy train which transported the children in imagination from one to the other. Fred never appeared on camera himself in Children's Corner. In 1961 we invited him to make a guest appearance in Junior Magazine. My intention was to persuade him to move to Toronto.

Having met Rogers several times, I became convinced that he would be a dynamic figure for children if he were to appear in person on television. His thoughtful conception and execution of the show led me to believe that on camera he could unify all of the elements and communicate directly to the children. While Josie Carey was unquestionably a talented performer, we felt that she lacked the capacity for immediate communication with young children. Like Homme, Fred Rogers became the writer, producer and performer of a new show entitled "Misterogers" and stayed at CBC for approximately two years. It was during this period that the format of the present show was developed.

Rogers' charismatic personality enabled him to relate immediately to children. Fred saw the program primarily as a vehicle for fostering a sense of self-worth among children. With his background in theology and psychiatric social work, he was able to articulate quite clearly his aims and objectives, which he wove into the script. Fred expresses his own feelings about his role in the following:

> In 1962, when I graduated from Pittsburgh Theological Seminary, I joined the Canadian Broadcasting Corporation in Toronto, where Dr. Frederick B. Rainsberry (head of CBC children's programs) told me, "Fred, I've seen you talk with children. I want you to translate that to television." I doubt if I would ever have "faced" a camera if it hadn't been for his encouragement. (I had stayed "behind the set" my first eight years of "being on television.") So I looked at the camera, remembered Mr. Hayes telling me about "one little buckaroo" ... and I've been communicating directly to families with growing children ever since.
>
> (It was also Fred Rainsberry's idea that the program should be called *Misterogers*. When I returned to Pittsburgh, we called the program *Misterogers' Neighborhood* and then later changed it to the present form, *Mister Rogers' Neighborhood*, out of a concern for viewers who were learning to read.)
>
> I knew that I wanted to use television the way I had used the piano and puppet play as a child: to communicate some things that I felt were important in our world. Since one can't be a communicator with equal impact on all segments of society, I guess I made an early decision somewhere inside of me to communicate with children--a decision I haven't regretted. With the help and counsel and support of many people, I've tried to help children feel good about being children and hopeful about who they can become. And I've tried to show them the wide range of artistry and feeling that make up a varied culture like ours. I've wanted to help children learn to discover worth

> in little things, in things that had no price tag, in people who might have outer handicaps and great inner strength. We've wanted every child to know that he or she was unique, valuable, and lovable, that everyone has limits as well as possibilities. We've wanted to engender feelings of responsibility toward the care of oneself as well as others.

Adult viewers frequently do not like his performance because he seems too rationalistic, and somewhat sentimental. The reason for this response is fairly clear. Most adults have developed conventions for social intercourse and defences for their own feelings of inadequacy to the point that they are embarrassed by the challenge of intimate communication and sharing of their anxieties. They are convinced that the world is not the lovely place which is Mister Rogers' Neighborhood. In their embarrassed response they manifest ridicule, hostility, or simple retreat. Children do not perceive Fred Rogers in this light at all. Rather, they relate to him directly as a person, almost like a Pied Piper. He is concerned about a child's sense of self-worth and about his feelings of security. He is also concerned to remove abnormal fears which a child might have about going to a dentist, to a barber shop or to a hospital. In each of these cases, Fred has produced some excellent work helping to reassure children about visiting these places.

I feel that Rogers is such a gifted performer that it is not always necessary for him to articulate these concerns as precisely as he does. His many talents, if left on their own, would effect the same relationships which he hopes to achieve by articulating his philosophy in the scripts.

Like Homme and Coombs, Rogers has served children's television for over twenty-five years. The durability of these shows is testimony to the creativity, intelligence and genuine concern for children which have characterized their performance. Fred Rogers describes in his new book his experiences with helping children to mature into adults: "It is because we parents are the holders of a priceless gift, a gift we received from countless generations we never knew, a gift that only we now possess and only we can give to our children. That unique gift, of course, is the gift of ourselves. Whatever we can do to give that gift, and to help others receive it, is worth the challenge of all our human endeavour" (Mr. Rogers Talks with Parents, Fred Rogers and Barry Head, with drawings by Jim Prokell. New York: Berkley Books, 1983, p. 256).

The quality of puppets in children's programs is a source of contention. Some performers feel that artistically designed puppets are unnecessary; it is the intention and the words put into their "mouths" that matter. Hence, Fred Rogers (Mister Rogers), Bob Homme (The Friendly Giant) and Judith Lawrence (Mr. Dress-Up) place a low value on the art of puppetry. On the other hand, Noreen Young (Hi Diddle Day), the Marquettes (Howdy Doody), the Keoghs (Razzle Dazzle, Mr. O, etc.) and Jim Henson (Sesame Street) have each made significant contributions to the art of puppetry in children's shows. Conscious of this problem, the CBC introduced George and Elizabeth Merton with their puppets in The King's Cupboard (1958, Paddy Sampson, producer). The scriptwriter, Phyllis Reid Duncan, did a good job of building meaningful relationships among the several characters. Perhaps the very number of puppets prevented the show from developing a significant identity or perhaps it was the inability of the Mertons to respond easily to the demands of television; in any case the show failed to win the confidence of the production unit.

Telestory Time

Telestory Time, which began in January 1953, was the earliest program contribution for pre-school and primary school children. Designed by Pat Patterson and Dodi Robb, the 15-minute presentation consisted of Pat Patterson as storyteller and songstress and featured original stories and songs written by Pat Patterson, Dodi Robb and Doug Sackfield. Musical accompaniment was provided by Doris Orde Fonger at the electronic organ, and the late George Feyer sketched witty and attractive drawings as the story unfolded.

The stories were centered on simple everyday experiences of an average Canadian child. Pat Patterson was a fresh and energetic storyteller. The problem with the show was that there was too much activity for a young child. It was confusing for the young viewer to establish direct relationships with the storyteller when there was visual interruption to watch George Feyer create his drawings and the organ was demanding the attention of the ear. These were the early days of television when we had much to learn about mobility of camera and the value of close-ups to strengthen relationships--in this case, between the storyteller and the viewer.

The show was withdrawn after a two-year run chiefly because of the cost of three writers and three performers. We had not yet realized that the indirect costs of production were actually far higher than talent fees. With more experience we would have reviewed the format to make the program more suitable for young children. As we learned more about production techniques, we were able to implement our policies about child development and its relationship to the use of television for children. It became a challenge to integrate the native talents of performers, writers and producers into more effective children's programs.

Maggie Muggins

A good example of this method for the realization of policy was the development of *Maggie Muggins*. The author, Mary Grannan, had established herself as a noted writer and performer on radio with both *Just Mary* and *Maggie Muggins*.

Possibly because Mary was not comfortable in the role of presenter for *Just Mary*, we chose to develop a television presentation of *Maggie Muggins*. Early in the planning, it was realized that the essential relationship in the stories was established in the real world, with Maggie sharing her fantasies with Mr. McGarrity. The show would open with Maggie greeting Mr. McGarrity, whereupon she would run off to explore the world of fantasy--in this case her relationship with the imaginary, talking animals Fitzgerald Fieldmouse, Grandmother Frog, and others. At the end of the show Maggie would return to report on her adventures, say good-bye, and end the show with her legendary line, "I don't know what will happen tomorrow!"

In contrast with the earlier days of television, we worked hard to establish high standards of showmanship. It was Joanne Soloviov who identified Mary Grannan's professional skills as a writer. With Michael Spivak as producer, production problems were solved with increasing skill. The problem of visual relationships between Maggie and the beautiful puppets made and manipulated by John and Linda Keogh was solved, as Michael Spivak records below:

> What bothered me a lot when I saw that show was that half the time Maggie was on ... there was a set which Maggie always approached with the camera directed towards the puppets--and Maggie's back. She'd always have to cheat. Consequently every sentence she'd have to say half of it to Fitzgerald Fieldmouse and then turn to address the audience, which meant that the audience felt patronized. The only way to solve this problem physically was to have Maggie behind the puppets. It didn't matter much if the puppets had to turn as long as Maggie always had her face to the camera. Looking back into the earlier development of Maggie Muggins I discovered that the whole environment had been a treehouse, and so they designed the set with a big knot hole in the tree. The look of the show changed from then on and you had a much greater chance to integrate the action because the puppets could go straight up to her face presenting the audience with a continuing uninterrupted relationship. The main reason for the change was that I hated the phony quality of her always turning to face the audience.

Such commitment and creative intensity characterized the work of many producers in those early days. Upon this foundation a tradition was built which gave the children's department its much deserved reputation.

Sing Ring Around

Sing Ring Around, devised by Joanne Soloviov, was a 15-minute playtime show for pre-school children which featured Donna Miller in a nursery in fantasyland. She played children's records, sang songs, told stories and talked with the puppets, Cheeky the monkey and Francis the clown. Mr. Starhopper danced and mimed in response to Donna's singing and storytelling. The aim of the show was to provide experience for young children in music and dance and to take advantage of the well-known interest of children in the wide variety of records available for them.

Most recently the CBC introduced a pre-school series starring Fred Penner in a show entitled Fred Penner's Place, a new 15-minute children's series. The young audience joins Fred in his own private place in a forest glade which he reaches through a hollow log. There they are entertained by Fred and his special guests in this very musical series designed to educate and entertain young viewers. Children learn, for example, how plants grow, or how instruments work. Some of Canada's best animation helps them learn French, the alphabet, and how to count. A special feature is the Word Bird, a magic talking bird who gives daily messages to the audience in a kind of "pre-school thought for the day." The show is produced by Randy Roberts in Winnipeg and Vancouver, with director Phil Kusie. Author, lyricist, composer and broadcaster Pat Patterson is the series writer.

Pre-School Shows on Private Television

The Uncle Bobby Show (1961) on CFTO featured Bobby Ash, who had begun his career many years ago as a circus performer. Originally, the show was known as Playtime with Uncle Bobby, which ran for 90 minutes with cartoons, live animals (pets and animals from zoos), singers, puppets, and magician Ron Leonard. Elena Jasechko took over as producer-director at the end of the first year. Except for those by George Feyer, the cartoons were eliminated in favor of a series of guests who stimulated the young audience with activities which would make them participants rather than passive viewers. The Uncle Bobby Show was the first children's show to introduce sign language for deaf children, using the skills of Bev Marsh. Over the many years the show was on the air, many talented performers made their start on it. Uncle Bobby was always a low-budget show, with many demands made upon Bobby Ash and the producer. It was later reduced to 30 minutes and was eventually terminated in 1980.

Kid's Corner (1979) was a spin-off from The Uncle Bobby Show, produced by Elena Jasechko. Whereas Bobby Ash had been the central character in his own show, in this production he became more the provider of continuity. In some ways the show was experimental, in terms of continuity and pacing. Faster paced children's shows, particularly from the U.S.A., appeared to be attracting audiences, so more

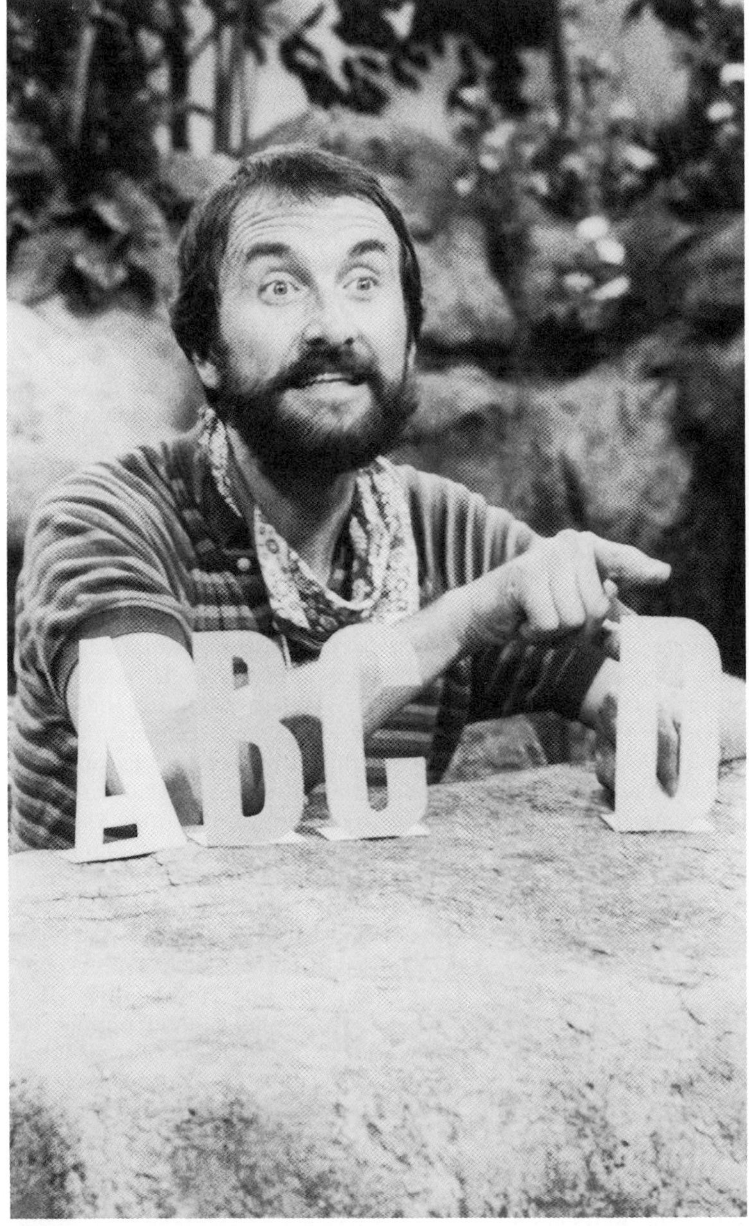

Fred Penner's Place, a CBC pre-school series. (Courtesy of CBC)

and shorter segments were used and the pace stepped up. The content remained the same, featuring the work of the policeman, the fireman, and other activities which would likely interest children. In all, some 81 episodes were produced. Like The Uncle Bobby Show, these run in a repeat pattern on CFTO.

The CTV network has carried a half-hour program for young children, Storytime (1980), produced at CFRN-TV in Edmonton. Each program centers on a puppet Pamela (the surrogate of the average 6-year-old) and her puppet friends Jinxo and Johnabec, all creations of the Kenuppets Puppet Troupe (Ken and Nelly Bishop). Pamela owns a scrapbook which comes to life with music and song. Each program has a story line which brings the puppets into relationship with hostess Esther Hudson and singers Dave and Andrea Spalding. The central character, Pamela, causes fun and some excitement by her frequent deviation from the story outline and her unpredictable responses to situations which arise. The show is directed by Ted Bartley of CFRN-TV.

The Silver Basketball is a good example of community cooperation to promote a good local children's program. Produced by Fred Barrie of CHEX-TV Peterborough, a 15-minute program is presented daily with host Ron Oliver (aged 22) as the basketball player. Oliver is a young magician who meets a small group of children on each show. The opening usually consists of Ron tossing the silver basketball in a park where he takes an interest in the children who play there. Each day, the children participate with a jogger (John van Leeuwen) doing his daily stretching exercises. They learn songs and rounds from singer Muriel Nicholls (who fixes the ferris whell) or hear stories from the story/costume lady Carol Walczak. The major segments of each show vary daily, conforming with a weekly theme. On day one, in the first of the segments, Ron uses a magic trick and a hand puppet to show small children how they may cope with problems that sometimes confront them. On other days, Oliver uses materials commonly available in homes to engage children in crafts, art forms and simple science experiments which he sometimes blends with his magic. On two days each week Ron and the children leave the park to visit with the costume lady, who helps the children to dress for parts in the story she reads. They sometimes meet a young policeman (John Zeyen) with whom they discuss safety and, for contrast, a bad boy (Brian

The Silver Basketball, with host Ron Oliver.

Eley) who is caught doing things he shouldn't do. Jane Chapman of the Peterborough Board of Education served as consultant and the Holiday Inn provided space for the production of some 260 shows.

Harrigan is a half-hour show produced by Barry Dale of CKWS, Kingston "for, and involving, children of all ages." Harrigan is a young-at-heart 209-year-old leprechaun who sings, dances, tells stories and plays his clarinet. He lives in a forest where every day Miss Sunflower delivers mail from the little people on her unicycle. Mr. Green, "who lives in a nearby mountain," drops in for a story. "Deblyn the Elf" has a "pot of gold" from which he draws works of art executed by his little friends across Canada and the northern United States. Guests drop in to demonstrate scientific experiments, to dance and sing, or to bring Harrigan up to date about safety rules. Marilyn and Maurine Yeates demonstrate crafts, making such things as an "egg-carton caterpillar" or a delicious "ice cream pizza."

The show also includes videotaped visits to a bakery, a boatbuilder, a cheese factory, and a fire or police station, allowing for a proper mix of fantasy and reality.

Heads and Tales, a series of eight half-hour programs for pre-school children produced by Rogers Cable TV of Calgary, Alberta, consists of stories and folk tales for children while a graphic artist draws posters to go with the narration. Each taping is preceded by a discussion about television production, and classes from schools are invited to see the live productions.

Size Small is produced by Stan Thomas for the Saskmedia Corporation in cooperation with station CKND-TV in Winnipeg, and features Helen Lumby as host with a teenage boy, Oliver, as her assistant. Designed for young children, it includes exercises in simple identification of body parts or other simple forms of information. Oliver is an older brother figure for the viewer, modifying Miss Helen's more authoritative role. Basic craft segments, storybooks and songs make up the half-hour. Much careful planning is given to the content and the pacing, and to the relationships between the people on the show as well as with the young viewers.

Size Small Country, a spin-off from Size Small, consists of a further 26 half-hour episodes in a country and western setting.

Curious George, the popular children's classic about an inquisitive little storybook monkey by Margaret and Hans Rey, was brought to the screen by Atkinson Film-Arts. Three of the four-minute segments, 104 in all, were presented in a 15-minute program format by CBC preceding The Friendly Giant.

Educational Programs for Pre-School Children

The earliest Canadian venture into "educational" pre-school programming was Nursery School Time, initiated by the late R. S. Lambert, the supervisor of Schools Broadcasts at the CBC. The scripts were designed and developed by Herta Fletcher and Phyllis Couse; Teddy Forman was hostess and Phyllis Reid Duncan performed at the piano. The show began in January, 1958, with Ms. Forman from Toronto alternating with Shirley Knight from Winnipeg. The next season, the show was scheduled in the early afternoon with three presentations from Toronto, Monday, Wednesday and Friday. On Tuesday and Thursday, Madeline Arbour hosted two shows as Maman Fonfon. The Toronto production featured Hoppy curricular goals or with an explicitly stated extension of them approved by the Canadian ad hoc advisory panel.

That the material is appropriate and of high quality within the framework of Canadian culture.

Further negotiation with the Workshop has resulted in an increase from seven to 15 minutes of original material produced in Canada. The dream is still held that "Sesame Street North" (or a Canadian Sesame Street) can be devised entirely by Canadian producers.

By 1986 the Canadian portions of the show constituted one-third of each program seen on the CBC. While the show continues to keep the basic concept of the Children's Television Workshop's bright and snappy format, the Canadian segments focus on Canadian culture, presenting multiculturalism, the learning of French, and an awareness of our native peoples.

Sesame Street is probably one of the most carefully researched children's programs in the history of Western television. There have been lengthy disputes about the fast pacing of the show and the strong emphasis on cognitive development, particularly in the show's early stages. Indeed, a controversy arose in 1979 between Gerald Lesser, the chief psychological adviser for Sesame Street, and Jerome and Dorothy Singer (Jerome J. Singer, Dorothy G. Singer and Gerald Lesser, "Children's TV: Does Fast Pacing Inhibit Imagination?" Psychology Today, March 1979, pp. 56-60), who asked whether fast pacing inhibited children's imagination. In my view, it was unfortunate that the issue of the importance of imagination in children's television should be reduced to the apposition of Mr. Rogers' Neighborhood to Sesame Street.

In Lesser's approach questions arose about the grounds used to differentiate creative imagination from cognitive development. One was left with the impression that they might be one and the same thing in his mind. At the same time, the Singers' article raised the question of whether imagination had to do with retaining new information regardless of the pace with which it was presented.

In my view, since behavioral scientists are concerned with the cognitive, physiological, neurological and emotional development of the child, they are inevitably concerned with the empirical evidence for their claims and for the proper scientific classification of this evidence. What constitutes empirical evidence for creativity, fantasy and imagination? How does one categorize a child's response to affection or beauty? What criteria does one employ to assess the importance of significant gestures in interpersonal communication?

In the case of Mr. Rogers, there is no doubt about his conviction and the rightness of his approach. More importantly, he doesn't build his show upon the single proposition that slow pacing is better than fast pacing. His concern is for a one-to-one relationship with his young audience. The esthetic, social and developmental factor here is existential response. What happens when the adult performer approaches the child with respect for the uniqueness of his selfhood--"as someone very special"? I doubt that Fred Rogers has any exclusive concern that a child shall learn facts and make inferences. He is concerned with a child's sense of physical and social security and with helping the child to understand the nature of his physical and social environment, so that he will have the confidence to explore the world around him. He is concerned with that paradox of learning, being oneself while also accommodating oneself to the external world.

One can certainly agree that slow pacing gives the child an opportunity for reflection and hence develops his imagination What concerned me about the Singers' examination of this problem was their attempt to use scientific categories to prove their point.

The Role of TVOntario in the Development of Television Programs for Early Childhood

When TVOntario went on the air, they took *Sesame Street* as a second play from the CBC on a two-week delay. Along with this, they took ten programs from the BBC's *Playschool* to fill in the two-week gap. They then began to build segments into what later became *Polka Dot Door*. As the shape of the show emerged, original material was introduced and the title changed. Peggy Liptrot was the first producer of the series and it was she who suggested changing the title from *Playschool* to *Polka Dot Door*. Pat Patterson wrote the original theme song and Dodi Robb wrote the continuity. At the outset,

In the meantime, Bouchard was anxious to extend the range of *This Living World*. He found the limitations of the studio somewhat restrictive and often problematical. On one occasion they were presenting a baby hippopotamus; in the process of bringing the hippo from the Granby Zoo to the old studios in the Ford Hotel building in Montreal, the hippo became frightened in the elevator and when the doors opened it refused to move. How does one dislodge a 1000-pound creature from an elevator? The show was held up for three hours, as was the elevator, until everybody had gone to lunch and quiet reigned. Hank Hedges, who had been participating in the show, was quick-witted enough to take advantage of the silence of the noon hour. He turned out the lights, the door was slowly opened and the hippo moved quietly out to his appointed place in the studio.

Amusing as the story may be, there were hazards of various kinds which made any extension of the show in the studio fairly difficult. To overcome these problems Bouchard eventually procured some land in Northern Québec so that he could film the animals more easily. In later years, after he had left Radio-Canada, Bouchard became interested in underwater photography of sea animals and did much undersea filming, both in the St. Lawrence River and off the Atlantic coast of the United States. The spectrum of the show, then, ranged from its beginning with stuffed animals and puppets, to simulated environments in the studio, to sophisticated photography of animals in their natural environments.

A show of this kind underlines the kind of relationship which is possible between the two networks and remains to this day probably the most successful exchange ever developed between them. Throughout his tenure at Radio-Canada, Doré and I maintained this relationship. During the summers we presented *Caravan* (1960), a live network production of a circus with ringmaster Guy Mauffette as Monsieur Loyal, who would set out in his caravan to bring the circus to children across Canada. Two circus rings permitted scene changes and enabled viewers to see the usual spectacles of lion tamers, daring feats of highwire trapeze artists, precision drilled horses and a troupe of chimpanzees. The 60-minute program was presented in both French and English. Such a show, by itself, would be a mere token for building communication between two cultures, but in the context of a show like *This Living World* and other shared programs, *Caravan* became part of the policy to establish increasingly meaningful relationships between the two networks.

Pierre DesRoches, presently the General Manager of Société Radio-Canada and formerly Executive Vice-President with President Al Johnson, was the successor to Fernand Doré. He extends great praise to Doré for his thoughtful planning and development and claims that his policies still prevail. The Children's Department for him was by far the most dynamic center in Radio-Canada at the time he became head, in 1962. He continued in this role for some four years. During his tenure he gave great attention to pre-school programming and extended his conviction about the service to young people by emphasizing late-teens and his concern that the culture of Québec should be a meaningful experience for them. He believes that this commitment, which is so necessary to educate, entertain and inform bright young people in Québec society, was effective because the present audience for a show like Le Temps d'Une Paix was built largely on the quality of previous children's programs. DesRoches was succeeded by Claude Caron and Roland Guay. More recently, Robert Roy took over and it was during his regime that the present arrangement of programs was confirmed, with morning programs for small children, the 4:30 p.m. slot for children of the middle years, and evening for older children when the schedule permitted. He became interested in the development of dramas, or télé-romans, for young people as a means of winning the audience. At the same time, he worked through the European Broadcasting Union to develop animation and documentary films which could easily be shared both with the English Services Division of the CBC and with the English-speaking members of the European Broadcasting Union.

Because there was no consistent policy or persistent intention to develop significant relationships between the two networks at the management level, the success or failure of this ideal in children's programming depended largely upon the good intentions and camaraderie of the two supervisors of children's programs. With the advent of Schools' Television, Chez Hélène, with Hélène Baillargeon, was produced in Montreal for the English network. Chez Hélène was essentially a nursery school program scheduled five days a week and designed to introduce basic French vocabulary and general orientation to a second language. Mme. Baillargeon was a most engaging host for young children and the show had a long series: Téléjeans and Salut Santé. So what are they turning to?

They are turning to U.S. products, U.S. music, U.S. records, U.S. songs, and U.S. lifestyles. And this is a great danger for the small group of North American francophones. So what's to be done? It is this challenge which must become the mission of Radio-Canada.

If the Corporation does not create new talent, who is to do it? Obviously, we are not alone in confronting this invasion: the educational system is better structured and people are more aware of the dangers, but on the other hand television is extremely intrusive; it is also a taskmaster listened to carefully, and a closely watched dispenser of culture. What reflection of today's world can the young see in television? They can still see pictures of their world on the Radio-Canada screen, but the images of another world come through on the other 39 channels offered by the converter. But if adequate financial resources cannot be found to establish a program schedule with producers, programmers, craftsmen, and creative staff possessing the necessary drive, then in a few years Radio-Canada Television will become a quaint aspect of folklore.

With these problems in mind, in the fall of 1981 an attempt was made to simplify the programs in the schedule. Two new, lighter programs were produced, with public participation, and produced live in a shopping center: a game format in which children were required to demonstrate their physical and intellectual skills, and a program entitled Clowneries, a light mini-drama using figures and with children also taking part. The youth magazine Téléjeans has been revised, with the program being broadcast live before a studio audience with shorter, more forceful items, moving away from a strictly informational format toward a more "fun-oriented" format. The program is now broadcast at a more convenient time for young people: at 5.30 p.m. on Tuesdays. Likewise, there has been an updating of the program Bobino (on the air for 25 years now), intended to identify more closely with the preschool audience watching this program.

In brief, when it comes to in-house and outside productions, as well as foreign purchases, formats which are more cheerful, light-hearted, and competitive will be favored, so as, we hope, to recoup the lost audiences.

A recent development in French programming for children is the endeavor of the Franco-Ontarian section of TV-Ontario. They have developed a pilot program entitled Terrarium, primarily for home viewing. The series is about two young people, Pivoine and Aquarelle, who uncover the mysteries of science with the help of a knowledgeable M. Valmont. With the aid of a computer, they communicate with the Rium, very intelligent little puppet people who live in the terrarium. Careful formative research was undertaken to determine the children's interest in the show and as a result several changes will be made in the series. The program is mounted in short segments which deal with such subjects as blowing up a balloon the question of atmosphere on the moon, the properties of hot and cold air, etc. All of these phenomena are explained by the Rium, known severally as Bernard, Délirium, Aquarium, Planetarium, Geranium and Solarium. The series is written by André Tassé and Gilles Charest and produced by Michel Beriault.

Chapter X

PRIVATE TELEVISION AND CHILDREN'S PROGRAMS

Most stations seeking a Canadian broadcasting license commit themselves to the production of some children's programming as part of their Canadian content requirements. To meet this need, as is the case in most broadcasting corporations, only limited facilities are made available for production. In spite of this handicap, the diversity of children's programs, both in quantity and quality, is wide indeed. Because of this immense diversity and volume of programs for children, I had to be selective in discussing private broadcasting. My criteria for inclusion were: all programs carried by more than one station or carried on a network; any prize-winning programs; and all programs seen in the metropolitan Toronto area. Cable programs were included only when they had been singled out for special awards or distinctions.

In viewing a considerable number of programs shown on local private stations in the Toronto area, I concluded that most people who have undertaken production are sincere in their intentions. The basic problem arises from the fact that many producers and performers are not well trained in dealing with children and do not have time or money to find source materials which would generally improve the quality of their endeavor. In most instances, the producers and performers have little opportunity to share experiences with others producing quality programs for children. At conferences, one generally meets program directors or senior personnel of the private stations; one rarely meets the performers or producers themselves. Almost anyone, talented though he or she may be, will be bound to commit errors in judgment or develop patterns in production and performance which need the correction achieved by interaction with one's peers.

Immediately the whole question of the use of puppets comes to mind. Naturally, the quality of the puppets will vary depending upon the talent available in the local community. I am not suggesting that an attempt should be made to abandon puppets, but I think considerable care should be given to their selection, since they become surrogates for children. They take on the proportions of human character and children interact with them in a very meaningful and significant way. A classic case in point is the care taken by TVOntario when they discovered that Sam, the nightwatchman in Today's Special, was not engaging the attention of children. With careful investigation and research they modified both the puppet and the character to achieve a more meaningful response from children. Another obvious problem in the use of puppets in the productions from private stations is the lack of attention to good voicing. In many instances, the voice for an otherwise handsome puppet is unpleasant, exhibiting a certain stridency and harshness that in my view will fail to evoke sympathetic responses from children. In most cases, the puppeteers do the voicing as a means of saving money. Usually, those who make puppets and manipulate them lack the skill to modulate their voices and develop character in sound--a skill unique to trained and experienced actors. The Ontario Puppetry Association has published two excellent works which provide professional guidance to producers: Kenneth B. McKay's Puppetry in Canada and Robert Tilroe's Puppetry and Television (see bibliography).

Another difficulty encountered with both puppets and live characters is the age-old problem of treating children as little adults who deserve condescension and patronage. Children are very quick to react, often negatively, to these attitudes. Program directors, in choosing someone to present material for children, should therefore be extremely careful to see that children are treated as individuals worthy of respect for their integrity. I have seen programs in which ethnic groups have been treated with a certain condescension, as though they were inferior. Often the guest is not allowed to impart information of equal value and significance to any kind of experience which the average native Canadian might have.

Then there is the problem of pacing and continuity. Earlier we have discussed the immense importance of attention to the sequencing of information in a magazine program. In programs like *Junior Magazine*, *Today's Special*, *Going Great* or *The Silver Basketball* great care was taken to provide meaningful visual continuity. Also, rapid pacing and harsh voices do not necessarily command enduring attention. These are negative elements in so many commercial programs and could easily be eliminated if thought were given to the needs of children being entertained. In the case of cartoons and films, again, price or availability should not be the first criteria. Surely it is worth the time and trouble to see what is available for a given sum of money? Then at least the program director can say with a clear conscience that, given the amount of money, this is the best material available.

Reference has already been made to the lack of a sense of community among the producers of television programs for children in private stations. When a local program director assigns a producer to undertake a children's program, he will naturally muster his resources and start thinking in terms of what he believes to be "good for children." An outgoing, somewhat extroverted personality with adult mannerisms having been selected, the content of the program then frequently focuses on elements of didacticism which are common parental rules. Heavy emphasis is given to safety and basic hygiene, e.g., brush your teeth and wash your hands frequently, be respectful to adults and kind to others. They tend to be "motherhood" doctrines with which few can quarrel. Such behavior by children is really more a function of their good disposition towards their own friends and towards adults as well; morals and social conventions cannot be imposed upon individuals if they are going to be an essential part of their nature. Rather, moral education and awareness of social cooperation are brought about through a feeling of self-worth. Such strong injunctions to follow the conventions of good behavior are more pleasing to adults than they are to children. Nevertheless, when the host is able to establish meaningful relationships with his young viewers, both on camera and off, there is an immediate positive response which almost certainly results in the kind of behavior that didactic injunctions are intended to achieve.

In order to make the most of the good intentions of those who undertake independent local productions for children, two recommendations come to mind. First of all, I think it is imperative that the private stations, through the Canadian Association of Broadcasters or through their network if they have one, should appoint an ombudsman, a supervisor--someone with sufficient knowledge and authority to take the time to screen programs regularly, to visit the stations and provide help and advice to those who do local productions. The failures or weaknesses of a children's television program are rarely the result of any malicious intention or indifference by the station. Rather, they stem from a simple lack of knowledge, an unawareness of what is consistent with and in the best interests of child growth and development.

At the outset, the producer must realize that children are not adults. Their growth is enriched by the information presented on television if it challenges their minds and stimulates their curiosity. The producer must be concerned about the accuracy and the truth of the information he presents. He should choose presenters who are authoritative rather than authoritarian. Regardless of the genre of the program--drama, storytelling, information or light entertainment--care should be taken to present the performers in meaningful relationships, respectful of one another as well as of their audience. Only in such an atmosphere will genuine humor and playfulness be possible. Only with these considerations in mind will television be a worthwhile experience for young viewers.

The cost of maintaining an officer to provide this service and the support system necessary would be minimal compared to the benefits which would accrue to the stations. Canada is a large country, and some regional cooperation might be necessary among the stations. Of course, the appointment of one person to service all private stations in Canada would have only a minimal effect. Nevertheless, limited monies already being spent on children's programs among private stations can be better used by attending to some of the criticisms already mentioned.

Another suggestion is that private stations pool their resources so that they become aware of the quality of programs being made. Since every station must provide some children's programming, there is often a tendency to reach for the most available program without carefully considering the mix of programs they may schedule. A poor program may therefore get wider distribution than a good one. By more careful reviewing of the qualities of good children's programs, the private stations will win bigger audiences, get more for their broadcasting dollar, and avoid the common criticism about indifference in the scheduling of children's programming.

4. Set an example

There is little point in telling his child to cut down on TV viewing if the parent spends hour after hour in front of the set. Under those circumstances he can't expect the child to develop discriminating tastes in terms of TV programming. Set an example by being selective in terms of the amount and type of programming watched.

5. Talk back to your TV set

If you have a complaint about program or commercial content or scheduling, please let the station know. This is often the only way producers know what they're doing wrong _or_ right. (Don't forget to acknowledge good programming when you see it, as well.) Even the youngest viewer enjoys sharing his feelings with the people behind the screen.

6. Visit a TV station

Does your child wonder how people get inside the TV set? Visit your local cable company or TV station and find out. A new perspective on what television is all about results. It's important that we all find ways of stepping back from the TV shows we watch to appreciate how they influence us. Your child will have dozens of questions about TV production. We teach our children to read and write by going back to the basic tools of the trade. Why not do the same for television?

7. The TV room

Families spend a great deal of time in front of the TV set. Parents who want to cut down on the number of hours their children spend watching television should make the experience less desirable by placing the set in an uncomfortable or out-of-the-way room.

8. Play road hockey

Or go bowling, or dust off the Scrabble board or visit the zoo. A simple way to combat the "Saturday morning glued-to-the-set" syndrome is to offer kids a non-TV alternative. Many children watch the same programs over and over because there's nothing better to do.

9. Plan ahead

How do you decide what the kids should watch? Many parents plan a week of TV viewing in advance. Sit down with the TV listings at the beginning of the week and decide with the kids which programs you will watch. This helps the child understand what your values are and gives him a chance to make his own critical judgments. Somehow, by making this process a family affair, the kids seem more willing to listen.

10. How much is too much?

There is no hard and fast rule. The average Canadian child between two and 11 years of age watches two and a half to four hours of television each day. Some children can cope with this amount and still have time for reading, sports and other activities. But for others, even a single hour may be unwise. It really depends on the child and the family. To help you decide how much TV is enough you should first determine how many hours he spends in front of the set.

The TV schedule on pages 8 and 9 is a handy guide to fill in with your child. You may find he spends much less (or more) time with TV than you had thought. After the timetable is completed, sit down together and determine which programs you want to cut back on. This is one more way of exerting control over the set and ensuring that family TV viewing is enjoyable and profitable.

These services, provided by the CBC and the Children's Broadcast Institute, show the concern which professional people have for the welfare of young people who use television for entertainment and education.

In the seventies the Children's Broadcast Institute continued to give professional service to parents, teachers, and others concerned with the welfare of children in their "Power of Television" project under the leadership of David and Janis

Nostbakken. This project was established on a much broader public and extensive national basis. The issues have remained the same through three decades of television. The Power of Television consisted of a series of workshops which, as the Nostbakkens say in _Talking Television_, the final report of the Power of Television Workshop Project (Toronto, 1983),

> were designed around the premise that the television experiences of the young can be positive and beneficial provided that parents, teachers and programmers properly support that experience.

The aims and objectives of the workshops were stated as follows:

> to discuss some of the issues (both positive and negative) on the lives of children;
>
> to assist parents and teachers in learning more about their children through television;
>
> to discuss potential guidelines for parents who want to make their family TV viewing a more positive experience;
>
> to explore current concerns and areas of interest to parents, teachers and children in the realm of television;
>
> to provide information about the state of children's television programming in Canada.

With the support of private enterprise, foundations, and government agencies, it was possible to organize 139 workshops under specially selected leaders across Canada, involving nearly 4000 participants over a five-year period. Each workshop included verbal introduction by the leader, a videotape presentation of questions and answers about television, and another videotape of an interview with a family trying to cope with television. Following a discussion, the participants were given hand-outs including the _CBI Membership Brochure_, _Questions and Answers about Children and Television_, and _Is Your Child a TV Junkie?_

There is little doubt that the project was a national

success. At present the CBI is reviewing the project to determine where its leadership should go from here. The combination of this public endeavor with a curricular emphasis on visual literacy in the schools is essential if progress is to be made in the development of critical viewing of film and television.

The more formal study of the problem of children and television has come to be known as "visual literacy," which comes under the jurisdiction and concern of education and research. The impact-cause-effect relationships between television and children has been a continuing challenge to behavioral scientists. Educators and broadcasters have taken a broader view which includes the esthetics of television production and appreciation of its social and cultural uses. This concern is now generally discussed under the heading of visual literacy.

Much parental and professional concern about the impact of television on children could be alleviated if both adults and children knew more about the nature of visual media. Many of the complaints about commercial television (both its commercial messages and its program content) arise from our ignorance of the medium's technical and esthetic dimensions. The perception of many educated middle class people that visual media are inferior to print again reflects ignorance of esthetic properties and the potential of visual media for creative expression. The activities of pressure groups like Action for Children's Television may have moderated some of the extremities of commercial TV for children but their confrontational approach has not changed the basic attitudes of the commercial broadcaster.

The endeavor of the behavioral scientists to measure the impact of television on children in relation to such factors as violence, stereotyping, modeling and overstimulation has produced relatively inconclusive results. Indeed, much of the controversy revolves around questions of taste and the sociocultural orientation of both producer and viewer. Since there has never been a tradition of responsible criticism for television programming in the press, no distinguished critics have emerged. Unaware of the properties of visual media, newspaper critics use their columns to express their own opinions and prejudices, or to win readership, rather than engage in meaningful criticism.

2. Understanding how children experience television viewing necessitates taking their perceptions of that experience into consideration. Researchers must converse with and ask children about their television viewing experiences in order to gain access to their perceptions. Researchers should not depend solely on their own observations of and inferences about the connections between television content and children's lives.[7]

Although this perspective seems to be newly emergent among purely academic researchers it has a long tradition among researchers linked to program development for children's television.

In 1965 CBC's Audience Research Department (Toronto office) collaborated with the Schools and Youth Department in a pioneering effort to systematically measure detailed responses to a weekly network program for teenagers, Time of Your Life. A nationwide, scientifically-selected panel of teenage viewers was created. Panel members were asked to complete and return questionnaires covering specific elements in each week's program.

This joint project called for unprecedented cooperation between researchers and program producers. The project was expensive and required a significant proportion of the entire Toronto audience research budget. Both the researchers and producers involved felt the project was a success. The producers were given detailed audience reaction to elements in each program in the series ten days after it was televised. As the TV season wore on the producers could see concrete results in audience appreciation of program elements that were refined and strengthened as a result of the research panel reports.

The program panel created for Time of Your Life in 1965 was the forerunner of the current national program panel maintained by CBC Audience Research.

It was also in the mid-1960s that the Children's Television Workshop made program-oriented research a vital factor in the development of the Sesame Street series. Gerald Lesser, the educational director of CTW, has outlined some of the problems inherent in the link-up of researchers and television producers in formative research.

> Research on how well we appealed to children would be of no value unless it was used to continually improve the programs. This would demand close collaboration between researchers and the creative staff; yet traditionally producers have relied exclusively on their own instincts, rarely seeking the reactions of children. Television producers have not only ignored this source of information, but often have vigorously rejected it, almost as if checking with children were a sign of cowardice--and admission that they did not trust their own intuitions. Yet without research on the children themselves, producers and writers simply cannot know, in time to permit changes, if they have hit upon an appealing approach, how to build on it, or when to abandon it and start over. The value of child-testing seems so obvious that one would expect it to be routine. Actually it is almost never done.[8]
>
> Research in children's development is encrusted with traditions. If collaboration was going to work, the researcher would have to modify, abandon or even violate several parts of his standard paraphernalia. The researchers' most familiar role in education is to police programs after they have been completed, evaluate how well they have met their professed goals.... To collaborate with producers, the researchers first had to give up the role of policeman; then they had to find ways to work with producers to improve the programs before broadcasting began.[9]

Backed by a start-up budget of $1.2 million, the pioneering research undertaking by the Children's Television Workshop was a critical factor in the design and success of the Sesame Street series. According to Lesser, CTW's research experience has pointed to the need for long-term research efforts "to correct our total ignorance about how children learn from visual media."[10]

> Television provides vivid visual portrayals of the world beyond classrooms and neighborhoods, and children respond to them as they have never responded to verbal and abstract education. Yet we are ignorant about how children do learn from the visual media. This understanding certainly will come in part from experiences such as Sesame Street, but long-term

research must extend beyond any single series of programs.[11]

The need for well-funded, long-term research on children and television is now being met, in part, through the partnership of CTW and Harvard University's Center for Research in Children's Television. In Canada, TVOntario has conducted extensive research to formulate and produce its new children's series, Today's Special.

These events and others point to a new collaboration between the social science research community and children's television producers and policy-makers. The attitudes that once divided these two communities are changing. A beginning has been made that will require continued financial support and nurturing if we are to fully understand the dimensions of the role television plays in the lives of children.

References

1. Comstock, G., "The Evidence So Far," Journal of Communication, Autumn 1975, vol. 25, no. 4, p. 25.

2. Television and Behavior, vol. 1, Summary Report, National Institute of Mental Health, Rockville, Md., 1982, p. iii.

3. Honig, A. S., "Television and Young Children," Young Children, May 1983, vol. 38, no. 4, p. 64.

4. Comstock, G., "Against the Grain," in J. F. Esserman, ed., Television Advertising and Children (New York: Child Research Services, 1981), p. 2.

5. Television and Behavior, op. cit., p. 4.

6. Atwood, P., Allen, R., Bargett, R., Proudlove, S., Rich, R., "Children's Realities in Television Viewing: Exploring Situational Information Seeking," in M. Burgoon, ed., Communication Yearbook 6 (Beverley Hills, Ca.: Sage Publications P87.CS974, 1982), p. 605.

7. Ibid., p. 606.

8. Lesser, G., Children and Television (New York: Random House, 1974), p. 132.

9. *Ibid.*, p. 134.

10. *Ibid.*, p. 150.

11. *Ibid.*

Chapter XIV

CONCLUSIONS AND RECOMMENDATIONS ABOUT THIRTY YEARS OF CHILDREN'S TELEVISION

What can and should be done if the CBC is to continue its role as a leader in television programming for children? The funds for programming must be redeployed so that a basic foundation for the development, planning and execution of children's programs can be undertaken in-house. Along with this reestablishment of adequate funds, a major studio must be provided for regular production of children's programs for all ages. Only in this way will the Corporation be able to make the best use of highly trained and competent producers of children's programs who can constitute a community of dedicated personnel working in the context of a clear, dynamic policy for our times.

It has already been pointed out that, with proper funding and with careful planning, the CBC has produced some of the world's finest public affairs programming. If Canadians are to accept the notion that they have a separate cultural identity within the context of North America, they must allot greater sums of money for full expression of our culture in every area of our lives. We cannot hope to develop the creative genius of young Canadians if we do not provide them with the fullest opportunities for expressing their gifts in writing, composition, production and performance. Especially in children's programming, we must devote fuller attention to children and make a certain sector of the television medium theirs and theirs alone. We have already referred to the vanishing line between adulthood and childhood. To pursue this social trend without critical awareness is to produce a generation of immature adults for the future.

Indeed, the "adult-child" or "hurried child" is a topic

of concern for some contemporary sociologists and psychologists. "The adult-child may be defined as a grown-up whose intellectual and emotional capacities are unrealized and, in particular, not significantly different from those associated with children" (Postman, p. 99).* Such children are forced into patterns of adult behavior before they are ready to cope with the tensions of adulthood. As a result,

> hurried children seem to make up a large portion of the troubled children seen by clinicians today; they constitute many of the young people experiencing school failure, those involved in delinquency and drugs, and those who are committing suicide. They also include many of the children who have chronic psychosomatic complaints such as headaches and stomach aches, who are chronically unhappy, hyperactive, or lethargic and unmotivated. These diseases and problems have long been recognized as stress-related in adults, and it is time we looked at children and stress in the same light. (David Elkind, The Hurried Child (Growing Up Too Fast, Too Soon (Reading, Mass.: Addison-Wesley, 1981), pp. xii-xiii.)

As far as television is concerned, the result of such a trend confirmed by programming policy will tend to produce a whole generation of adults who are totally uncritical viewers. Moreover, there will be a further tendency for such adults to be unable to discriminate between the values they cherish as Canadians on the one hand, and those often worthwhile values of the United States which, while worthy of our viewing, should not constitute full fare in prime time. Moreover, with the new technologies making available a wide selection of programming from satellite selection to home video, network programming as we have known it is not likely to be the major determinant in recreational viewing. Instead, great emphasis will now have to be placed upon increasing the volume of production and preparing programs for dissemination through several different technologies. This does not preclude the possibility of selling some of our programs abroad, but that should not be the primary intention.

---

*See bibliography for complete references in all cases where abbreviated citations are given in parentheses in this chapter.

At present, the Children's Department of the CBC has focused its main attention upon drama, for reasons given above. Since there are no available studios, the use of outside facilities is necessary to make the most of the limited funds available. Not enough programs can be produced to create a critical mass of Canadian content that will be a significant force in shaping social and cultural attitudes of young Canadians in the future. In stressing the necessity for preserving an area in the television schedule as it presently exists, or in setting aside sufficient monies for the production of children's programs on VCR and film to meet the increasing demands of the new media, I am not in any way suggesting a perpetuation of childhood. Rather, I am seeking ways in which children can be provided with outside material which will enable them to know more about themselves and to live in a realm where they feel comfortable and secure. Without this security, and without this opportunity to explore the world of childhood, they will be forced out of it long before they have known what it means to be a child. Adulthood on these terms is immature: the wrong dimensions of childhood are preserved on the one hand, while on the other hand, as adults, they will be mere imitators of conventions which have become jaded and have fallen into disrepute. It is the death of any kind of creativity; it kills the initiative for leadership and it destroys the possibility of full personhood.

While everyone has great admiration for the work of Ernie Coombs and the team of Mr. Dressup, and for Bob Homme and The Friendly Giant, the time has come to invest further in new children's programming for the pre-school group. Sesame Street is currently 25 per cent Canadian in content. The team which has developed the animation and the French segments for this program are top-flight, and represent some of the best talent for production of children's programming in Canada. It is now time for a major promotional campaign to launch a new children's series which is exclusively Canadian. The public needs to be apprised of the fact that they will not be losing the values of a show like Sesame Street, which will be readily available via satellite and cable on several other channels in most parts of the country. We now need to expand the current Canadian element of Sesame Street into a full-fledged Canadian show. It is now time for Canada and the CBC to demonstrate to itself and to the world that we are more than capable of producing a top-flight pre-school children's show without contractual accommodation to a children's production from a foreign country. Depending on popularity and commitment of funds, the length of the show can vary from its present 15 minutes to 30 or 60 minutes.

As has already been discussed, TVOntario does careful formative research for its productions, especially those planned for younger viewers. Clearly articulated educational objectives motivate the planning of *Polka Dot Door* and *Today's Special*. Planning for *The Friendly Giant* and *Mr. Dressup* is somewhat more personal and intuitive. The mix of educational planning with charismatic performers like Bob Homme (*The Friendly Giant*), Ernie Coombs (*Mr. Dressup*) and Fred Rogers (*Mister Rogers' Neighborhood*) make up the complement with programs like *Polka Dot Door* and *Today's Special*. *Romper Room*, seen on the CTV network, also has clear educational objectives with Canadian input from CTV's consultant, Janis Nostbakken. As the CBC looks forward to the development of more pre-school programming, it is to be hoped that they will retain the "playful" and "intuitive" element which has made the work of Homme and Coombs so successful.

Sesame Street, for all its quality as a television production, reminds one of the early days when programs like *Hidden Pages* were used to encourage children to use the library. There is more concern for the didactic element than for the esthetic dimension of television for children. As the CBC looks ahead, I would like to see the talents of the production team for the Canadian segments of *Sesame Street* turned to a more appropriate and significant use of the television medium. Let us not prostitute one medium (the visual) to another (the art of reading), but concentrate on providing the most creative visual experience possible for children. How can television itself be used to help young people to be more discriminating about techniques of television?

> With television, many of the conceptual and logical barriers to extending children's experiences posed by the other media are effectively swept away. Children no longer have to read or be able to translate a broadcaster's words in order to experience events that are happening simultaneously around the world. Television to a child now is what radio is to the adult. With radio the adult has access to news, drama, and enter-

> tainment at home without the intermediate stage of reading. With television, children have access to news, drama, and entertainment without having to translate words into images. The images are already there. (Elkind, pp. 72-73.)

Since many children watch television for more hours than they read, it is time that we presented television fare which alerts them to the "grammar" and "syntax" of this powerful visual medium. When Neil Postman asked what Leonard H. Goldenson, Chairman of the Board of the American Broadcasting Company, means when he claims that visual literacy--i.e., electronic literacy--"will be as much of an advance over the literacy of the written word we know today as that was over the purely oral tradition of man's early history," he fears that the great traditions of logic, science, education and civilité will be lost (Postman, pp. 118-119). He does not see the great awakening which can be realized by visual media if we would take advantage of their unique esthetic qualities to share our most noble feelings and ideals. The plea for visual literacy is a plea to raise the consciousness of the viewing public to an awareness of the opportunities for creative expression provided by film and television. Instead of reducing the medium to the service of the commercial advertiser, the educator or the advocate of conventional mores, let us develop programs which invite creative responses from young viewers and a critical awareness of what they see and hear. There is no necessity for one medium to displace another; each has its proper use as a tool of understanding and imagination.

It will be difficult to realize these objectives all at once. Nevertheless, by the establishment of a strong unit a sense of community will develop among those responsible for the production of children's television. Only by this means will public confidence be restored in the ability of the Corporation to meet the needs of children in our time. Only in this way will a sense of high morale develop among members of the production unit and be an inspiration to all others in the private sector.

The Canadian Broadcasting Corporation is a national programming agency, committed to representing all the regions of Canada. Throughout its 30-year history in television there has always been tension between the major network center of

Toronto and the regional centers, each of which wishes from time to time to produce a children's program. The national ideal should never be abandoned, but it does entail a great deal of communication between the regions which participate and the network center where the policies for good children's television are being developed. The regional center should not be made to feel that its creative endeavor is being interfered with; rather, in the light of the policy described above, each station should in its own way strive to produce material which will realize the goals which that policy sets forth as clearly as possible. Indeed, the community at the network center is as significant as the community of regional producers who cooperate with it. Frequent intercommunication is necessary if this ideal is to be realized.

In order to provide a full schedule of high-quality children's programs in film and television, a number of options should be considered. The CBC should continue the pre-school programs as scheduled in morning time. Since TVOntario schedules the pre-school programming from 6:00 p.m. to 7:00 p.m., young children in Ontario have good programs available both in morning and early evening time.

Programming for children in the 8-12 age group is presently scheduled at 4:30 p.m. Monday to Friday. The programs scheduled include What's New and Going Great, along with other series procured from outside sources. The period 4:00 p.m. to 6:00 p.m. should be reserved for network children's programming. The period from 4:00 to 5:00 should be scheduled for pre-school and primary-age children. From 5;00 to 5:30 there should be a daily magazine made up of elements contained in programs like What's New and Going Great. Indeed, Chris Makepeace could easily become the central host, along with a team of two or three regulars who would interact on various topics of interest to young viewers.

The present format of Going Great, as the title indicates, focuses on the energy and talents of dynamic and creative young people across Canada. It depends on program elements being developed on film, and includes information segments on such topics as sport, science, crafts, or computer technology. What is missing is the integration of performances by young musicians, actors, dancers, etc. As well, comic sketches reflecting the attitudes of young people could provide light relief. Above all, the show is presently scheduled only one day a week. Instead, it would be good if the show could be a daily show, making use of the talents of Makepeace and his co-hosts, creating a regular hour's opportunity for young people to learn more about themselves and to interact with their peers. Such a daily show would make much of the art of continuity--the creation of meaningful and creative visual sequences so necessary for a magazine of this kind. As was the case with both Razzle Dazzle and Junior Magazine, such a program builds up a loyal and continuing audience. Because of its flexibility, such a format has potential for a long and productive run.

In keeping with the recommendations of Nostbakken and Caron in their report to the federal policy review committee, the author would underline their deep concern about the perpetuation of the strip show/magazine show on a daily basis for children. Indeed, as they looked at scheduling, they isolated three important issues already referred to in this report: (1) children require ... a regularly, clearly identified daily pattern of children's programs; (2) children's programs need to be scheduled in time periods when children are most likely to be viewing television, e.g., 4:00-6:00 p.m. and Saturday and Sunday mornings; (3) prime-time children's and family specials should be carried early enough in the evening (before 8:00 p.m.) to enable young children to see them before bedtime. In keeping with the spirit of the recommendations here,

> it is particularly important that long-term budgeting take place to ensure continuity and longevity of programs meant to develop a constant and faithful viewership of children, who thrive on familiarity and daily companionship. The several commissioned studies and governmental reports that argue the importance of long-term budgeting should be taken seriously and acted upon by the appropriate government bodies and regulatory authorities, especially as they relate to children's television.

In reference to the great importance of daily magazine shows for children, Nostbakken and Caron emphasize again that it

> is constantly pointed out by children's specialists, by spokespersons of the children's department of the

> CBC, and in research of children's viewing habits, children benefit from and prefer continuity in programming. Strip show formats such as the pre-school programs now available on weekday mornings, such as Mr. Dress-Up and Passe Partout ... and as was demonstrated in the afternoon hours by the popular series such as Razzle Dazzle and Felix et Ciboulette, provide daily participation and familiarity. A weekend morning magazine series with a friendly host has shown to be extremely popular in French programming.

From 5:30 to 6:00 p.m. I propose investment in a dramatic situation comedy centered on the life of young people: their relationships, their problems and their happiness with their peers and with adults. Young Canadians are fascinated by the new technologies in media, science and engineering. With a team of good researchers and writers, an imaginative and humanistic series could be developed which would enrich the genre of sci-fi adventure and readily win a large audience of young people and their families. In order to win a good audience, such a series would have to be of the highest quality and, like the previous half-hour, the project would have to be well funded. The most experienced and well-known writers would have to be enlisted--e.g., Bernard Slade, whose success as a writer of plays for Broadway (Same Time Next Year) and for Hollywood comes to mind because he has an interest in young people and could realize the possibility of such a series. Or the current stable of writing talent for children's drama on Seeing Things could be considered. Perry Rosemond (whose success with the King of Kensington might well ensure the success of this proposed series) was, of course, the producer of Through the Eyes of Tomorrow, the CBC's major youth show in the '60s. And there is Denis Hargrave, for many years a producer in the Children's Television Department, whose success with children's drama, the pilot of The Stowaway, and documentary (Countdown to a Gold Medal) has been internationally recognized. At present, CBC is cooperating with Playing with Time, Inc., the Public Broadcasting System of the U.S. and Telefilm Canada in the production of a new series for young teen-agers, DeGrassi Junior High, which will be an important addition to drama series for young people in the English-speaking world.

The realization of these proposals for the 5:00-6:00 p.m.

period represents a major commitment of funds and a reallocation of priorities within the CBC's program budget. Studio space would have to be regularly available, especially for the pre-school and magazine program proposal. Indeed, planning should ensure that adequate facilities be available for all children's programs. Production of drama series to fill the 5:30-6:00 p.m. slot afford an excellent opportunity for independent producers and Telefilm Canada to work with the CBC and other networks to provide a steady flow of good Canadian dramatic programming for children. Such a series should be conceived in a way that would make it attractive to a French-speaking audience. With the cooperation of Société Radio-Canada, the series could be shot both in French and English (as was the case with Empire Inc.), and therefore could become a truly national series seen in every province of Canada.

This use of the 4:00-6:00 p.m. period would restore basic in-house production for the Children's Television Department, providing a model for any future productions undertaken with the private sector. Contributions both in information programming and in drama from the private sector would extend and enrich the CBC in-house productions and not require CBC studios to meet the schedule. Currently, the episodes of Kids of DeGrassi Street, produced by Playing With Time, Inc., are being scheduled in weekly sequence along with several other co-productions under the title Just Down the Street. A similar repeat of the dramas produced for CBC by Atlantis Films could be scheduled as part of the proposed magazine at 5:30 p.m. once a week. Both of these series have been scheduled individually once a month in prime time. There is merit in continuing this pattern as a means of winning the family audience.

But the proposal for a regular daily dramatic series would have far greater impact and would eliminate the necessity to carry Three's Company on the English network and Grizzly Adams dubbed into French on the French network at 5:30 p.m. Nostbakken and Caron, in a document submitted for the federal task force on broadcast policy, have recommended that the CRTC should provide a program of incentives to both public and private broadcasters to produce children's programs. Their recommendations include suggestions that broadcasters should be credited with advertising time not used during children's broadcasts. In this way, broadcasters would

Niki Kemeny (r.) and Nicole Skoffman in DeGrassi Junior High. (Courtesy of CBC)

then be allowed to exceed the maximum advertising time per hour allowed now for use on other time periods. The amount of credit to be allowed should be subject to adjudication by a CRTC Quality Control Council on the basis of a program meeting a 10/10 Canadian content schedule, and on the program's ability to meet an acceptable quality standard. In no instance should less than 40 per cent of the revenue generated by the credited advertising time be dedicated by the broadcaster for the production of children's programs. They urge further that the CRTC Quality Control Council, in its capacity of reviewing programs for Canadian content, and quality standards, may on this basis of 10/10 Canadian content criteria and high quality standards grant up to 200 per cent Canadian content ratings to qualifying programs. Since it is generally recognized that the market for advertising to children is a small market at best, such an incentive would encourage private broadcasters to present more and better children's programs, and would discourage the CBC from treating children's programming as a financial liability, since the policy at present prevents advertising to children. In this way both public and private broadcasting would be given both a challenging and creative incentive to improve their contributions to the needs of children on television.

In planning for the future, considerable attention should be given to more intimate cooperation with the Children's Department of Société Radio-Canada. There have been several quite successful attempts in the past. At present it is difficult to establish connection because so little material is produced in studio. We do have the model of Empire Incorporated which was double-shot and therefore available in both French and English at the same time throughout its run. The high cost has to be put up against the importance of using the television medium to achieve a higher degree of mutual understanding between the two cultures.

Referring back to the schedule described above, the magazine segment proposed for 5:00-5:30 p.m. could readily include segments from Québec as well as the other regions of Canada. In each case the planning should include elements of animation which come from Québec, and other information segments that can easily be given a French or English voice to provide the commentary. In some situations the show would have to be double-shot, and there will be occasions, I am sure, when English-speaking children with French as a second language could speak French to their peers in Québec and vice versa. It would take a great deal of care in planning plus imaginative and sensitive development, but this could be a most worthwhile endeavor. Very early in the development of children's television Fernand Doré expressed the concern that more than a redeployment of funds was necessary to bring about more dynamic cooperation between the two networks. Along with Pierre Desroches (who was Doré's successor as head of children's TV for Société Radio Canada), he would agree that commitment to the sharing of our cultures must be central policy for all programs and services. There must be deeper creative commitment involving program planners from both English and French services in the conception and development of programs in every department--especially the Children's.

The sitcom provided for the 5:30 period could be double-shot if funds were available. In pre-school programming, we already have the precedent of Chez Hélène. The proposed substitute for Sesame Street would provide a renewed opportunity to develop creative bicultural and bilingual responses among younger viewers.

In 1980, in response to a call from the CRTC, TVOntario submitted a proposal for a children's channel with a service of children's programs entitled Galaxie. It was to be distributed by Anik C3 using two half-Canada spot beams. Service on the eastern beam would begin at 7:00 a.m. Eastern Time Monday to Friday, and would run until 7:00 p.m. on Saturday and Sunday, when it would run until noon. Service on the western beam was to be delayed by two hours: it would begin at 7:00 a.m. Mountain Time and follow the same schedule as in the east. The motivation for the application came from the program service entitled Galaxie, which was a cooperative effort between TVOntario, the cable satellite network, and Rogers Cable Systems. The original service was four hours a day, seven days a week, with a package of programs comprising a number of TVOntario series, selected Canadian and foreign acquisitions in both English and French. The package was distributed by video cassette only to a limited number of cable companies. Almost half a million dollars was realized for reinvestment in the production of two new Canadian series, Today's Special at TVOntario and La Maison Magique through an independent producer. The participating cable companies offered Galaxie to their subscribers as part of their augmented basic service, enabling some 1.7 million subscribers in six provinces to enjoy Canada's only television service dedicated to children.

In spite of the care taken in the preparation of the proposal, TVOntario's application was turned back by the CRTC, as were several other applications for specialty services. Clearly, the CRTC had had second thoughts about its original call for applications for special services, probably because of its concern about unsatisfactory subscription levels for the two pay-TV channels.

Since that time, the CRTC has reviewed its policies and once again called for applications for pay-TV channels, as of 1984. In its original application TVOntario had undertaken very careful market analysis. It recognized, as ironically the CRTC did when it turned the application down, that the application was filed

> in a climate of great uncertainty, in both the economic and the regulatory environments. The rules of the game are not clear and therefore the application is based on a number of critical assumptions and premises. If these assumptions and premises are not fulfilled, the viability of this application is in jeopardy.

TVOntario went ahead with its application in spite of this uncertainty, because of private encouragement of the CRTC to proceed with an application on a semi-discretionary basis. Unlike pay-TV--a subscriber-discretionary service available at the option of the individual subscriber--the cost of a semi-discretionary service is cable-discretionary. Any costs not covered by advertising revenue to the cable company would be absorbed in the basic cable charge, and unless otherwise subsidized would be paid by all subscribers whether they wanted the service or not. TVOntario's research revealed that although a subscriber or totally discretionary service was not economically viable, there was sufficient acceptance of the Galaxie service by the cable operators to ensure its economic viability on the semi-discretionary basis.

Nostbakken and Caron, in dealing with the issue of new

applications for a children's channel, set forth basic principles on which decisions might be made for the licensing of a children's channel. At the outset they insisted that the service should reach as many Canadian children as is technically possible. They furthermore emphasized that there was no point in licensing a Canadian specialty service for children unless the programming was of the highest quality and with a minimum of 60 per cent Canadian content. With these two principles in mind, they proceeded to make recommendations. At the outset, they recognized that the service could not be a pay service or discretionary service to householders, since this would discriminate against those not able to pay and would restrict the reach of service. For this reason, they urged that the service should be non-discretionary to the householder, with a small pass-through fee allowable, with a maximum percentage of the pass-through dollar going into the production of Canadian programming. They urged that regulatory pressure should be brought to bear on cable services to carry the specialty children's service. A mandatory policy should be brought to bear if cable companies proved uncooperative in carrying the service. They emphasized that the service should be on the basic or extended-basic service, and should be non-profit. They further urged that no commercial advertising should be allowed within the service, a policy consistent with that already adopted by the CBC. At the same time they did allow for corporate sponsorship of programming of the service, as a device to bring in extra revenue. They recommended the service should be licensed for at least a five-year period. Expectations for a full and adequate service to be in place within the first or second year may not be realistic. At least a five-year period should be provided to allow for growth and maturity.

As part of the promised performance,

> the license service should provide for a strong statement of program policy and a governing board should be in place that will ensure quality control. Programs imparted should reflect the diversity of cultural traditions and viewpoints, and should not be dominated by any one cultural source.

Care should be taken to ensure that the programming should be diverse in order to meet the age differences of young viewers ranging within ages of two to 12. They recommended strongly co-productions with the CBC and other public broadcasters; and that private broadcasters be encouraged to insure continued program offerings through those broadcast outlets, particularly within those regions not reached by cable.

It is clear from the outset that the licensing of any children's channel in Canada would be effective only if strong support is given by other agencies capable of production of children's programs, namely the CBC, the private broadcasters, and the National Film Board.

In countries like Canada which have a national, publicly-owned broadcasting corporation, it has been natural to think of that body as the logical provider of special programs for children, schools, agriculture and fisheries, religion, etc. Where the national broadcasting service is a monopoly, the issue of who will provide what service never arises. In the early days of television in Canada, there were no challengers to the CBC's pre-eminent right and obligation to provide a daily program service for children both at home and at school. In the case of schools programs, there was the National Schools Advisory Council to lend approval to the CBC's service to schools. The various religious denominations and sects (all those whose adherents exceeded 500,000) were represented on the National Religious Advisory Council. Because children's programs were part of the general broadcasting service, there was no advisory council since none of the agencies committed to the service of children had vested interests to represent to the CBC as far as broadcasting was concerned.

The first challenge to the CBC's provision of a service to children came with provincial educational television in Ontario and Quebec. Because education is a provincial responsibility, the more affluent provinces inevitably assumed the job of educaitonal television.

Concurrently, when the CBC surrendered its original role as both broadcaster and regulator of the federal law concerning the licensing of broadcasting, another break came in its traditional universal authority. It became the responsibility first of the Board of Broadcast Governors and finally of the Canadian Radio, Televison and Telecommunications Commission to grant licenses to independent stations and networks, and to regulate their conduct. Broadcasting to children became one of the minor conditions required to receive and retain a license.

We have already discussed the issue of entertainment versus education in broadcasts to children. Children now have access to alternative programming from CBC, from the CTV and Global networks, from independent stations, from the provincial networks (especially Ontario and Alberta), and occasionally from cable and pay-TV stations.

Just as such diversity has become a reality chiefly in urban areas, advancing technology has broadened the alternatives and the diversity of media themselves. Increasingly, home video machines enable families to select their own programs for adults and children. Satellite dishes are becoming more economical, thus widening even farther the accessibility of programs from many sources.

The problem then arises about quality and quantity of children's programs. From what sources and from what funds will good programs originate? Who will do the planning to ensure a balanced schedule? What will be the range of alternatives? Since random selection from many sources is possible, these questions have a certain meaninglessness. The only guarantee of quality will come from the producers of the programs themselves. It therefore becomes increasingly necessary that more funds should be available to the traditionally responsible agencies--the CBC and the provincial educational networks--to set standards for others who undertake the production of children's programs.

Since the advent of the Canadian Broadcast Program Development Fund (Telefilm Canada) in 1980, there has been significant development in the support for new Canadian television and film products. Many of these productions are single films or videos, of varying length, from a half-hour to full-length feature films. These programs are all listed with brief descriptions in the _Canadian Children's Film and Video Directory_, edited by Dr. Deborah Bernstein for the Children's Broadcast Institute. As the CBC had done with its series _Just Down the Street_, Sullivan Films created three anthologies in order to make independent programs more attractive for scheduling in the television market. The series entitled Golden Tales and Legends includes Kevin Sullivan's film *The Fir Tree* and *Megan Carey*, along with Ariadne Ochrymovich's *The Juggler* and *Billy Goat's Bluff*, along with John Kozak's *The Golden Apple*. They packaged another series entitled *Against All Odds*, ten half-hour episodes by various producers such as *Flowers in the Sand* and *Claire's Wish* by Ikon Kino Films, *God Is Not a Fish Inspector* by Alan Kroker, *New Tomorrow* and *Jimmy Luke* by Film Arts Incorporated, *The Highway* by Keith Lott, *City Survival* by Red Snapper Films, and *Corletto and Son* by Cineflics. Atlantis Films, some of whose programs had been included in the series presented by the CBC entitled Just Down the Street, have packaged several of their programs in two series entitled *Rainbow* and *Northern Lights*. The *Rainbow* series consists of 12 shows done in association with the CBC Children's Television Department and Telefilm Canada. Each episode features a young protagonist who encounters certain moral and physical dilemmas which provide a glimpse of the world beyond childhood. Each experience enables the young hero to deal in a positive way with life's complexities and challenges. The dramas are based on stories and poems from Canadian authors such as Alice Munro, Margaret Laurence, Lucy Maud Montgomery, and Earle Birney.

In the pro-social vein, the series *Northern Lights* is similar to *Rainbow*, with each episode focusing on the simple truths and universal themes of community and family life. Overall, a combination of contemporary, period, urban and rural settings are featured. The dramas are based on stories by authors such as Mordecai Richler, Guy Vanderhaeghe, Morley Callaghan, and Sinclair Ross.

While this collection of programs into several anthologies with a generic title is useful for marketing purposes, it also meets the critical need in the children's area of providing them with a signal of the nature of a program series. While one would have no argument with the support of independent producers by Telefilm Canada, the fund is not sufficiently great for them to be able to take over the entire responsibility for children's television. Initiative must still remain with major producing agencies such as the CBC. At the same time, it has been argued elsewhere in this report how very important it is that there be a strong children's department in the major broadcasting agencies which is responsible for the development of program policy as a guide for production which will meet the needs of children in their creative growth and development. To achieve this end, the recommendation of Nostbakken and Caron is heartily endorsed that money should be set aside by whatever agency--the CBC, Telefilm Canada, etc.--to provide support for training and development of producers who can make a career out of leadership in the field of children's television.

The attention of young people has now been diverted to video games and computers, introducing a totally new language of communication. It is certainly important that children become familiar with computer technology and that responsible leadership be given to ensure that they are used properly. If computers are used only for video games, the same criticisms can be made about this new technology as were made about radio and television. CBC with _Mister Microchip_, TV-Ontario with its _Computer Academy_, and ACCESS with _Computer Literacy_ have taken the initiative in familiarizing both young people and adults with the many dimensions of computer technology.

So, from the days when the CBC was solely responsible for quality program production in radio and television, the responsibility is now more widely distributed. From the time when television was a dominantly external force shaping sociocultural attitudes and thereby constituting (for good or bad) a unifying force, the media are increasingly individualized and fractionated. This in no way lessens the responsibility of production agencies for leadership in quantity and quality of programs, but it does demand a new strategy to coordinate the creative, financial and administrative endeavor of writers and producers, private and public corporations, and government to meet the challenges of the rapidly changing technology. It is therefore valuable to compare the role of the CBC and TVO's proposal in the light of a third model.

Faced with problems similar to these described above, Australia took up the challenge in a totally different way. At a meeting of the Children's Television Advisory Committee to the Australian Broadcasting Control Board in 1972, the concept of an independent children's authority originated. It was suggested

> that the Commonwealth government should consider

> means of encouraging the production of suitable programs, for example, by offering grants, subsidies or tax concessions as financial assistance to those programs.
>
> Perhaps it should also consider ways in which to support the establishment of an independent foundation to produce film and television programs especially designed for children. [booklet on The Australian Children's Television Foundation.]

The committee was very aware of the need for adequate training of personnel for children's program production. To this end, they recommended

> that many organizations which work to develop the creative, critical and intellectual resources of children (which is likely to contribute to a growing maturity of judgment and responsiveness to good quality children's television programs)

should cooperate more fully. The proposal for a children's television foundation was reiterated by the committee in its final report in February of 1973. Proposed funding of the foundation was to be by a levy on stations' gross revenue. Other measures were proposed to improve the quality of programs seeking accreditation for the school-age quota. But the committee saw the institution as an independent foundation, as the ultimate response if other measures failed to improve the quality of children's programs--which they had. In 1976 the Australian Broadcasting Control Board had noted that it had attempted to encourage stations by establishing quotas and the point system for Australian content; however, these attempts had not been effective.

In 1977, the Australian Broadcasting Control Board was replaced by the Australian Broadcasting Tribunal. In its initial surveys it found that the criticisms of children's programs uttered by the Control Board's Advisory Committee were still true. As more and more bodies became concerned about the quality of programs for children, the cry for the establishment of an independent foundation to produce quality programs gained in momentum.

In 1978, a Senate Standing Committee on Education in the Arts stated vehemently,

> We believe that children's television is a crucial social issue, and that if we are genuinely concerned to protect the interests of the child viewing audience from possible harmful effects and to see to it that the medium is used to enrich and enlighten their lives, then the responsibility for producing programs for children should be removed from the arena of industry economics.

Finally, early in 1979, the Australian Children's Television Foundation Steering Committee was established with a grant of $2500 from the New South Wales government. This grant was later matched by the government of the State of Victoria. The committee's purpose was to gain support for a foundation which would be incorporated as a national association. The committee had reached the point of incorporation proceedings when the Australian Educaiton Council established a working group. It therefore halted its work but remains an active committee interested in the foundation.

In May 1980, the Minister for Post and Telecommunications stated in Parliament that he would endorse any effort that would improve the conditions indicated in the report of the Senate Standing Committee on Education in the Arts. Finally, at a meeting of the commonwealth and state ministers with responsibility for the arts in Canberra on February 13, 1980, it was unanimously agreed that the ministers for arts and education proceed to set up a children's television foundation to improve the quality of television programs for young people. Over a period of ten years the Australian people gradually recognized that children have special needs as television viewers and require special treatment. It was noted that

> the failure to achieve satisfactory results has been due partly to the absence of concerted and continued action by networks and advertisers; partly to a paucity of leadership on this issue by governments; and partly to there being insufficient public action. The main factor, however, has been that no one has acknowledged that a substantial improvement in the quality and availability of children's programs requires the spending of large amounts of money.

It was noted that children's drama is not cheaper than adult drama, but the revenue that realistically can be expected from it is considerably less. Good quality drama programs cost at least 84,000 Australian dollars per hour to produce. Other programs, such as magazines, cost about 17,000 dollars per hour. On a 50-50 mix, the average production cost per hour of Australian-made material would be 50,000 dollars per hour. It was recognized that no significant improvement in the quality of children's television programs would be achieved unless a massive effort was made by governments, networks, and other funding sources to cooperate in meeting this challenge.

The Children's Broadcast Institute is the major voluntary agency in Canada concerned with films and television for children. It was set up to promote more and better-than-ever TV programs for kids across Canada, and to encourage the positive use of television in the child's learning-entertainment experience. It presently holds a biennial festival of children's programs at which awards are given by a professional jury. The Institute has contributed to the development of media literacy by means of production workshops (viz. the handbook "Children's Television Programming," published in cooperation with the CRTC). Under the leadership of David and Janis Nostbakken, a series of workshops for parents were held across Canada with the cooperation of the Canadian Home and School and Parent/Teacher Federation and co-sponsored by Wintario (the provincial lottery enterprise of the Province of Ontario).

Annually, the Institute sponsors Parents' Viewing Month in September just as the various networks' fall schedules are launched. Across Canada, viewers are exposed to a creatively designed public service announcement urging parents to share the experience of watching television with their children. Advertising agencies have contributed these messages as a public service, urging parents to "Be your child's TV guide!"

The Institute represents on its Board a cross-cut of all agencies concerned with television and film for children.

The Association for Media Literacy professes to develop among young people "an individual response to all forms of the new visual and aural languages." The Association is concerned "to help young people respond to this new language as effectively and richly as possible, to increase their ability to understand themselves as well as others." The Committee defines media literacy as an awareness of how the media operate in terms of their form and content. Media literacy entails an understanding of the special skills required to analyze media. It also requires an awareness of the social and commercial implications of mass communication systems with their persuasive value messages. Above all, media literacy helps the viewer to be a discriminating critic, not only of the social forces at work in program planning and production but of the potential for creative expression which the media afford. To these ends the Association for Media Literacy is committed. At the present time, in cooperation with the Ministry of Education of Ontario, the Association is producing a Media Literacy Resource Book for Grades K-12 for Ontario schools.

The Canadian Centre of Films for Children was a federally-registered non-profit corporation, established in 1977, promoting the production, exhibition and distribution of films by, for and about children. It was the national member of the International Centre of Films for Children and Young People set up by UNESCO in Paris in 1955. Like the international organization, the Canadian Centre was committed to the increase of quantity and quality of children's film and television in Canada. To achieve this end, the Centre aimed to establish a resource center of information on the production, distribution and availability of children's films and television in Canada and to publish a directory of such information. Its policy and program entailed the sponsorship of festivals, media literacy and the evaluation of scripts, treatments and completed films.

Because of the similarity of aims and objectives and because of difficulties in raising adequate funds for the Centre, amalgamation with the Children's Broadcast Institute was arranged in 1984. The Institute was enriched by the addition of some members of the Board of the Center. It also gave the Institute an international face since it became the Canadian constituent member of the General Assembly of the International Center. Unfortunately, owing to the financial difficulties facing UNESCO, the International Center has been considerably reduced in its function, making continued membership of Canada and of some other nations an uneconomical proposition. The International Center is unable to play an effective role on behalf of its members.

The Children's Broadcast Institute remains the most financially viable advocate for children's television in Canada. Because it is so important for there to be one national agency through which public opinion can be expressed to broadcasters and producers of film and television for children, I strongly urge the amalgamation of the Association for Media Literacy with the CBI, so that funds raised can be effectively put to work on behalf of children who need more and better programming in all media.

The Association for Media Literacy is at present centred in Toronto and does no have the funds to function on a national basis. The inclusion of the Association would bring in the professional endeavor of a group of creative teachers and media philosophers to extend the already significant public service given by the Institute.

In its new role, the Institute could maintain a file of Canadian talent (independent producers, writers and performers).

Four options have been presented: revision of the CBC's national network schedule; proposals for a children's channel; the model of the Australian Children's Television Foundation; and the use of new technology. If one were to allow each of these to develop without coordination and without a national policy, the costs would be exorbitant; it is also highly unlikely that any of the options would ever be realized. Therefore, I propose that some consideration be given to the route taken by the Australians in setting up their foundation. What is needed now is some agency which has the capacity to activate public interest and concern about the production and distribution of good material for children to see on television. To this end, I would like to see the Children's Broadcast Institute and the Canadian Council on Children and Youth meet with representatives of the Canadian Broadcast Program Development Fund to discuss the recommendations of this report along with those contained in Nostbakken and Caron's document for the federal policy review committee. Nostbakken and Caron repeatedly recognize how important continuity is to children in the program offerings that they see, and to this end series play an important part of their television diet. They argue that the position with respect to reduced funding for renewed series may readily hurt the children's program area.

> It may be desirable, in view of the importance of strong Canadian program offerings for children, and the likelihood that a new children's channel might lead to a greater participation of independent producers, and in view of the tendency within the Canadian Broadcasting Corporation to seek outside

> productions in the children's area, that some special considerations be accorded producers of children's programs.

The adoption of such a policy would greatly enhance the possibility of more series for children's programs and fewer individual programs which have no immediate connection one to another except as contrived under generic titles referred to above. After careful review of these recommendations, the group then should consider meeting with the Minister of Communications to request that CRTC set up a task force to investigate the media needs of children in Canada.

Special attention should be given to the recommendation of Nostbakken and Caron that consideration be given to the creation of a special children's governing group within Telefilm Canada.

> This group should have visibility so that young producers will know who and how to decisions will be made with respect to the 30 per cent of Telefilm funds allocated to the children's area. Accountability for the distribution and the administration of the funds relating to children should rest with this group.
>
> This group should be made up with individuals who know and understand children, are committed to the development of high-quality programming in this field, and who understand marketing of children's programs.

The establishment of such a group in no way denies the importance of the CBC's endeavor in children's programming. Since the beginning, the CBC has had a policy of hiring producers who have some commitment to the needs of children, and the policies established in the early years still to a large extent prevail in the building of schedules and in guidance for producers in making programs. Nevertheless, because of the diversity of partners involved in production, and with the existence of Telefilm Canada, it is necessary that producers who are not part of the CBC endeavor have some source of reference and consultation in order that their efforts may be in the best interest of the child audiences. I would urge that one of the primary recommendations of this group should be the establishment of a task force to investigate the media needs of children in Canada. While this report, along with that of Nostbakken and Caron, touches on many vital areas of concern, it is still important to obtain a grass-roots support for a movement that would enhance the development of children's television for the next decade.

Once the Children's Broadcast Institute, the Canadian Council on Children and Youth, and the Telefilm Canada group have concluded their deliberations, then the report should be referred to the Department of Communications of the federal government of Canada at Ottawa. The Department of Communications is the body ultimately responsible for public and private television sectors and the public funding mechanisms which serve and control them. From the Department of Communications should come clear guidelines, policies, and decisions which will affect the development of children's programming in the future.

The media cut across the lives of our children in many ways. In the first place, they often see a reflection of contemporary adult values as they are perceived by advertisers and broadcasters who are anxious to gain large audiences. We worry greatly about the negative impact of the values perceived on television, often not realizing that these in fact are the norm of adult behavior in a good part of our society. Secondly, the media play an important role in helping or hindering the development of a sense of national identity. Thirdly, television is a source of social, scientific, and moral information for children. Not enough care is given to providing sufficient alternatives for them to make creative use of television or the other media accessible to them. We are currently faced with a rapid development in computer technology, and the same pettern is occurring as did with television and radio: no one is making any preparation whatsoever for its creative utilization in society. We tend to be critical of the newer media without understanding their esthetic dimensions, and for this reason we need a central body that will concern itself with regular and significant information of use to parents, broadcasters, advertisers and the children themselves.

In choosing the Canadian Council on Children and Youth as one partner in the development of this proposal, I am mindful of the fact that the Council since its inception has been concerned with the needs of the whole child. In particular, the Council initiated the first national conference on Children's

Television, organized by volunteers in 1972. Out of this conference came the realization of the Children's Broadcast Institute, which represents the broadcaster, the advertiser, the product manufacturers, and the public sector.

It has already been recommended that a newly constituted Children's Broadcast Institute should be the voice and advocate of thoughtful public and professional concern for children's film and television in Canada. In recommending that the CRTC should conduct public hearings in order to obtain a true reading of the public needs for children's television, the following concerns should be examined.

I have urged a revitalization of the CBC's Children's Television Department that would give greater access to studios for in-house production and would guarantee an effective schedule for its programs. Should the former pre-eminence of the CBC as leader in the field of children's television be restored?

Regardless of the broadcasting agency to whom it may be given, in what ways would a children's TV channel serve the public need?

With the multifarious means of production and distribution available today, what is the best way to insure a continuing flow of high-quality children's programs on videotape and film? How do we insure that there is enough good programming available to independent stations, cable networks, and home video to provide good alternative viewing?

How do we provide everyone--the public, the broadcaster, the product manufacturers, the advertisers and the educators--with good research concerning the production, the use and the impact of television on children?

Does the Australian Children's Television Foundation provide a model which could be adapted to meet Canadian needs?

The necessity for a full national investigation of the problem of children and the media arises from many of the implications of this report. Underlying the whole enterprise throughout the 30 years lies the relationship between television and values, both esthetic and moral. Inevitably, all media reflect contemporary values. If this is the case, then to what extent can media be considered a negative external force? To be sure, media will be perceived as a negative external force if parents viewing television find that the values represented on TV are in conflict with their own. The difficulty is very often that we cherish an ideal set of values which we use to judge others, but we are victims of the very mores we would have our children reject. The time has come for a full investigation to relate contemporary values of western society to the realities of what we see on television.

Other areas of investigation requiring study are the uses which children make of television, and the whole question of media education. To what extent are we obliged as a society to help children use the new technologies creatively?

No systematic review of the proper financing of television for children has ever been undertaken. In Canada we have always left the problem to the CBC, hoping that it would regularly provide adequate service. With rising inflation and with increasing demands for sophisticated adult entertainment, budgets for children's programs have been shrinking. We therefore need a thorough investigation of the worth of children's television and all other media to the society in which we live, before we launch another enterprise for its improvement. We must know at the outset that it will cost a great deal of money to do the job properly. The question then remains as to where the money will come from and how it can best be spent.

Other recommendations which are contained in the Nostbakken/Caron report would be worthy of consideration by the task force proposed above. The Department of Communications (DOC) should be urged, in the use of its authority in the international exchange of programs and signals, to ensure that any program exchanges contain a minimum of 25 per cent children's content, and that promotional and support programs for international exchange should contain an optimal exposure of plans, personnel, and programs relating to children. They further argue that the DOC should ensure that the international TV5 agreement among francophone European countries and Canada should contain a provision for each country supplying programs to include an optimum proportion of children's programs.

Concerning the Broadcasting Act itself, Nostbakken and

Caron strongly recommend that any changes in the future for the Broadcasting Act should include direct reference to children and the importance of service to them, within Section 3 on broadcasting policy for Canada, within Part 2 on the objects and powers of the Canadian Radio and Television Telecommunications Commission, and in Part 3 in relation to the Canadian Broadcasting Corporation.

Since the cable industry in Canada would be responsible for carrying a children's channel, specific recommendations are important for consideration here. When TVOntario submitted its earlier proposal in support of a license for *Galaxie*, they argued that distribution on a subscriber discretionary basis of a specialty service of high standard designed specifically for Canadian children would not generate sufficient revenues for the service to survive. TVOntario, it will be remembered, urged that the Commission reconsider its policies with respect to the carriage of specialty services. The Canadian Broadcasting Corporation also strongly supported the universal mandatory system for the carriage of a children's channel in Canada on cable systems. To insure that the needs of children are met, policy control over the cable industry is contained in two recommendations made by Nostbakken and Caron.

> 1. CRTC should continue to regulate the American specialty services allowable in Canada. No specialty children's service should be allowed on a stand-alone basis.
>
> 2. Cable companies should be required with respect to a children's specialty service to allow a pass-through fee to subscribers. If necessary to universal mandatory system with respect to children's specialty service may be required if affiliation agreements do not materialize in sufficient numbers. Because of the priority importance of children's programming in this country of a Canadian nature, government regulation requiring the cable companies to carry a children's specialty service should not be regarded as a precedent for other specialty services, but as an exceptional, Canadian requirement.

This history concludes at a point when major changes in broadcasting policy for Canada are likely to take place.

At the outset, we have before us the Caplan/Sauvageau report. While Nostbakken and Caron had recommended a children's channel and had articulated very carefully the conditions under which it should be licensed, Caplan and Sauvageau recommended against specialty channels in favor of a second service to be known as TV Canada, which would combine children's shows, arts programming, and films from the National Film Board and other sources.

> We are not able to support the notion of a channel dedicated exclusively to young people. In our view, as legitimate as the need for children's programming is, there is also a need for more outlets for regional programming, for documentaries, for National Film Board productions, for many other sorts of specialized programming. The Canadian system simply does not have the resources to accommodate many new Canadian channels, unless they serve simply as vehicles to import more foreign programming. It is our judgement that the most viable and equitable way of providing more quality children's programming is through a sharing arrangement as part of the new public sector networks we are recommending. [Gerald Caplan and Florian Sauvageau, Report of the Task Force on Broadcasting Policy (Ottawa: Ministry of Supply and Services Canada, 1986), p. 351.]

A second player in the forthcoming changes is the chairman of the CRTC, Mr. André Bureau. His views about the future of broadcasting differ sharply from those recommended by Caplan and Sauvageau. Bureau sees the necessity for broadcasting to be established on a sound business foundation. He had set about licensing new independent stations even before the task force was able to submit its recommendations to the government. He has gone ahead with hearings for license renewal for the CBC, CTV, and the Global Television Networks. In pressing the private networks to give more time to Canadian programming, his accent was more on quality than on quantity. In some instances, stations have been allowed to reduce the amount of Canadian content provided that they increased the quality of the programming they provide. Nevertheless the Global Television Network was informed that it must double its spending on Canadian shows during the next five-year term of its license. The applications for licenses for specialty channels will be received up to March

12, 1987, and hearings will follow in the months thereafter. Regardless of the changes which the Minister of Communications might wish to make in the Broadcasting Act, the actions taken by the chairman in this critical time will largely shape the future of broadcasting in Canada.

Perhaps the greatest need in creating a permanent foundation for children's television in Canada is to insure sustained finances, continuing formative and summative research, and a continuing, uninterrupted flow of high quality productions. At present the leadership is uncertain. There is little value in licensing a children's channel if there is no clear policy governing both quality and quantity of production. While no one can argue with the need to give independent producers the opportunity to make children's programs, a central agency is needed to give guidance on the needs and preferences of children and young people. Some coordination of the program endeavor of the CBC, the independent producers, TVOntario, ACCESS, the independent stations, and the private television networks is necessary if a consistent, well-planned flow of children's programs is to be accomplished.

Appendix A

ANNOTATED REFERENCES

Applebaum, Louis, and Jacques Hébert. Report of the Federal Cultural Review Committee. Information Services, Department of Communications, 406 pp., Ottawa, Canada, 1982. A comprehensive review of the wide diversity of cultural activity in Canada rooted in the ethnic diversity of the peoples who came to share their cultural heritage and their creative endeavor in the building of a new nation. The Report describes the shape and future of cultural policies for Canada, making a wide range of recommendations to guide the government in its decision-making for cultural activity in the future.

Broadcast Code for Advertising to Children. Advertising Standards Council, 1240 Bay Street, Toronto, Ont. M5R 2A7. A publication of the Canadian Advertising Advisory Board designed to set standards for advertisers in preparing commercial messages for insertion into children's programs. The Code complements the general principles of the Canadian Code of Advertising Standard which apply to all advertising in Canada. Both codes are supplementary to all federal and provincial laws and regulations governing advertising. The pamphlet includes guidelines for advertisers and broadcasters designed to encourage creative and informative commercial messages which do not exploit young viewers.

The Canadian Children's Film and Video Directory. Toronto, Ont.: The Children's Broadcast Institute, September 1985. This is a completely updated directory of available films, videocassettes, and television programs available for children in Canada, covering specifically the period 1980-1985.

Children's Programs: CBC Background. Canadian Broadcasting Corporation, Ottawa, Ont., 1979. Published in response to the United Nations' celebration of the International Year of the Child, it sets forth the policy and descriptions of children's programs on both the English and French networks of the CBC. Details about research, distribution, and programming philosophy are described.

Communication Yearbook 6. Beverley Hills, Ca.: Sage Publications, 1982.

Elkind, David. The Hurried Child. Reading, Mass.: Addison Wesley, 1981. Elkind presents a convincing case for damage done to a child's creative growth and development by too much stress rooted in the compulsion for success, divorce, role conflict and the fear of failure.

Esserman, June F., ed. Television Advertising and Children. New York: Child Research Service, 1981. A collection of essays concerned with the impact of advertising on young viewers of television. The studies include examination of children's perceptions of realism in televised fiction, children's comprehension of television commercials, and a comparison of the impact of TV commercials on children in Australia and the USA.

Follow the Rule. This publication of the CBC, in cooperation with the Canadian Highway Safety Conference, was an integral part of the Canadian Howdy Doody Show. While there was a strong accent on the importance of traffic safety for children, young viewers were able to gain a deeper understanding through their identification with Timber Tom and the cast of the show.

Galaxie: A Summary of TVOntario's Application for a Specialty Children's Television Service. August 15, 1983. TVOntario presents its case for a children's TV channel. The document presents TV-Ontario's policy for the development of children's programs, along with a detailed description of its productions to date and the success of those productions with young viewers.

Hyne, Lynne, and Jack Livesley. "Let's Play TV in the Classroom." TVOntario, Toronto, Ontario. A comprehensive utilization unit for teachers and their students to improve their awareness of visual literacy. The unit describes production techniques, planning, writing, direction of a TV show. The aim is to encourage a critical viewing so that the viewer is aware of style and aesthetic quality in television production.

Journal of Communications. Vol. 25, no. 4, Autumn 1975. The journal is a publication of the Annenburg School of Communications, University of Pennsylvania. While the journal generally deals with broad issues of communication theory, this issue is devoted to a symposium on "The Effects of Television on Children and Adolescents." As well as the research report by George Comstock, articles deal with such subjects as the developing child as viewer, violence and behavioral disorders, positive social learning, identifying with television characters, etc.

Lesser, Gerald S. Children and Television. New York: Random

House, 1975. This book is a comprehensive record of the planning, development, production, and evaluation of Sesame Street. The study reveals how basic principles of child development, mastery of skills, and social relationships were expressed in the challenging medium of television. The book describes how children use the television medium and how producers provided a viewing experience which was both educational and entertaining.

Lesser, Gerald S., "Stop Picking on Big Bird"; and Singer, Dorothy and Jerome, "Come Back Mr. Rogers, Come Back." Psychology Today, March 1979, pp. 56-60. The two articles raise the issue of fast pacing in the children's production Sesame Street. While the Singers argue that the fast pacing in the program tends to shorten the attention span of young children and inhibits their ability to reflect on and retain new information, Lesser argues that research does not support the Singers' argument and that fast pacing can teach young children important intellectual skills.

McKay, Kenneth B. Puppetry in Canada. Willowdale, Ont.: Ontario Puppetry Association Publishing Co., 1980.

Monette, Pierre. "Policy Statement re Children's Programmes, Societe Radio-Canada," Montreal, Quebec (undated). Describes the philosophy of youth programming on the French network of the CBC from 1952 and its development with the expansion of available TV channels, particularly American ones, predicting the degeneration of French programming into quaint folklore if resources are not found to bolster French-language productions for children on the channels of Société Radio-Canada.

Nostbakken, David, and André Caron. Children and Television, Programs, People, Policies. Prepared for the Federal Task Force on Broadcast Policy, January 1986, unpublished. This study, prepared at the direction of Gerald Caplan and Florian Savageau, reviews television production for children during the past five years and analyzes public response. The study is based on information gleaned from interviews with broadcast executives, producers, distributors, and carriers of children's television. Policy options and suggestions are made for future action.

Nostbakken, David and Janis. "Is Your Child a TV Junkie?" Children's Broadcast Institute, Toronto, Ont. 1978. Helps the parent to take a positive and constructive approach towards children who tend to be addicted to television viewing.

Nostbakken, David and Janis. Questions and Answers About Children and Television. Children's Broadcast Institute, Toronto, Ont. 1979. Provides a quick and ready reference for concerned parents about common questions related to program content, policy, and production and accessibility to good children's programs.

Nostbakken, Janis and David. Talking Television: Final Report of the Power of Television Workshop. Toronto, Ont.: Children's Broadcast Institute, 1983. This is a report on a series of workshops on the subject of children's television over a period of seven years. The workshops were conducted across Ontario. Eventually, with the aid of a training manual, print and video materials, and a large grant from the Department of Communications at Ottawa, 150 workshops were conducted across Canada.

Postman, Neil. The Disappearance of Childhood. New York: Delacorte Press, 1982. The author stresses the great importance of fostering a sense of self-identity and self-worth among children, encouraging them in their creative growth and development instead of forcing adulthood upon them before they have reached emotional maturity. He identifies forces in contemporary society that contribute to "the disappearance of childhood" in Western society.

Rainsberry, F. B. Children and TV: The Moral Concern. Canadian Broadcasting Corporation, Toronto, Ont. 1965. This pamphlet outlines the general policy and guidelines which determined the direction of children's programs for the English network of the CBC in the 1960s. The text reveals common concerns of parents and educators regarding values both cultural and moral, and basic principles concerned with the creativity, growth, and development of children.

Razzle Dazzle News. A publication of the CBC to establish contact with the audience for this daily show for pre-teen viewers. It contained profiles of the main hosts of the show, a telequiz, groaners, riddles and jokes sent in by young viewers. Printed on newsprint in a tabloid format, the paper was published occasionally to meet the needs of the show as changes took place in its cast and format.

Rogers, Fred, and Barry Head. Mister Rogers Talks with Parents. New York: Berkley Books, 1983. The author is the creator, writer, and performer in the long-running children's television program Mister Rogers' Neighborhood. In this book, he records his philosophy about programming for children. He deals directly with many common problems of parent-child relationships attempting to resolve tension and anxiety. He demonstrates how he deals with these problems from a child's point of view in his television programs.

Solberg, Janet. Children's Television Programming. Toronto, Ont.: Children's Broadcast Institute, October 1977. This work was written with the needs of children's television producers in mind. The contribution of research in the planning stages, during production and post-production, is presented in nontechnical terms. In the same manner, principles of child development, target audiences for programs content, and typical responses to television by various age group contribute to more meaningful presentations by producers for children.

Television and Behavior: Ten Years of Scientific Progress and Implications for the Eighties. Vol. I: Summary Report. National Institute of Mental Health, Rockville, Maryland. 1982. This report, written under the supervision of Dr. David Pearl, Project Director and Chief of the Behavioral Sciences Research Branch of the National Institute of Mental Health, reviews research on children and television commencing with the Surgeon General's Scientific Advisory Committee Report of 1972. The areas reviewed deal with such subjects as television's influence in fostering violence and aggression; cognitive and emotional functioning; imagination, creativity, and pro-social behavior, family and interpersonal relations, etc.

Tilroe, Robert D. Puppetry and Television. Willowdale, Ont.: Ontario Puppetry Association Publishing Co., 1981. This book is intended to provide puppeteers with an introduction to the use of puppets on television. The author demonstrates how puppetry can enhance television production and contribute to the education of children, especially since puppets become surrogates for children by means of which they "distance" problems and resolve them through the interaction.

The TVOntario Method: Nine Steps to Superior Children's Programs. A publication of TVOntario. The pamphlet is written to inform parents and teachers about the care taken to plan and produce good children's programs. Using the series Readalong as a case study, the steps taken from the initial program idea are developed in nontechnical language to the final presentation and evaluation.

Young Children. Vol. 38, no. 4, May 1983. A publication of the National Association for the Education of Young Children, Washington D.C. Contains viewpoints on a wide range of current issues with respect to child development and education of young children. This issue contains the article by A. S. Honig dealing with common concerns about the average child's use of television.

Appendix B

LIST OF INTERVIEWEES

Interviewees included a sample of writers, performers, and producers, along with former supervisors and heads of children's television at CBC. As well, representatives of provincial television and independent television are included. The numbers at the right of the names indicate the sides of the audiotapes. All audiotapes are stored with the National Public Archives at Ottawa.

ANDREWS, Neil (Aug. 12, 1982) 99-102
TV Producer
Razzle Dazzle, Time of Your Life

ATTRIDGE, BRUCE (Dec. 5, 1982) 1
deceased, Dec. 19, 1982)
former Executive Producer, Junior Magazine
Supervisor of Children's Programs

BELLEW, RAY (telephone interview) 154
Host
Razzle Dazzle

BLOOMER, Stephen (Jan. 17, 1983) 142
Performer
This Living World (the English edition of La Vie Qui Bat)

BOUCHARD, Adelin (Jan. 18, 1983) 149
Producer
La Vie Qui Bat (This Living World)

BRAGGINS, Cliff (Dec. 2, 1982) 64-68
Senior Writer, Composer
Howdy Doody and Razzle Dazzle

CAMPBELL, Norman K. (CAMPBELL, Elaine) 38
First Producer
Uncle Chichimus

CANDOW, David (Oct. 4, 1982) 21
Producer
Skipper and Company (St. John's, Nfld)

CHAPMAN, Francis (Sept. 14, 1982) 103, 104
Producer
Misterogers

CHERCOVER, Murray (Mar. 14, 1983) 164-166
President, CTV Network
CBC Producer, Space Command

CHETWYND, Arthur (Oct. 8, 1982) 44
Film Producer
President, Chetwynd Films

CLARK, John (Dec. 14, 1982) 9
Original host
Junior Magazine

CLEE, David A. (Aug. 22, 1982) 105, 106
Research and Continuity
World Passport and Junior Magazine

CLOTHIER, Robert (Dec. 6, 1982) 60
The Beachcombers

CONEYBEARE, L. H. (Ted) (Jan. 6, 1983) 39
Producer
Polka Dot Door

CONEYBEARE, Rod (Dec. 20, 1982) 4, 5
Voice for Rusty and Jerome
The Friendly Giant

CONWAY, John (Nov. 23, 1982) 34
Writer, Puppeteer and Voice
Uncle Chichimus

COOMBS, Ernest (Sept. 28, 1982) 41
Mr. Dressup

CROSBY, Laurel (Sept. 22, 1982) 37
Administrative Assistant,
TV Children's

DAVIDSON, Douglas (Sept. 29, 1982) 45-47
Film Producer and Professor,
York University

DAVIDSON, William (Sept. 2, 1982) 107-112
Executive Producer
Razzle Dazzle

DAVIS, William A. (Dec. 8, 1982) 72
Studio Director
Children's TV

DESIGN DEPARTMENT (TORONTO) (Nov. 26, 1982) 27, 28
Peter Garstang (Head)
Laurie McVicar
Glen Kono
John Hall
Stephen Finnie
Richard Knowles
John King

DESROCHES, Pierre (Jan. 17, 1983) 146
General Manager, Société Radio-Canada
Former Chef du Service des Emissions Jeunesse

DEVERELL, Rita (Dec. 17, 1982) 7
Communications Consultant
Children's TV

DOOHAN, James M. (Dec. 9, 1982) 74
Selected as first host Timber Tom
Howdy Doody

DORE, Fernand (Jan. 18, 1983) 147, 148
Former Chef du Service des Emissions Jeunesse

ELDER, Donald (Jan. 19, 1983) 151, 152
Executive Producer
Coming Up Rosie and Dr. Zonk and the Zunkies

ELLIS, Ralph C. (Aug. 30, 1982) 113, 114
President, Ralph Ellis Enterprises Ltd.
Film Procurement, Children's TV

EVANS, Trevor (Oct. 8, 1982) 42, 43
Producer
Coming Up Rosie

FICE, Frank (Oct. 17, 1982) 87, 88
First Producer
Howdy Doody

GIBBONS, Robert (Aug. 27, 1982) 115, 116
Producer
Drop-In

GILCHRIST, Stuart (Aug. 3, 1982) 132
Producer
Butternut Square and *Mr. Dressup*

GILLANDERS (BEACH), Beth (Dec. 3, 1982) 61, 62
Hostess
Hidden Pages and *Storytime*

GLENN, Bill (Jan. 11, 1983) 52
Producer
Razzle Dazzle and *The Mystery Maker*

GRANNAN, Helen J. (Oct. 10, 1982) 51
Sister of late Mary Grannan

GREENFIELD, Shirley (Nov. 19, 1982) 22
Producer
Mr. Dress-Up

HACKETT, Robert J. (Sept. 29, 1982) 48
Writer and Performer
Private TV

HAGON, Rex (April 22, 1983) 76, 76A
Actor
Aubrey and Gus, *Drop-In*, *Whistletown*, *Science Alliance*

HAMEL, Alan (Dec. 8, 1982) 73
First Host
Razzle Dazzle

HAMILTON, Barbara (and Jacqueline WHITE) (Nov. 9, 1982) 25
Willow in *Howdy Doody*

HARCOURT, Nada (Aug. 25, 1982) 29-32
Present Head, Children's TV, Toronto

HARGRAVE, W. Denis (Sept. 9, 1982) 125, 126
Drama Producer, Children's TV

HAZZAN, Ray (Oct. 13, 1982) 77
Executive Producer
What's New

HEDGES, "Hank" (Dec. 30, 1982) 53
Science Editor
Junior Magazine

HOLMES, Rod (and Noreen YOUNG) (Nov. 23, 1982) 33
Producer, Ottawa
Pencil Box, *Reach for the Top*, *What's New?*

HOMME, Robert (Aug. 19, 1982) 117-120
The Friendly Giant

JEWISON, Norman (Mar. 8, 1983) 163
(telephone interview)
Producer
Uncle Chichimus

JOHNSTON, Stan (and John NOWLAN) (Oct. 19, 1982) 85, 86
Switchback, Halifax

KEATLEY, Philip (Dec. 6, 1982) 19
Producer, CBC Children's, Vancouver

KENNEDY, John H. (Jan 12, 1983) 139
Area Head, Television Drama, CBC

KENNEDY, John L. (Aug. 27, 1982) 121-124
Producer and Head, Children's TV

KRANTZ, Ronald (Sept. 27, 1982) 57, 58
Writer
Razzle Dazzle

KUZMIKAS, Nijole (Dec. 6, 1982) 2
Present Producer
Switchback, Vancouver

KYNE, Terry (Dec. 9, 1982) 20
Studio Director
Howdy Doody

LAWRENCE, Judith (Jan. 10, 1983) 16
Writer and Puppeteer
Mr. Dressup

LIPTROT, Peggy (Aug. 24, 1982) 133-136
Producer
Let's Make Music, etc.
Children's TV, Toronto

LUMSDEN, A. P. (Sandy) (Oct. 20, 1982) 49, 50
Producer
Children's TV, Halifax

MATHER, Jack (Nov. 5, 1982) 35
Voice

Howdy Doody (Dilly Dally and Flubadub),
Nursery School Time

MAXWELL, Douglas D. 150
Sports Editor and Quizmaster
Junior Magazine Sportstime

McCARTHY, Dan (Aug. 5, 1982) 127-131
Former head, Children's TV
Producer, Sesame Street

McCURDY, Ed (Oct. 18, 1982) 78
Performer
Ed's Place and Ed and Ross Show

McKEOWN, Madrienne (Dec. 21, 1982) 11, 12
Producer
Misterogers, etc.

MEWS, Peter (and Alfie SCOPP) (Oct. 29, 1982) 13, 14
Timber Tom
Howdy Doody 15: Confidential

MILLER, Maxine (Nov. 24, 1982) 63
Princess Heidi
Howdy Doody

MONETTE, Pierre (Jan. 17, 1983) 145
Present Chef du Service des Emissions Jeunesse,
Société Radio-Canada

MOSS, Sylvia (Oct. 10, 1982) 23, 24
Program Organizer
Children's Radio & TV, Toronto

NOSTBAKKEN, Janis (Jan. 14, 1983) 141
Editor, Chickadee Magazine
Broadcast Consultant

NOWAKOWSKI, Vera M. (Jan. 4, 1983) 54
First Head, Children's Programs,
TVOntario

NOWLAN, John (and Stan JOHNSON) (Oct. 19, 1982) 85, 86
Switchback, Halifax

PRICE, Roger (Nov. 22, 1982) 36
Producer, CJOH-TV
You Can't Do That on TV

RAE, Claude (Jan. 11, 1983) 40
Voice
Howdy Doody, Razzle Dazzle, Whistletown

ROBB, Dodi (Oct. 18, 1982) 79, 80
Head, Children's TV
Writer, Telestory Time

ROGERS, Fred M. (May 15, 1983) 157, 158
Writer, Producer, Performer
Mister Rogers' Neighborhood

ROSEMOND, Perry (Aug. 19, 1982) 93, 94
Producer
Through the Eyes of Tomorrow

ROY, Robert (Jan. 17, 1983) 143, 144
Former Chef du Service des Emissions Jeunesse, Société Radio-Canada

ROSENZWEIG, Mervyn (May 10, 1983) 167
TV Producer, CBC Montreal

SAMPSON, Robert J. (Paddy) (Sept. 1, 1982) 91, 92
Producer, Toronto
Junior Magazine and Howdy Doody

SANDORFY, Sybil (Dec. 13, 1982) 8
Producer
What's New

SCOPP, Alfie (and Peter MEWS) (Oct. 29, 1982) 13, 14
Clarabell
Howdy Doody 15: Confidential

SEYMOUR, Ethel (Feb. 3, 1983) 153
Hal (deceased) and Renée Marquette, puppeteers for Canadian Howdy Doody Show

SIMONS, Joy (Dec. 3, 1983) 69, 70
Writer
Mr. Dressup

SLADE, Bernard (Dec. 14, 1982) 10
Understudy for Clarabell
Howdy Doody

SNETSINGER, Ross (Dec. 20, 1982) 3
Writer, Performer
Ed and Ross Show, Junior Magazine

SOLOVIOV, Joanne (Aug. 4, 1982) 95, 96
Producer and Writer, Children's TV
Hidden Pages, *Time of Your Life*, *Sing Ring Around*

SPIVAK, Michael (Oct. 4, 1982) 55, 56
Producer, Children's TV, Toronto
Maggie Muggins, *Razzle Dazzle*

STEVENS, Wm. (Nov. 22, 1982) 26
President, Atkinson Films
Producer, children's films

STEWART, Sandy (Oct. 9, 1982) 81-84
Executive Producer
Reach for the Top

TARNOW, Toby (Dec. 14, 1982) 6, 7
Hostess, *Nursery School Time*
Princess Summer Fall Winter Spring, *Howdy Doody*

THOMAS, David (Mar. 7, 1983) 162
TV Producer, CBC

THOMAS, Richard (Mar. 7, 1983) 161
Writer
Aubrey and Gus

THORNE, Jack (Dec. 6, 1982) 59
Executive Producer, Children's TV, Vancouver

TREBEK, Alex (Dec. 10, 1982) 17, 18
Host
Reach for the Top

TWOMEY, John E. (Aug. 25, 1982) 97, 98
Executive Producer and Assistant Supervisor, Children's TV, Toronto

VANDERBURGH, Clive (Jan. 12, 1983) 138
Executive Producer, Children's Programs, TVOntario

VERNON, Ruth (Jan. 12, 1983) 137
Superintendent, Children's Television, TVOntario

WATSON, Patrick (Oct. 13, 1982) 89, 90
Host
Junior Magazine

WHITE, Gloria (Dec. 3, 1982) 75, 76

Producer, Children's TV, Toronto
Toby, The Marbles

WHITE, Jacqueline (and Barbara HAMILTON) (Nov. 9, 1982) 25
Howdy Doody in Howdy Doody

WHITEHOUSE, Ray (Dec. 6, 1982) 71
Drama Producer, CBC, Vancouver
Tidewater Tramp

YOST, Elwy (Jan. 14, 1983) 140
Project Director, Film Features, TVOntario

YOUNG, Noreen (and Rod HOLMES) (Nov. 23, 1982) 33
Puppeteer, Ottawa
Pencil Box, Reach for the Top, What's New

STANLEY HOUSE CONFERENCE (June 27-July 1, 1983) 168-189
Participants:
Cliff Braggins
Georges Noel Fortin
Gayle Jabour
John L. Kennedy
Dan McCarthy
Lee Polk
Fred Rainsberry
Dodi Robb
Joan Soloviov
Peggy Stevenson
John Twomey

Appendix C

SOURCE COMPANIES AND ASSOCIATIONS

ACCESS Alberta, the Alberta Educational Communications Corporation, established by an act of the legislature of the Province of Alberta in 1973. Its purpose was to bring together under one corporation all the activities of the Alberta government with respect to educational television. It is also charged with the preparation and distribution of programs designed to meet curricular needs for the schools of Alberta and for adult education. As time goes on, the Corporation will explore newer technologies as these are developed and become available.

Association for Media Literacy. This organization was formed as a result of an invitational conference sponsored by the National Film Board of Canada and the Canadian Filmmakers' Distribution Centre. Its purpose is to advocate visual literacy among teachers and professionals working with children and, to a broader extent, members of the adult community. Since its foundation, three major conferences have been held, along with some 15 workshops. Its membership consists of some 400 individuals and 41 school boards, primarily in the Province of Ontario. Presently the Association is working as a task force with the Ministry of Education of Ontario to produce a resource book for the teaching of media literacy across the curriculum of the schools of Ontario.

ATEC (Agency for Tele-Education in Canada) is an association of organizations which are empowered by a provincial statute or by the Lieutenant-Governor in Council of a province, to produce and broadcast media-designed educational materials. The purpose of the organization is to promote and advance generally the interests in educational communications of its members, and to establish relations with other broadcasting organizations or groups of such organizations. The association aims to promote co-operation in economic, technical development, acquisition, production, distribution, exchange, utilization, and evaluation of media-designed educational projects and materials.

The Australian Children's Television Foundation (ACTF) was incorporated as a company limited by guarantee in March 1982.

The registered office is in Melbourne, and supporters' groups exist in each state, the northern territory, and the Australian capital territory. Recognizing the demand from the community for better-quality Australian children's programs, the ACTF was created to invest in the innovative, but costly, high-risk stage of the production process--program development--and then to attract the industry to make the programs it has developed. The Association also conducts workshops and training sessions.

The CTV Television Netowrk is Canada's only privately operated, fully national television network. It is also the only affiliate-owned, commercially funded national television network in the world. At the present time it operates in cooperation with some 16 privately owned and operated affiliated stations, 5 supplementary affiliates, and 218 rebroadcast transmitters. At present it utilizes a 7,900-mile microwave system in addition to 8 organization facilities and delay centers necessary to adjust to the time-zone requirements across the country. The network was established on October 1, 1961, as a major-market commercially funded national television network under private ownership. The network is complementary to the CBC network and reaches 97 percent of the population of Canada.

The Canadian Advertising Foundation, which in 1981 superseded the Canadian Advertising Advisory Board (founded in 1957), is an all-industry body, funded on a voluntary basis by advertisers, media, and advertising agencies. The Foundation has two operating divisions, the Standards Division, which works with a volunteer Advertising Standards Council and administers codes of advertising ethics; and the Advertising Division, the public relations-advocacy arms. The equivalent French-language bodies are Le Conseil des Normes de la Publicité and La Confédération Générale de la Publicité.

The CBC (Canadian Broadcasting Corporation) was established by act of Parliament November 2, 1936. It became the national broadcasting facility, taking over the staff of the former Canadian Radio Broadcasting Commission along with eight publicly owned or leased stations and 14 affiliates. The CBC is a Crown corporation designed to meet the needs of Canada as a nation while providing regional service across the country. Television service began in 1952. At present CBC outlets total 99 owned stations, 48 private affiliates, and 1,395 owned or affiliated rebroadcasters.

The Children's Broadcast Institute (CBI) was founded in 1974 by a group of parents, broadcasters, producers, advertisers, educators, researchers and child advocates who were concerned about the state of children's television in Canada. At the present time the CBI is the only national voluntary organization working exclusively in the interests of children to improve the quality of their TV experience. The Institute aims to ensure that as many Canadian children and youth as possible are regularly reached with high-quality programming. Another aim is to increase public awareness of the influence of television and to encourage its positive use by both children and parents. The Institute promotes media literacy through workshops conducted with parents, teachers, and other community groups to explore the nature of television and its creative use in the school and at home. Annually it supports Family Viewing Week to encourage parents to guide their children's viewing experience. Public service announcements are designed to promote responsible viewing and are produced and distributed by the CBI for use in TV stations across Canada. Video cassettes for family viewing are also listed to provide parents with guidelines for the seleciton of family viewing from the home video market.

The Global Television Network began in January 1974. It is Canada's third largest television system, covering 94 percent of Ontario. With headquarters in Toronto, Global Television serves half of English Canada, or approximately 8.5 million people, by means of five simultaneous transmitters strategically situated across the province. Global Television has a mandate to create alternative Canadian drama, variety and children's programming, working in conjunction with the country's independent production community. Global News, backed by its Ottawa bureau/studio, produces 20 hours of live news programming each week. For further information, please contact Averill Maroun, Media Relations Department, Global Television Network, 416-466-5320.

The National Film Board of Canada was founded in 1939 by an act of Parliament "to initiate and promote the production and distribution of films in the national interest and in particular ... to interpret Canada to Canadians and to other countries." The Board maintains distribution offices which provide films and videos to any individual or organization. The NFB also reaches audiences through television broadcasts, public screenings and commercial outlets for its features and theatrical shorts. In recent years, the NFB has also created production studios in different regions of the country in order to have access to the best film-making talent as well as to encourage the Canadian film industry nationwide. Since its inception, the Board has produced over 4,000 original films. In recent years, production has averaged more than 100 new titles annually, in both official languages. The Board's Technical Operations Branch handles all the requirements of film production, including full laboratory services for processing film and videotape. A technical research section publishes information about its findings regarding new techniques and developments, to the benefit of the entire film industry. The operational headquarters of the Board are located in Montreal: National Film Board of Canada, P.O. Box 6100, Station A, Montreal, Quebec, H3C 3H5.

TVOntario was created in 1970 by an act of the provincial legislature, and is legally known as the Ontario Educational Communications Authority. The OECA Act describes TVOntario's primary objectives, which include the acquisition, production, and distribution of programs and materials in the educational broadcasting and communications fields, and the conduct of research that contributes to the achievement of such objectives. TVOntario is best known as the educational television network for the Province of Ontario, and is the only educational network in Canada to produce and broadcast regularly in both the English and French languages.

Addresses

ACCESS National
Alberta Communications and Educational Authority
16930 - 114 Avenue
Edmonton, Alberta T5M 3S2

AMTEC
Association for Media and Technological Education in Canada
500 Victoria Road
North Guelph, Ontario N1E 6K2

CTV Network
42 Charles Street East
Toronto, Ontario M4Y 1T4

Canadian Advertising Foundation
1240 Bay Street, Suite 302
Toronto, Ontario M5R 2A7

Canadian Broadcasting Corporation
Head Office
1500 Bronson Avenue
Ottawa, Ontario

Children's Broadcast Institute
234 Eglinton Avenue East, Suite 405
Toronto, Ontario M4P 1K5

Global Television Network
81 Barber Greene Road
Don Mills, Ontario M3C 2A2

National Film Board of Canada
P.O. Box 6100
Montreal, Quebec H3C 3H5

Société Radio-Canada
C.P. 6000
Montréal, Québec H3C 3A8

Telefilm Canada
130 Bloor Street West, Suite 901
Toronto, Ontario M5S 1N5

Head Office
Tour de Banque National
600, rue de la Gauchetière Ouest, 25e étage
Montréal, Québec H3B 4L2

TVOntario
2180 Yonge Street
Toronto, Ontario M4T 2T1

INDEX

ACCESS (Alberta Educational Communications Corporation) 82, 89, 90, 92, 106, 135, 137, 138, 161, 260, 272, 287, 290

Action for Children's Television, (A.C.T.) 230

ACTRA (Association of Canadian Radio and Television Artists) xi

Adam, Denyse 141, 149

Adventures in Rainbow Country 134

Adventures of Chich 9

Adventures of Snelgrove Snail 116

Advertising Standards Council 217

After Four 95, 144

Against All Odds 259

Against the Grain, G. Comstock 241

Agoos Foundation for Character Education 224

Aiken, Steven 157, 158

Albert's Place 119

Aldwinckle, Eric 49

All for Fun 154

All in a Tube 112

Allen, R. 241

Along the Way 76

Alphabet Soup 97

Amadio, Norm 144

Amateur Naturalist, The 86

Amato, Julie 135

American Broadcasting Company 247

AMTEC (Association for Media and Technological Education in Canada) 290

Andrews, Neil 57, 72, 73, 278

Anne of Avonlea 132

Anne of Green Gables 132, 133

Anne of Green Gables--the Sequel 133

Anne of the Island 132

Anne of Windy Poplars 132

Ants Don't Leave Footprints 72

Applebaum, Lou 72

Applebaum-Hébert Report 29, 31, 273

Arbour, Madeline 180

Archie and His Friends 154

Ark on the Move 86

Art in Auction 102

Artscape 102

Ash, Bobby 176

Association for Media Literacy 263, 265, 287

Atkinson Film Arts 127, 131, 180

Atlantis Films 155, 251, 259

Attridge, Bruce 68ff, 73, 79, 103, 106-7, 168, 278

ATV-CJBC, Sydney, Nova Scotia 155

Atwood, P. 241

Audience Research Department 239

Austin, Joe 12, 13, 48, 56, 129

Australian Broadcasting Control Board 260, 261

Australian Broadcasting Tribunal 261

Australian Children's Television Foundation 261, 265, 268, 287

Australian Children's Television Foundation Steering Committee 262

Australian Education Council 262

Avenue Television 150

Babar and Father Christmas 131
Bagatelle 199
Baillargeon, Hélène 182, 198-99
Baker, Ace see Baker, Don
Baker, Don 56, 57
Baldaro, Barry 59
Bambi 52
Banana Splits, The 146
Bananas, The 145
Barclay, Robert 117
Barge, Ron 153
Bargett, R. 241
Barney's Gang 97
Barrager, Stephen 82
Barrie, Fred 178
Bartholomew, Grace 104
Bartley, Ted 178
BCTV, Vancouver, B.C. 115
Beachcombers, The 121
Beaton, Brian 96
Beaver Valley 66
Beethoven, Ludwig van 58
Beker, Jeanne 144
Bellew, Ray 57, 148, 278
Bellings, Ray 170
Bello, Lisa dal 148
Bellours, Mary 147
Beloshisky, Vera 148
Bériault, André 206
Bernardini, Mario 71, 107
Bernstein, Dr. Deborah 258
Bessada, Wilod 135
Bigras, Jean Yves 128, 194
"Billy Breaks the Chain" 124
Billy Goat's Bluff 259
Bird in the House, A 121
Birney, Earle 127, 259
Bishop, Ken and Nelly 178
Bits and Bytes 92
Black, Terry 142
Blackford, Gordon 140
Blazuk, Julia 135
Bloomer, Steve 195, 278
Bluster, Phineas J. 41
Board of Broadcast Governors 257
Bobino 205
Boisvert, Reginald 5, 194
Bookshop 17
Bookstop 81
Bonas, Carol 83
Boomer, Barney 95, 122
Booth, Dr. Charles 109
Boss, Valentine 122
Bouchard, Adelin 195, 278
Bourne, Tommy 98
Boys and Girls 127
Broggins, Cliff 37, 41-2, 50, 57, 67, 278, 286
Braithwaite, Dennis 222-3
Broadcast Code of Advertising to Children 216-18
Broadcasting Act 269, 271
Broadfoot, David 49
Bromfield, Vabri 148
Brown, Sid 135
Bruce, Angelo 14, 30
Bruce Raymond Ltd. 97
Bruneau, Trevor 98
Brunhoff, Jean de 131
Buckshot Show, The 153, 154
Budgell, Jack 144
Buffalo Bob 43
Bugs Bunny 52
Bureau, André 271
Busy Fingers 101
Butternut Square 168

Callaghan, Morley 259
Calling All Safety Scouts 115
Camp Caribou 156-7
Campbell, Averil 140
Campbell, Jerome 155
Campbell, Norman 103, 278
Campbell, Rick 83
Canada Council Explorations Program ix, 3
Canada Cup Sailing Race 58
Canadian Advertising Advisory Board 213; see also Canadian Advertising Foundation
Canadian Advertising Foundation 288, 290
Canadian Association of Broadcasters 209
Canadian Association of Broadcasters Code of Ethics 33
Canadian Broadcast Program Development Fund 29, 30, 31-2, 258, 265
Canadian Broadcasting Corporation

Levy, Eugene 148
Leonard, Ron 176
Lesser, Gerald 27, 187, 239, 240, 246, 274, 275
Let's Build a Town 71, 106
Let's Go 142, 149, 211
Let's Go to the Museum 14, 100
Let's Look 100
Let's Make Music 13, 18, 104, 105
Let's Play TV in the Classroom 231
Let's See 5
Levitch, Gerald 86
Liberty Award 50
Library Storytime 17, 81
Lightfoot, Gordon 58
Liimatainen, Walter 132
Linder, Cec 117
Lindsay, Deborah x
Liptrot, Peggy Nairn 9, 66, 188-89, 282
Lisa Makes Headline 124
Livesley, Jack x, 231, 235, 274
Lott, Keith 259
Louie, Linda 95
Lowry, John 117
Lucarotti, John 128, 194
Lumby, Helen 180
Lumley, Skip 92
Lumsden, A. P. (Sandy) 100, 282
Lund, Alan and Blanche 103
Lynn, Ball 123, 147
Lynsky and Co. 152

M & M Productions 150
MacAndrew, Heather 93
MacDonald, Brian 103
MacKay, Jed 62
Maggie Muggins 119, 174-75
Magic Lie, The 81, 121
Magic of Music, The 105
Maison Magique, La 254
Maitland, Alan 146, 147
Makepeace, Chris 77, 248-49
Malenfant, Gail 147
Mallett, Jane 124
Maman Fonfon 202
Man from Tomorrow 119
Man in Space 66
Man in the Moon 66
Manitou Productions 129, 134
Mann, Larry 5, 39, 44
Marbles, The 147
Marc's Grab Bag 147
Marcuse, Kitty 119
Marquette, Hal and Renée 39, 284
Marsh, Bev 176
Martin, Jerry 95
Martin, John 145
Martin, Tom 9, 81
Mason, Mendel Mantelpiece 41
Mather, Jack 41, 56, 181, 282
Matt and Jenny on the Wilderness Trail 129-30
Maufette, Guy 197
Maxwell, Doug 71, 98, 282
Maxwell, Lois 135
Maxwell, Roberta 71
Mayer, David 123, 147
Mayerovitch, David 60
Mayoh, Leonard 120
McCaffery, Margaret x
McCarthy, Dan 14, 96, 185, 282, 286
McCurdy, Ed 12-13, 82, 104, 283
McCutcheon, Ian 74
McDonald, Bob 87
McDonnell, Arch 123
McDougal, Ian 130
McEwan, Virginia 95
McGillivray, Susanne 157-58
McInnes, Neil 85
McKay, Kenneth B. 208, 275
McKeever, Kay 90
McKeown, Madrienne 283
McLachlin, Lorne 85
McLean, Quentin 39, 41, 42
McLean, Ross 110
McLear, Michael 77
McNamara, Ed 56
McNea, Frances K. 153
McNea, Kathy Lynn 153
McNea, Michael 153
McNea, Robert J. 153
McNeil, Robin 100
McNichol, Kristy 95

McPhail, Marnie 130
Meek, Billy 59
Meek, Mendel 56
Melançon, André 201
Menotti, Gian-Carlo 28, 108
Meraska, Ron 144, 201
Mercel, Ed 57
Mercer, Ruby 109
Merrythought, The 58
Merton, George and Elizabeth 173
Mews, Peter 39, 283
MG Film Production 116
Michie, Dave 142
Mickey Mouse Club 66, 67, 95
Mighty Mites, The 91
Milestone rock band 58
Miller, Donna 68, 135, 175
Miller, Marjorie 41, 283
Mills, Alan 104, 199
Mirage, The 58
Mister Dressup 30, 34, 76, 162, 168-70, 245-46, 250, 279
Mister I-Got-It 56
Mister Microchip 92, 260
Mister O 18
Mr. Peaceable Paints 108
Mister Piper 105
Mister Rogers' Neighborhood 19, 170-73, 187-88, 246
Mister Rogers Talks with Parents 173, 276
Mister Sharpy 56
Mister X 43-44, 46
Mitchell, W. O. 121
Mollin, Fred 62, 122
Mollin, Larry 62, 122
Mon Ami 76, 199
Monette, Pierre 200, 275, 283
Monk, Rosalee x
Monkey Bars 79, 159
Montgomery, L. M. 121, 127, 132, 259
Moonstone, The 117
Moore, Mavor 4
Moore, Teddi 96
Morency, Helen 148
Morris, Maggie 147
Morse, Barry 124
Moss, Sylvia 283
Muir, Roger 111
Muller, John 151
Munro, Alice 127, 259
Munro, Marce 109
Music Box 105
Music Hop 142
Music Inc. 105
Music Machine, The 142
Mystery Maker, The 122

Nagler, Eric 148
Nairn, Peggy (Liptrot) see Liptrot, Peggy Nairn
Nas, Jimmy 120
Nash, Knowlton 185
National Academy of Television Arts and Sciences 224
National Association of Broadcasters 224
National Council of Churches of Christ of the U.S.A. 224
National Educational Television 96
National Film Board 257, 271, 289, 290
National Gallery of Canada 101
National Institute of Mental Health 236
National Museum of Canada 100
National Religious Advisory Council 257
National Schools Advisory Council 257
National Youth Orchestra 73
Nature of Things, The 83, 86, 196
Nature's Half Acre 66
Neill, A. S. 139
Nelvana Pictures 92, 130, 134
New Majority, The 73
New Music, The 144
New Tomorrow 259
News from Zoos 83
Nibbles 92
Nic et Pic 199
Nicholas, Cindy 95
Nicholls, Muriel 178
Nickerson, Betty 101
Nigrini, Ron, and the Gentle Rock Band 58
Noel Buys a Suit 124

Northern Lights 259
Northey, Stuart 60
Noseworthy, Beth 148
Nostbakken, Dr. David ix, x, 228, 249, 253, 255, 259, 263, 265, 266, 269, 275, 276
Nostbakken, Janis x, 151, 155, 156, 183, 211, 226, 228, 246, 263, 275, 276, 283
Nova Scotia Museum of Science 100
Nowakowski, Vera 283
Nowlan, John 148
Nursery School Time 180-81

Ochrymovich, Ariadna 125, 259
Odyssey 81
O'Hara, Catherine 60
Old Testament Tales 119
O'Leary, Brian 57
O'Leary, Sean 140
Oliver, Fergie 111
Oliver, Ron 178-79, 211
Olson, Bobby 140
Omega Productions 128
On My Own 126
Ontario Ministry of Education 97
Ontario Ministry of Education Guidelines for Education in the Primary and Junior Divisions 231
Oopsy the Clown 153
Oral History Project 2-3
Ouchterlony, David 18, 102, 105
Owl TV Show 30, 90

Pallegrini, Maria 95
Pan of the Forest 41
Pappert, Pan 183
Parade 76
Parents' Viewing Month 263
Park, William 67, 95
Parr, Kate 124
Pascu, Margaret 110
Passe Partout 250
Passport to Adventure 68
Paterson Ferns 86
Patrick, Doug 4
Patterson, Pat 97, 108, 173, 176
Patti's Picture House 66, 95
Paul Hanna and Friends 154
Peanut Gallery 41, 43
Peanuts and Popcorn 76
Peck, Gregory 95
Pencil Box 26, 28, 122
Penfield, Dr. Wilder 182
Penner, Fred 30, 176, 177
Pepinot et Capucine 4, 194
Peppermint Prince, The 119
Percival, Lloyd 4
Percival Parrot 44
Percy Kidpester 56
Perth County Conspiracy rock band 58
Pet Corner 10, 83
Petawabano, Buckley 135
"Pete Takes a Chance" 124
Petrie, Susan 123
Phelps, Ann x
Piccadilly 17
Pictures with Woofer 66, 68, 95
Pieces of Eight 120
Pinsent, Gordon 73, 128-29
Pinvidic, Margot 144
Pirate's Gold 108
Pitman, Bruce 124
Planet Tolex 12, 119
Playing with Time Inc. 123-24, 125, 251
Pogo 52
Polk, Lee 286
Polka Dot Door 34, 79, 160, 188-89, 190, 246
Pollock, Jeremy 137
Popcorn Man, The 28
Postman, Neil 244, 247, 276
Potts, Barney 97
Power of Television Project 228
Precious, Lorraine 144
Prew, Richard 141
Price, Flo 114
Price, Roger 139, 211, 283
Primedia Ltd. 86
Princess Haida (in Howdy Doody Show) 41, 46
Princess of Tomboso, The 122
Prix Jeunesse International 74
Productions Prisma, Les 201
Proudlove, S. 241
Proveau, Guy 195
Public Archives of Canada 2

Puppetry and Television, Robert D. Tilroe 208, 277
Puppetry in Canada, Kenneth B. McKay 208, 275

Quadramedia Management Corp. 84
Questions and Answers About Children and Television 22, 29, 62, 275
Quiz Kids 112

Raccoons--Let's Dance, The 127
Raccoons and the Lost Star, The 127
Raccoons on Ice 127
Raddall, Thomas 117
Radio Guide, CBC 235
Radisson, Pierre 128, 194
Rae, Claude 41, 284
Rainbow 259
Rainsberry, Frederick B. 171, 219, 276, 286
Rainsberry, Linda 81
Rampen, Leo 110
Ranger Bob 39
Rank, J. Arthur see J. Arthur Rank Organization
Raymond, Bruce see Bruce Raymond Ltd.
Razzle Dazzle 50, 95, 249, 250
Razzle Dazzle Club 50, 53, 54
Razzle Dazzle Daily 53, 54
Razzle Dazzle News 276
Reach for the Top 109
Reaching Out 125
Read All About It 81, 136-37, 234
Readalong 80, 136, 233
Red Balloon, The 66
Red Snapper Films 259
Reed, Fiona 124
Reiniger, Lotte 135
Reiter, Bill 115
Report of the Federal Cultural Review Committee 273
Restless Years, The 73
Rey, Margaret and Hans 180
Reynolds, Tom 152
Reynolds-Long, Peter 132
Rich, R. 241
Richler, Mordecai 259
Rin Tin Tin 52
Robb, Dodi 28, 29, 30, 173, 284, 286
Roberge, Jean-Jacques 123
Roberts, J. D. 144, 145
Roberts, Pete 95
Roberts, Randy 176
Robertson, Lloyd 110
Robinson, Carol 111
Robinson, John 148
Robson, Gary 149
Rochon, George 112
Rocket Boy 134
Rockett, Paul 49
Rodgers, Nancy 183
Roger Sudden 117
Rogers, Fred 19, 20, 23, 72, 108, 246, 276, 284
Rogers Cable Company (Toronto) 190, 254
Rogers Cable Systems 254
Rogers Cable TV Calgary 180
Roland, Herb 72
Rolling Stones, The 143
Romper Room 183, 211, 246
Ronning, Chester 72
Rookie of the Year 76
Rooney, Ted 152, 153
Rope Around the Sun 104
Rose, Patrick 89
Rosemond, Perry 72, 73, 250, 284
Rosenberg, Barney 135
Rosenzweig, Mervyn 196, 284
Ross, A. W. ix, 2
Ross, Jerry 57
Ross, Sinclair 259
Ross the Builder 82
Roth, Michael 56
Roundup Goes Camping 49
Roy, Robert 199, 284
Royal Ontario Museum 100
Russell, Brian 142
Rustler and the Reindeer, The 122

Sabiston, Andrew 130
Sackfield, Doug 173
Salter, Brian 141
Saltzman, Deepa 96, 99
Saltzman, Paul 72, 96
Saltzman, Percy 9, 49, 84-85
Salut Santé 205
Salzman, Glen 125
Same Time Next Year 250
Sampson, Paddy 141, 173, 284
Samuels, Maxine 128
Sandorfy, Sybil 284
Saskmedia Corporation 180
Saturday Morning Camera Clubs 75
Saunders, Michael x
Savath, Phil 62, 122
Schneider, Bob 150
Schuyler, Linda 123
Science All Around Us 85
Science Alliance 87
Scopp, Alfie 41
Scott, Marilyn 135
Scott, Rich 149
Scuttlebut, Captain 39
Seal Island 66
Second City Revue 59
Secret of the Samurai, The 100
See For Yourself 82
Seeing Things 250
Senate Standing Committee on Education in the Arts (Australia) 261
Sesame Street 26, 30, 34, 184-88, 240, 245, 246-47, 254
Sewer, The 72
Seymour (Ethel) (Renée Marquette) 39, 284
Shadow Puppets 135
Shantytown 155
Shatner, William 39
Shaver, Calvin 153
Shiner, Alan 148
Sills, Paul 136
Silver Basketball, The 178, 209, 211
Silver, Rhonda 142
Simard, René 95
Simmons, Al 93, 154
Simon, Dayna 92
Simons, Joy 16, 219, 284
Sing Ring Around 68, 175
Singer, Dorothy and Jerome 27, 187
Siren, Valerie 96, 141
Size Small 180
Size Small Country 180
Skeena Broadcasters Ltd. (CFTK-TV) 132
Skipper and Company 148
Skippy the Bush Kangaroo 66
Skoffman, Nicole 252
Skolnick, Norman 72
Slade, Bernard 41, 162, 250, 284
Small Fry Frolics 5, 13, 140
Smallwood, Joey, Premier of Newfoundland 148
Smith, Bob 43
Smith, Clive A. 134
Smith, Donald A. 58
Smith, Eileen Taylor 117
Smith, Dr. H. Ward 141
Snetsinger, Ross 48, 82, 284
Snow Queen, The 122
Société Radio-Canada 251, 253-54, 290
Solberg, Janet 276
Soloviov, Joanne Hughes 9, 66, 68, 71, 72, 174-75, 285, 286
Somers, Harry 107
Somerville, Cathy 183
Song Shop, The 104
Sons and Daughters 127
Sophie Minds the Store 124
Space Command 117
Spalding, Dave and Andrea 178
Spalding, John and Maggie 113
Speakeasy 137
Speaking Out 74
Spiess, Fritz 120
Spirit Bay 130
Spivak, Michael 50, 174-75, 285
Sports College 4
Sportstime 98
Spread Your Wings 96, 99
Spring Thaw 39
Springbett, David 93
Springford, Ruth 122
Stamp Club 4
Standard Broadcasting Company (CJOH Ottawa) 139, 211

Stanton, Jean 148
Star Trek 39, 117
Starbuck Valley Winter 121
Stardate 151
Stationary Ark, The 86
Stephens, Paul 131
Stevens, William 285
Stevenson, Peggy x, 286
Stewart, Nonie 119
Stewart, Sandy 50, 285
Stocker, John 60, 144
Stormy the Thoroughbred 66
Story of Robin Hood 66
Story Seat 119
Storybook 119
Stott, Margaret 140
Stowaway, The 28, 77, 250
Strange, Mark and Susan 121
Stratas, Teresa 72
Stren, Patty 126
Stuart, Al 90
Stuart, Joan 85
Sugar Shoppe, The 142
Sullivan, Ed 50
Sullivan, Fred 71
Sullivan, Kevin 132, 259
Sullivan Films 258
Summer Camp 75
Survival in the Wilderness 76
Suzuki, Dr. David 85, 86
Swaffield, Bob 151
Swan, Stan 28
Swartz, Bob 115
Swing, Catherine 111
Swing Your Partner 104
Swingaround 110
Swinton, Prof. George 102
Swiss Family Robinson 211
Switchback 63, 148
System, The, rock band 58

Tabachnik, Michelle 200
Take III Productions 93
Tales of the Riverbank 120
Tales of Wesakechak 136
Talking Television 229, 276
Tan-Gau Method 182
Tarnow, Toby 41, 56, 181, 185
Tassé, André 206
Tavenuik, Bill 85
Taylor, Dr. Bryce 98
Taylor, Samantha 154
Taylor, Susan 95
Teacher, Rosie 59
Telecultura 154
Telefilm Canada (Canadian Broadcast Program Development Fund) 33, 77, 150, 251, 258, 259, 266, 291
Téléjeans 205
Telestory Time 11, 173-74
Television Advertising and Children, June F. Esserman 241, 274
Television and Behavior: Ten Years of Scientific Progress and Implications for the Eighties Vol. I, Summary Report, National Institute of Mental Health 255, 270, 277
Templeton, Jean 49
Temps d'une Paix, Le 198
Tennant, Jan 98
Tennant, Veronica 95
Terrarium 206
Terrible Ten, The 56, 66
Terry, Chris 151
Tesar, Graham 147
Things We See, The 101
Think Again 79
This Living World 83, 195
Thomas, David 60, 285
Thomas, Ralph 142
Thomas, Richard 285
Thomas, Stan 180
Thompson, Betty 185
Thompson, Drew 41
Thompson, Wayne 72
Thorne, Jack 199, 285
Thrasher, Sunny 130
Three Plus One 76
Three's Company 214, 251
Through Children's Eyes 101
Through the Eyes of Tomorrow 57, 72, 73, 250
Tidewater Tramp 49, 121
Tilroe, Nikki 135
Tilroe, Robert D. 208
Timber Tom 39, 43, 46
Time for Adventure 66, 75

Time of Your Life 57, 72, 95, 122, 239
Timothy T 119
Tiny Talent Time 151
Toby 122
Today's Special 79, 246, 254
Toes in Tempo 103
Toronto Daily Star 6-7
Tranquility Base 142
Trapper Jack 132
Trapper Pierre 47
Travellin' Time 96
Treasure Island 66
Trebek, Alex 111, 142, 143, 285
Treehouse Club, The 113, 152
Trinity Television 114
Trott, Vern 140
Troupers 155
Tully, Peter 129
Tune-Up Time 106
Turtleshell Players 56
TVOntario x, 75, 79, 80, 92, 94, 102, 105, 115, 136, 159, 160-161, 190-93, 206, 208, 215, 231-32, 233, 234, 241, 246, 248, 254-55, 260, 270, 272, 290, 291
TVOntario Method, The 80, 233, 277
Tweed, Tommy 58
Tween Set 141
Twenty Thousand Leagues Under the Sea 9, 117
Twomey, John x, 214, 285, 286

U-Titky Kuitky 155
Ukrainian Folk Tales 135
Uncle Bobby Show, The 176
Uncle Chichimus 5-9
Undersea Adventures of Captain Nemo 76
UNESCO 44, 71, 235, 264
UNICEF 96
United Nations 70
U.S. Department of Health and Welfare 224
Usher-Sharp Inc. 155

Vacation Time 76
Vancouver Children's Festival 93
Vanderburgh, Clive 159, 285
Vanderhaege, Guy 259
Van der Veen, Milton 89
Van Horne, Sir William 58
Van Leeuwen, John 178
Varon, Frank 195
Velleman, Leo and Dora 10
Verne, Jules 117
Vernon, Ruth x, 285
Vickers, Hetty 65
Vid Kids 150, 151
Video Hits 154
Video I 74
Vie Qui Bât, La 83, 195

Waldman, Marion 103
Walk with Kirk, A 97
Wallace, Clarke 98
Walsh, Jim 112
Ward, Christopher 144
Ward, Robin 111
Wargon, Alan 105
Waterville Gang, The 135
Watson, Patrick 285
Watson, Whipper Billy 141
Way I See, The 90
Waynes, Jamie 98
We Live Next Door 115
Weisgard, Leonard 108
Welcome to My World 77
Westgate, Murray 49
What's New? 93-94, 248
When Knighthood Was in Flower 66
Whipper, David 144
Whistletown 48-49, 82
White, Gloria 122, 285
White, Jackie 41, 285
White Mane 66
White Stone, The 76
Whitehouse, Ray 121, 286
Wilcox, Rose 71
Wilcox, Victoria x
Williams, Penny 141
Willow 39
Willy and Floyd 151
Wind in the Willows 66

Winkler, Henry (The Fonz) 95
Winter, Charles 96
Wipper, Kirk 97
Wise, Sidney 2
Wonder, Stevie 95
Wonderful Stories of Professor Kitzel, The 116
Wonderstruck 87, 130
Wood, Kerry 104
Woodman, Steve 103
Working Summer, A 73
World According to Nicholas, The 124
World Passport 65, 67, 196
World's Children, The 93
W.O.W. (Wonderful One-of-a-Kind Weekend show) 28, 75, 106, 108
Wright, Gordon 97

Yates, Rebecca 125
Yeates, Marilyn and Maureen 179
Yes, You Can 98, 127
Yost, Elwy 286
You Can't Do That on Television 139, 211
Young, Noreen 98, 121, 286
Young, Norman 119
Young, Peter 123
Young, Trudy 57, 95
Young Children (magazine) 277
"Young Juggler, The" 124; see also Juggler, The
Young Naturalist Foundation 90
Yours Truly rock band 58
Youth Choir, The CBC 71
Youth Confrontation 74
Youth ' 60 141
Youth Takes a Stand 140

Zenon, Michael 129
Zeyen, John 178
Zig Zag 114
Zigzags 201
Zoo Factory, The 144
Zucchini Alley 155